# Artificial Intelligence Annual Volume 2024

*Edited by George A. Papakostas, Marco Antonio Aceves-Fernández and Mehmet Emin Aydin*

Published in London, United Kingdom

Artificial Intelligence Annual Volume 2024
http://dx.doi.org/10.5772/10.5772/intechopen.1008722
Edited by George A. Papakostas, Marco Antonio Aceves-Fernández and Mehmet Emin Aydin

Contributors
Ali Akbar Firoozi, Ali Asghar Firoozi, Antonis Konstantinos, Aziz Makandar, Efren Gorrostieta-Hurtado, Eleni Vrochidou, Evangelos Georgakoudis, George A. Papakostas, Hannes Allmaier, Igor Agbossou, Jesus Carlos Pedraza-Ortega, Jose Luis Maciel-Jacobo, Marco Antonio Aceves-Fernández, Michail Marinis, Nayan Jadhav, Ragazou Vasiliki, Sophia Bastidas



First published in London, United Kingdom, 2024 by IntechOpen
IntechOpen is the global imprint of INTECHOPEN LIMITED, registered in England and Wales, registration number: 11086078, 167-169 Great Portland Street, London, W1W 5PF, United Kingdom

For EU product safety concerns: IN TECH d.o.o., Prolaz Marije Krucifikse Kozulić 3, 51000 Rijeka, Croatia, info@intechopen.com or visit our website at intechopen.com.

British Library Cataloguing-in-Publication Data
A catalogue record for this book is available from the British Library

Artificial Intelligence Annual Volume 2024
Edited by George A. Papakostas, Marco Antonio Aceves-Fernández and Mehmet Emin Aydin
p. cm.

This title is part of the Artificial Intelligence Book Series, Volume 31
Series Editor: Andries Engelbrecht

Print ISBN 978-0-85014-939-5
Online ISBN 978-0-85014-938-8
eBook (PDF) ISBN 978-0-85014-940-1
ISSN 2633-1403

IntechOpen Book Series

# Artificial Intelligence

Volume 31

## Aims and Scope of the Series

Artificial Intelligence (AI) is a rapidly developing multidisciplinary research area that aims to solve increasingly complex problems. In today's highly integrated world, AI promises to become a robust and powerful means for obtaining solutions to previously unsolvable problems. This Series is intended for researchers and students alike interested in this fascinating field and its many applications.

# Meet the Series Editor

Andries Engelbrecht received the Masters and Ph.D. degrees in Computer Science from the University of Stellenbosch, South Africa, in 1994 and 1999 respectively. He is currently appointed as the Voigt Chair in Data Science in the Department of Industrial Engineering, with a joint appointment as Professor in the Computer Science Division, Stellenbosch University. Prior to his appointment at Stellenbosch University, he has been at the University of Pretoria, Department of Computer Science (1998-2018), where he was appointed as South Africa Research Chair in Artifical Intelligence (2007-2018), the head of the Department of Computer Science (2008-2017), and Director of the Institute for Big Data and Data Science (2017-2018). In addition to a number of research articles, he has written two books, Computational Intelligence: An Introduction and Fundamentals of Computational Swarm Intelligence.

# Meet the Topic Editors

George A. Papakostas received the Diploma, M.Sc. and Ph.D. in Electrical and Computer Engineering in 1999, 2002 and 2007, respectively, from the Democritus University of Thrace (DUTh), Greece. He has 15 years of experience in large-scale systems design as a senior software engineer and technical manager. He is the Head of the Machine Learning and Vision (MLV) Research Group. He is a Tenured Full Professor in the Department of Informatics at DUTh, Greece. Prof. Papakostas has (co) authored more than 250 publications in indexed journals, international conferences, book chapters, one book (in Greek), three edited books, and eight journal special issues. His publications have over 4900 citations with an h-index 38 (Google Scholar). He has been included in the World's Top 2% of Scientists' Stanford list for 2022 and 2023 years in the field of "Artificial Intelligence & Image Processing". His research interests include machine learning, computer/machine vision, pattern recognition, and computational intelligence.

Dr. Marco Antonio Aceves-Fernández obtained his B.Sc. (Eng.) in Telematics from the Universidad de Colima, Mexico. He received both his M.Sc. and Ph.D. from the University of Liverpool, England, in the field of Intelligent Systems. He has been a full professor at the Universidad Autonoma de Queretaro in Mexico and a member of the National System of Researchers (SNI) since 2009. Dr. Aceves-Fernández has published more than 80 research papers as well as a number of book chapters and congress papers. He has contributed to more than 20 funded academic and industrial research projects in artificial intelligence, ranging from environmental, biomedical, automotive, aviation, consumer, and robotics applications. He is also an Honorary President of the National Association of Embedded Systems (AMESE), a member of the Mexican Academy of Computing (AMEXCOMP), a senior member of the Institute of Electrical and Electronics Engineers (IEEE), and a board member of many institutions and associations. His research interests include intelligent and embedded systems.

Mehmet Emin Aydin is a Senior Lecturer in Computer Science at the University of the West of England. He obtained a B.Sc, MA, and Ph.D. from Istanbul Technical University, Istanbul University, and Sakarya University, Turkey, respectively. His research interests include machine learning, intelligent agents and multi-agent systems, metaheuristics, swarm intelligence, resource planning, scheduling and optimization, and combinatorial optimization. He has served as guest editor for special issues of peer-reviewed international journals. In addition to being a member of the advisory committees of many international conferences, Dr. Aydin is an editorial board member for various journals. He is currently a fellow of the Higher Education Academy, a member of the Engineering and Physical Sciences Research Council (EPSRC) College in the UK, and a senior member of the Association of Computing Machinery (ACM) and Institute of Electrical and Electronics Engineers (IEEE).

# Contents

# Preface

With the advent of deep learning, computer vision has emerged as one of the most transformative research and application areas within artificial intelligence. As a result, computer vision has penetrated a multitude of applications in both people's daily lives and professional workplaces in many disciplines. The ability of machines to analyze and understand visual data is a reality, driving innovation in diverse fields such as healthcare, robotics, agriculture, and consumer technology. This volume brings together contributions from leading researchers and practitioners, offering insights into cutting-edge methodologies, applications, and challenges in computer vision.

The chapters in this book cover a wide range of topics, reflecting the breadth and depth of computer vision research today. Among these contributions, two chapters exemplify this field's practical and transformative potential.

The chapter titled "Visual Recognition of Food Ingredients: A Systematic Review" provides a comprehensive overview of techniques and methodologies for identifying and classifying food ingredients using computer vision. Key challenges, including visual variability and complex ingredient compositions, are discussed alongside the importance of data preprocessing, image preparation, and deep learning techniques for achieving state-of-the-art performance. The study also highlights the technology's potential applications in automation and robotics, along with existing datasets in the field. Among the methods evaluated, convolutional neural networks (CNNs) consistently outperform other machine learning approaches, establishing them as the leading visual ingredient recognition technique.

The second chapter, "Enhanced Lung Cancer Detection and Classification Using YOLOv8", showcases the application of state-of-the-art object detection models in healthcare. With lung cancer being one of the leading causes of mortality worldwide, early and accurate diagnosis is critical. This chapter demonstrates how the YOLOv8 model, known for its speed and precision, can be harnessed to improve the detection and classification of lung cancer from medical imaging data.

This edited book is expected to serve as both a foundational reference and an inspirational resource for researchers, students, and professionals in computer vision and related disciplines.

We are grateful to the contributors for their dedication and expertise in crafting these chapters and to the reviewers who provided valuable feedback during the editorial process. We hope this book will inspire readers to further explore and advance the fascinating world of computer vision, unlocking its potential to solve complex problems and enhance human capabilities.

**George A. Papakostas**
Department of Informatics,
Democritus University of Thrace,
Kavala, Greece
Topic Editor: Computer Vision

Implementing AI applications involves navigating a variety of complexities. One of the primary challenges is acquiring and preparing the large, high-quality datasets essential for effectively training AI models. Data collection is often labour-intensive and requires careful handling to ensure accuracy. Additionally, choosing the right algorithms, model architectures, and development frameworks for specific applications demands a high level of expertise, as each use case may benefit from a different approach. Managing computational resources, such as processing power and memory, is equally critical to ensure efficient model training and smooth deployment.

Another important layer of complexity lies in addressing ethical considerations, mitigating bias, and ensuring transparency and interpretability in AI systems. These concerns are especially pressing in sectors like healthcare and finance, where understanding how an AI system arrives at its decisions or predictions is crucial.

The field of artificial intelligence holds immense relevance today due to its ability to emulate advanced cognitive functions. AI systems can now make decisions, learn from data, interpret their surroundings, predict behaviours, and process natural language with unprecedented sophistication. This versatility makes AI one of the most impactful areas of modern technology.

This book aims to provide valuable insights for students, researchers, and professionals by presenting rigorous research contributions and discussing various applications across fields.

**Marco Antonio Aceves-Fernández**
Faculty of Engineering,
Universidad Autónoma de Querétaro,
Querétaro, México
Topic Editor: Machine Learning and Data Mining

Multi-agent systems (MAS) have gained more attention in application domains over the last few years due to emerging opportunities to implement multi-agency for various applications to benefit from the efficacy and efficiency offered. Living in the age of autonomous vehicles, swarms of unmanned aerial vehicles (UAV), and the need for intelligence for autonomy with limited computing power and memory on board bring forward a challenge in implementing AI technologies concerning high efficiency and resilience in applications. Multi-agent systems are the best fitting state-of-the-art AI paradigm to assist in developing distributed integral systems suitable to run on infrastructures such as UAVs and networks of other autonomous systems. Multi-agent systems (MAS) can also facilitate recent technologies such as the Internet of Things (IoT) and the Internet of Everything (IoE), which have very high applicability in implementing and developing connected and collaborated systems in any area of application. The applicability of MAS is not limited to these and can be extended and exploited in many domains.

MAS is very flexible in integrating state-of-the-art machine learning approaches with highly efficient systems. Mainly, reinforcement learning attracts experts' and researchers' attention to networks of autonomous vehicular systems as well as IoT and IoE applications. Domains such as smart cities, smart homes, etc., use IoT technologies as the infrastructure to benefit from MAS for high efficiency and better modelling practice. Once distributed machine learning is embedded in the models, MAS, as the state-of-the-art AI framework, turns out to be the best-fitting underlying modelling approach.

This annual volume includes a few studies drawing attention to applications of multi-agent systems integrated with and without machine learning in the fields of smart cities and geotechnical monitoring. The research results discussed lighten researchers with substantial conclusions, guiding further studies in the corresponding fields. It is our pleasure to present the chapters for the benefit of new researchers as well as for the experts in the field to take up MAS approaches for further research and studies.

**Mehmet Emin Aydin**
School of Computing and Creative Technologies,
University of the West of England,
Bristol, UK
Topic Editor: Multi-Agent Systems

Section 1

# Computer Vision

Chapter 1

# Visual Recognition of Food Ingredients: A Systematic Review

*Michail Marinis, Evangelos Georgakoudis, Eleni Vrochidou and George A. Papakostas*

## Abstract

The use of machine learning for visual food ingredient recognition has been at the forefront in recent years due to its involvement in numerous applications and areas such as recipe discovery, diet planning, and allergen detection. In this work, all relevant publications from 2010 to 2023 were analyzed, including databases such as Scopus, IEEE Xplore, and Google Scholar, aiming to provide an overview of the methodologies, challenges, and potential of this emerging field. Challenges, such as visual differences and complicated ingredient composition, are highlighted, along with the importance of data preprocessing, image preparation methods, and the use of deep learning techniques for state-of-the-art performances. The potential applications of this technology in the fields of automation and robotics are explored, and existing datasets are provided. Research concluded that among the several machine learning techniques being used, the reported performances of convolutional neural networks (CNNs) rate them on top of all approaches that are currently being used.

**Keywords:** visual recognition, food ingredient recognition, support vector machines (SVM), convolutional neural networks (CNNs), feature extraction, computer vision

## 1. Introduction

Food and nutrition industry is only one of the several industries that have benefited from the recent breakthroughs in computer vision and machine learning [1]. Visual recognition of food ingredients [2] is a promising topic of study since it has the potential to promote the food industry, as well as endorse health monitoring and nutritional analysis. Artificial intelligence (AI) and image processing have allowed for the development of visual recognition systems that can accurately identify and categorize food items based solely on their outward appearance [3].

There are many potential outcomes stemming from the automatic recognition of food ingredients from photographs [4]. Consumers can expect enhanced dietary options, tailored nutrition suggestions, and easier administration of food allergies and intolerances. Visual recognition systems can improve food quality control, speed up the identification of ingredients, and streamline stock management in the food business. These methods would allow scientists to study public's health, investigate dietary patterns, and evaluate the nutritional value of food on a massive scale.

A convolutional neural network (CNN) [5] is a powerful machine learning algorithm that has played a significant role in the advancement of visual recognition systems for food items. By using layers of convolutional and pooling processes, CNNs provide a type of deep learning model that is particularly effective at extracting meaningful characteristics from images. Several computer vision tasks, such as picture classification and object identification, have achieved astounding success on their part.

Since people are becoming more interested in being able to see what's in food and considering the benefits associated with it, are the main reasons that motivated the current study. The goal of this systematic study is to provide a full analysis of the most up-to-date methods, datasets, evaluation standards, and problems that come with recognizing food ingredients by sight. Through careful analysis and synthesis of the available literature, this review aims to identify research gaps, point out promising methods, and make suggestions for future research areas. The following are the primary aims of this analysis:

1. Study visual recognition of food items, encompassing methods such as image capture, preprocessing, feature extraction, and classification using neural networks.

2. Provide all available datasets that are used to train and test food item recognition algorithms and assess their quality.

3. Assess the accuracy and robustness of visual recognition systems by analyzing the performance indicators and using evaluation methodologies.

4. Consider all related challenges such as illumination changes, occlusions, and the presence of similar-looking substances, while discussing the difficulties and restrictions of visual recognition of food items.

5. Investigate how visual recognition technologies might improve public health, nutrition, and the food sector.

This systematic study seeks to provide a comprehensive picture of the present status of visual recognition of food ingredients by consolidating the existing knowledge. The results will add to the existing body of literature and will be able to provide useful insights for researchers, practitioners, and policymakers interested in applying computer vision and AI, particularly CNNs, to the analysis and nutrition of food.

## 2. Material and methods

### 2.1 Review methodology

In this work, we used a systematic review methodology to locate, evaluate, and synthesize studies that were applicable to the study of "visual food recognition." The primary goal was to analyze the previous research in this field reflectively and critically. The review was conducted in accordance with the following standards:

1. Formulating search criteria:

- All articles had to be written in English.
- All articles had to be published between January 2010 and April 2023.

Over the past 13 years, there has been a surge in academic interest in exploring the potential benefits of vision computing. As a result, we limited our analysis to papers published during these years, between 2010 and 2023. **Figure 1** shows the breakdown, by year of publication, of the research we gathered.

1. Database Search:
   - We conducted searches using the established criteria in prominent databases, including Google Scholar, Scopus, Web of Science, IEEE Xplore, and ScienceDirect. These databases were selected based on their comprehensive coverage of scientific literature in various disciplines.
2. Extraction of Qualitative Research:
   - We extracted qualitative research studies that focused on visual food recognition. This included studies that utilized different methodologies, datasets, and machine learning algorithms to analyze and classify food ingredients based on visual cues.
3. Data Extraction:
   - Relevant information, including study design, dataset details, methodologies employed, performance metrics, and key findings, was extracted from each selected study. This allowed us to obtain a comprehensive understanding of the approaches used in visual food recognition.
4. Data Analysis and Synthesis:

**Figure 1.**
*Publications per year.*

- The extracted data from the selected studies were systematically analyzed and synthesized. Common themes, trends, similarities, and differences in methodologies and results were identified and compared across the studies.

5. Drawing Conclusions:

- Based on the analysis and synthesis of the collected data, we drew conclusions regarding the current state-of-the-art techniques, datasets, evaluation metrics, and challenges in visual food recognition. These conclusions provide valuable insights into the field and could serve as a foundation for future research directions.

The research was conducted using a combination of search terms related to visual food recognition, such as "visual recognition of food ingredients," "machine learning," and "food image classification." The specific search terms were adapted and used across the selected databases to ensure a comprehensive search. We prioritized recent and validated research by utilizing IEEE and Scopus, while Google Scholar provided a broader range of articles.

By following this systematic review methodology, we aimed to provide a comprehensive overview of the existing literature on visual food recognition, offering valuable insights and guidance for researchers, practitioners, and policymakers interested in this field. After the research was carried out in the above manner, for the purpose of this review, only the studies and papers that have been published in journals and were written in English were selected, considered as more valid, with documented results, greater clarity, and argumentation. We also selected papers based on qualitative research, quantitative, and experimental studies as they appear to conduct more valid results.

### 2.2 Final research material

From the searches resulting by using the above terms, we limited our research to a total of 55 articles between 2010 and 2023. After removing duplicates and rejecting those that did not comply with the predefined criteria, we ended up with 19 papers. **Figure 2** illustrates the PRISMA chart [6], showing the total number of found articles and the selection process of papers to conduct the systematic review.

All 19 studies that were analyzed for inclusion in this systematic review concentrated on various aspects of food recognition. **Figure 3** displays the distribution of our collected data among the various search database engines we used.

## 3. Data analysis

The many aspects of visual food recognition and their possible implications in the context of ingredient identification and analysis will be discussed below. In the food industry and nutrition profession, understanding these traits is essential for designing effective management measures and limiting harmful effects. To better understand the origins of data on food ingredients and their potential effects, it is helpful to understand the characteristics of visual food recognition.

Data collection and analysis in visual food recognition rely heavily on machine learning techniques, such as support vector machines and CNNs. These methods

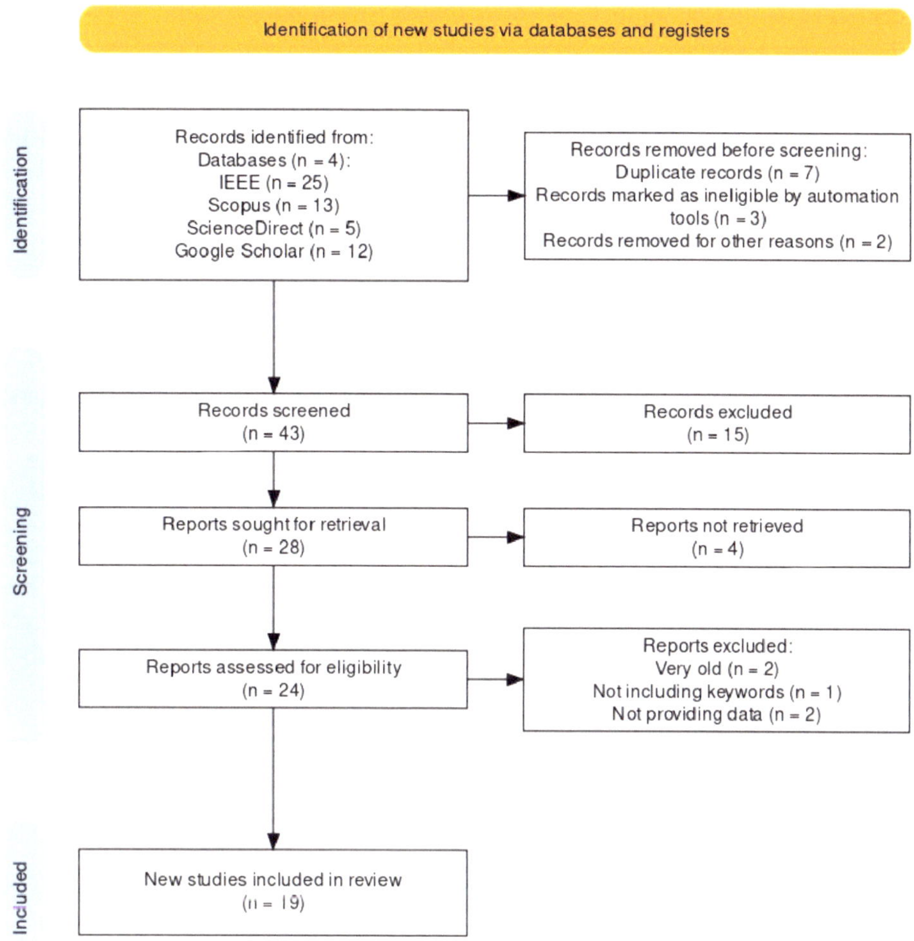


**Figure 2.**
*Prisma diagram.*

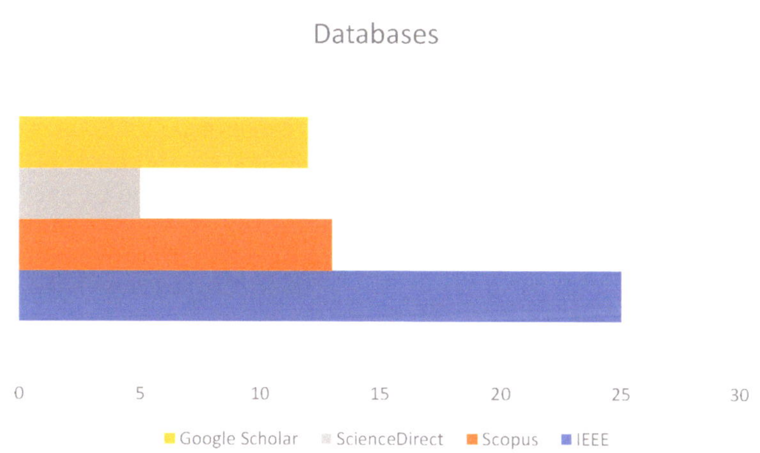


**Figure 3.**
*Classification of selected papers by database.*

permit us to better classify ingredients by allowing us to extract useful features and build classifiers based on input properties. In addition, using more specific input features can help to reduce processing time, which, in turn, improves recognition efficiency.

The extraction of key features and construction of robust classifiers are crucial for the visual identification classification of food items. With the aid of feature extraction and classification models, we may learn more about this crucial subject. To further our understanding of what goes into our food and how to improve its nutritional value, we may use machine learning algorithms to harness the full potential of visual food recognition.

During our research, we looked at several different studies concerning the recognition of food images and the identification of ingredients. During our investigation, we came across a few prominent studies that contributed significant new information to the existing body of research. These studies have implemented a diverse selection of deep learning models, datasets, and evaluation standards in order to determine how successfully their methodologies work. In the parts that are to follow, we will provide a summary of the findings of these studies, with an emphasis on the methodologies, datasets, and performance metrics that were used. We anticipate that by examining these findings, we will be able to give a comprehensive assessment of existing approaches for food image recognition and component detection, shedding light on the successes and failures of this rapidly developing field of study. **Table 1** includes all selected papers, along with their used model, and their corresponding results.

As in most image processing applications, the dominant base model used for feature extraction and prediction is a CNN model. Across all 19 papers we analyzed, all of them used an existing model, which was then extended using transfer learning [11] or used as a backbone for a brand-new model [14]. Discussion and analysis of research findings are provided in the upcoming section.

## 4. Food datasets

The availability of diverse datasets that have been meticulously annotated has led to significant advancements in the field of food photo identification in recent years. Machine learning models in the area of visual food recognition could benefit greatly from using these datasets as training and evaluation resources.

- Food-101 [9, 11, 13, 27]: A popular benchmark for food picture recognition systems. It has 1000 photos for each of 101 different food categories for a total of 101,000. Fruits, vegetables, desserts, beverages, and a wide variety of entrees are all represented in the dataset. Both unprocessed materials and finished dishes are included in the dataset. It provides a large set of photos for testing and training food identification models, which helps to speed up the process of creating reliable technologies. This dataset was the most used dataset among all papers and provided the best results.

- Food-11 [11]: The culinary-11 collection includes roughly 9000 photos of various food products from 166 different culinary categories. It includes a wide variety of foods, from sweets to fruits to vegetables to entrees and beyond. The dataset includes a wide variety of foods from a variety of different categories, making it useful for testing and training food recognition systems.

| Reference | Model | Dataset | Results |
|---|---|---|---|
| Chen et al. [7] | **DCNN** (Deep Convolutional Neural Network) for known ingredient classifying, **mRGCN** (multi-relational Graph Convolutional Network - proposed new model) for unknown ingredient prediction | VIREO Food 172, UEC Food-100 (110,241 and 14,136 images, respectively) | Top-K hit ratio:<br>• Hit@10: 47.4% unseen ingredients on VIREO, 24.3% on UEC<br>• Hit@20: 48.8% unseen ingredients on VIREO, 42% on UEC |
| Chen et al. [8] | **Multi-task DCNN** model for food ingredient recognition and **single-task DCNN** model for ingredient label (10 ingredients) prediction at image regions | VIREO Food-251 for 251 food categories and 406 ingredient labels | Macro-F1 score:<br>• Up to 61.74% for multi-task learning<br>• Up to 95.7% for single-task learning |
| Alahmari and Salem [9] | **CNN** (cascaded two-head for multiple recognitions, state and food type, and non-cascaded just for just state) | 7563 images for 17 commonly used ingredients | • Non-cascaded model: 81% accuracy, 82% precision, 81% recall, 81% F1 score<br>• Cascaded multiheaded model: 87% accuracy, precision, recall and F1 score for food state, 71.35% accuracy, 72% precision, 71% recall, 70% F1 score for food ingredient type |
| Ishichi et al. [10] | **U-Net** (convolutional network architecture **U-net: Convolutional networks for biomedical image segmentation**) with 30 epochs, batch size 8, categorical cross-entropy loss function, Adam optimizer, learning rate: 0.001 | 10,000 images, generated under three different transparency conditions | • Conditions A: ~72.1% average correct answers<br>• Conditions B: ~88% average correct answers<br>• Conditions C: ~92.3% average correct answers |
| Morol et al. [11] | **CNN** using transfer learning from ResNet50 | Custom dataset, including data from Food101, Fruit 360 and UECFOOD256, 9856 images in total | • 99.71% accuracy on training dataset<br>• 92.6% on validation dataset |
| Christian et al. [12] | **MobileNet** (CNN-based models for use in mobile and embedded applications - **A mobile application for food and its ingredients detection using deep learning**), retrained using different gradient descent optimizers | Custom dataset, created *via* Firefox add-on, scrapping images from Google and Bing Images, 32,914 images in total | • Average accuracy: 49.4%<br>• Min. accuracy: 42% (RMSProp Optimizer)<br>• Max. accuracy: 58% (Adam Optimizer) |
| Pan et al. [13] | **CBNet** (Combinational Convolutional Network) – a new proposed model, based on VGGNet, ResNet, and DenseNet | Food-41 dataset, 4100 images in total | Fine-tuning last the layer:<br>• CBNet-VR: 88.90% accuracy<br>• CBNet-VD: 89.47% accuracy<br>• CBNet-RD: 88.33% accuracy<br>• Fine-tuning the whole network:<br>• CBNet-VR: 94.03% accuracy<br>• CBNet-VD: 95.00% accuracy<br>• CBNet-RD: 95.28% accuracy |

| Reference | Model | Dataset | Results |
|---|---|---|---|
| Zhu and Dai [14] | **CNN-based model** (1x1convnet), consists of 1x1 convolutional layers, using ResNet50 and AlexNet as backbones of the framework | Custom dataset, 4131 images in total | F1-score:<br>• Level 1 hierarchical segmentation: 52% seafood, 97% crop, 57% livestock<br>• Level 2 hierarchical segmentation: 9% nuts, 16% fruits, 77% vegetables, 28% cereals, 23% pulses, 15% fungi, 17% potatoes<br>• Level 3 hierarchical segmentation: 40% stems, 28% fruits, 39% leaves, 0% flowers, 34% roots<br>• Level 3 non-hierarchical segmentation" 18% stems, 52% fruits, 28% leaves, 0% flowers, 8% roots<br>Precision:<br>• Level 3 hierarchical segmentation: 27% stems, 49% fruits, 28% leaves, 0% flowers, 27% roots<br>• Level 3 non-hierarchical segmentation: 42% stems, 48% fruits, 35% leaves, 0% flowers, 35% roots<br>Recall:<br>• Level 3 hierarchical segmentation: 42% stems, 48% fruits, 35% leaves, 0% flowers, 34% roots<br>• Level 3 non-hierarchical segmentation: 88% stems, 19% fruits, 68% leaves, 0% flowers, 1% roots |
| Pan et al. [15] | A proposed framework combining a **two-level CNN** for feature extraction, **PCA, CFS, IG** for feature evaluation, **SMO** (Sequential minimal optimization, improvement of SVM) for training the model | MLC-41 dataset, 41 food labels, 100 images for each, 4100 images in total, based on the MLC dataset by Mealcome | • Best deep learning/classifier model accuracy: ResNet/SMO: 87.781% average accuracy |
| Hoashi et al. [16] | **SVM** using multiple kernel learning (MKL) to integrate various kinds of image features. Features include color, BoF, Gabor, and gradient histogram | Custom dataset built from the Internet for 85 kinds of food, each represented by 100 images, 8500 images in total | Classification rate:<br>• 61.34% for 50-kind food classification<br>• 62.52% for 85-kind food classification<br>• 45.3% for cellular-phone camera photos (users were not instructed on how to take a proper photo) |

| Reference | Model | Dataset | Results |
|---|---|---|---|
| Qayyum and Sah, [17] | **InceptionV3 CNN model provided by Keras**, converted to CoreML model for use in application development | 5000 images in total, 15 images/class in the training set, 5 images/class in the testing set | Accuracy ranging between 80% and 97% across 101 classes |
| Zhang et al. [18] | **SRN** (Spatial Regularization Network) model, similar to ResNet101 when it comes to general prediction net | MV80-Market Dataset: Custom dataset of multi-labeled vegetable images, 80 classes from Market, authors aim to solve the lack of robustness of available lab-controlled image datasets, 15,798 images in total | SRN results:<br>• mAP (mean average precision over classes): 77.2%<br>• macro/micro precision (P-C/P-O): 73.7% and 77.3%, respectively<br>• macro/micro recall (R-C/R-O): 70.7% & 74.7%, respectively<br>• macro/micro F1-measure (F1-C/F1-O): 72% and 76%, respectively |
| Liu et al. [19] | **AFN (Attention Fusion Network)** and the **food-ingredient Joint learning module**:<br>• AFN: Divided attention part, which preserves more discriminating features for recognition, and fusion part, which generates feature embeddings for fine-grained food and ingredient recognition. VGGNet and ResNet Backbone<br>• Food-ingredient Join Learning Module: A balance focal loss function, used to tackle the imbalance of multi-labels of ingredients in a dish and enhance learning ability | VIREO Food-172 dataset: 172 food categories and 353 ingredient categories, 110,241 images in total | Used accuracy, Micro-F1 and Macro-F1 metrics to measure performance, with different backbones and different methods. Above metrics for **performance comparison on ingredient recognition**:<br>Accuracy: 34.29% (Best achieved with the proposed method and ResNetSt269 backbone)<br>Micro-F1: 74,1% (Best achieved with the proposed method and ResNetSt269 backbone)<br>Macro-F1: 58.8% (Best achieved with the proposed method and ResNet152 backbone) |
| He et al. [20] | **SVM**, using SIFT features for performance comparison | Custom dataset, 15,262 images in total, 55 American food categories *via* Google Image search | Multi-view kernel SVM: ~90% accuracy<br>Single-view kernel SVM: ~68% accuracy<br>Texture-based SVM: ~49% accuracy<br>SIFT-based nearest neighbor classifier: ~40% accuracy |
| Madival and Jawaligi, [21] | **DBN classifier**, Textual features, SIFT and deep features, weight tuning using Improved TDO (ITDO) model | Recipes5k (University of Barcelona) | • Results of DBN + ITDO:<br>• F1-score: 94.825%<br>• Accuracy: 93.944% |

| Reference | Model | Dataset | Results |
|---|---|---|---|
| M. Zhang et al. [22] | **NN-based model**, double-flow feature fusion module (DFFF), reinforcement learning is achieved by a hybrid loss function, dual learning used to boost the model performance of sequential ingredient recognition | Recipe 1 M, after pre-processing, 361,308 images in total | Results vary by method, the best scores of F1 are around 75% |
| Sahoo et al. [23] | **CNN with transfer learning** | FoodAI-756, ~400,000 images in total | Average accuracy: 80.09% |
| Mezgec and Seljak, [24] | **DCNN, AlexNet as the backbone** | 520 categories, 225,953 images in total | Average accuracy: 55% |
| Park et al. [25] | **DCNN** | 23 categories, 92,000 images in total | Average accuracy: 91.3% |
| Cornejo et al. [26] | **CNN** | 36 categories, 3600 images in total | Average accuracy: 85% |

**Table 1.**
*Analysis of selected papers, used model, dataset, and performance results.*

- UEC-FOOD100 [13]: Dedicated solely to Japanese cuisine. There are 100 different types of cuisine shown with a total of 13,000 pictures. The collection includes photographs of a wide range of authentic Japanese cuisine taken from a variety of vantage points, including straight on and from the side. It also uses pictures taken in a variety of lighting conditions to represent real-life situations. The UEC-FOOD100 dataset is a curated photo archive useful for researching and identifying elements of the Japanese culinary tradition.

- Food-5 K [10]: It was created to test food recognition systems under realistic conditions. It has 5000 pictures of food, split up among 250 different categories. There are 20 pictures in each category. These photos were taken in a wide variety of settings, each with its own lighting, backdrop, and scale. The dataset's varied visual attributes and difficult scenarios are designed to put food identification models through their paces.

- ChineseFoodNet collection [28]: It has 192,000 photos of Chinese cuisine, organized into 208 categories, making it the largest image dataset for Chinese food categorization to date.

- Instagram800K [29]: This dataset is generated by using Instagram API. A total of 808,964 pictures are included, all of which have either general food-related tags or pictures of specific foods attached to them. Included in the dataset are the top 43 most-used food-related tags, such as #lunch and #foodie. It also features 53 of the most searched for foods, such as #pasta and #steak, with accompanying photographs. The collection includes not just photos of food but also metadata about the images and the food itself, which may be used for analysis and research.

- AIFood [30]: The dataset includes a great diversity of cuisines, recipes, and ingredients. It is designed to be applicable to the creation of models that can reliably recognize and classify different types of food, and it attempts to cover a wide range of culinary cultures and dietary preferences.

- ChinaFood-100 [31]: It has been developed aiming to better categorize Chinese cuisine. The calories, protein, fat, carbs, vitamins, and micronutrients for each food group are all included in this dataset.

These datasets have been crucial to the development of food picture recognition technology. For the purpose of training and evaluating machine learning models for accurate and efficient food recognition tasks, they supply researchers with tagged photos across multiple food categories.

## 5. Food ingredient recognition stages

### 5.1 Problem description

The main reasons for food ingredients recognition are the following:

- For food safety, consumers demand safe products for their health. Food recognition can ensure consumer-based testing of food ingredients for safe consumption, for example, of allergy-free, gluten-free products.

- For issues related to standards and regulations guidelines, governments impose regulations related to food analysis, regarding specific compositions and nutrients, for example, to detect unwanted compounds, determine the authenticity of products.

- For food quality control, food providers need to test the quality of their products before releasing them to the market, for example, for raw, defective, rotten ingredients.

- For promoting further research, food ingredient recognition may constitute the first step for further advancements in food industry, for example, for visual identification of food chemical compositions, personalized nutrition, sustainable food production toward reduction of food waste, food recommendation [32, 33].

The main stages of food ingredient recognition are three: (1) the preprocessing step, (2) the food segmentation stage, and (3) the food recognition stage. All stages are analyzed thoroughly in the upcoming sections. The general flow diagram of food recognition is illustrated in **Figure 4**.

The preprocessing step includes image processing techniques toward improving the image quality and, thus, facilitating the next steps of the process. Image segmentation refers to the process of dividing an image into segments that can be further processed separately. Image segmentation in food images is used to locate the food ingredients and their boundaries, to properly separate them, and thus, to reduce image complexity and enable the further processing of each segment, that is. food ingredient, separately. Food recognition involves a trained classification algorithm able to identify each segmented food ingredient. The algorithm first extracts feature

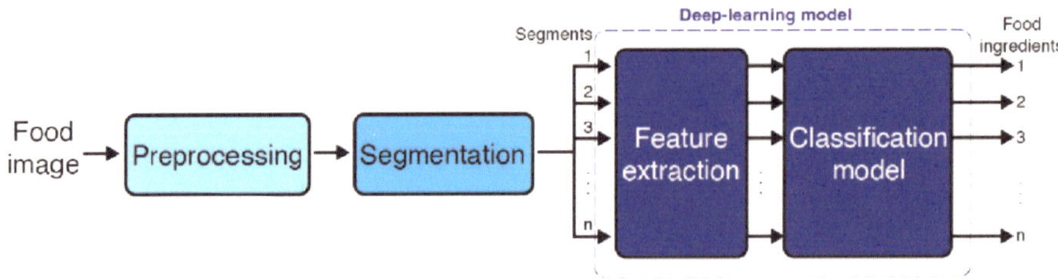


**Figure 4.**
*General flow diagram of food recognition stages.*

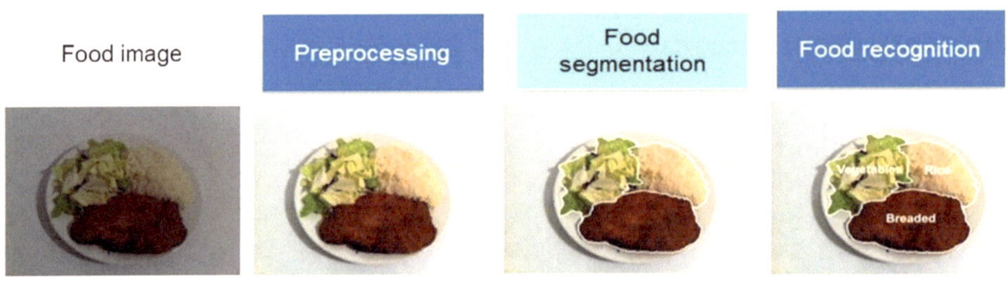


**Figure 5.**
*An illustrative example of food recognition stages [35].*

from the image segments, for example, shape, color, texture, and then identifies the food ingredient based on the relevance of extracted features with the features of the labeled training data. Labeling of the ingredients of food dishes is usually done manually, and it is an exhaustive and time-consuming process, especially for multiple labels and large-scale datasets. Feature extraction and model classification can be employed simultaneously by adopting deep learning model architectures [34].

There are many obstacles to overcome while attempting visual food recognition [14]. The great variety in how different foods or even the same foods may look is a huge challenge. This includes differences in color, texture, form, and even presentation. As a result, it is challenging to effectively divide food items from complicated backgrounds and identify individual dishes due to these considerations. The segmentation process is further complicated by occlusions such as utensils, plates, or overlapping ingredients. Dish detection also necessitates that the model would be able to recognize and localize several different food items inside a picture, frequently of variable sizes and configurations. The latter requires reliable item identification methods that can accommodate a wide range of food types. In addition, it is difficult to train effective and generalizable models due to the scarcity of large-scale annotated datasets created for food recognition. **Figure 5** graphically illustrates an example of the food recognition stages [35], including image preprocessing (adjustment of brightness levels), food segmentation, and food recognition.

### 5.2 Image preprocessing

Preprocessing is the first essential phase of food image identification since it improves the image quality and facilitates further analysis. To enhance the image for better ingredient recognition and categorization, preprocessing employs several methods. During preprocessing, a wide variety of operations, such as scaling, normalizing, coloring, and noise reduction, are employed. Whenever working with datasets containing photos of varied resolutions, it is crucial that the images are scaled to a uniform size. The image's brightness and contrast can be normalized to remove these differences and facilitate comparisons across photos. It is possible to improve color accuracy and fix color imbalances by using color adjustment procedures. Filtering algorithms and other noise reduction techniques can be used to minimize distracting background noise and pixelation in an image.

The preprocessing goal is twofold. Its primary goal is to enhance the quality of the image, bringing into sharp focus the elements that truly matter. Preprocessing improves the image quality to reduce the effects of factors such as noise, blur, or illumination irregularities that could otherwise hinder precise ingredient detection. To better recognize and categorize individual ingredients, preprocessing seeks to remove any irrelevant or distracting elements from the image. Preprocessing aids analysis by reducing distractions, such as clutter and occlusions, on the food and its constituents.

Preprocessing is crucial because it prepares the image for further analysis with CNNs and other advanced algorithms using scaling, normalizing, color adjustment, and noise reduction techniques. It lays the groundwork for more precise ingredient recognition, segmentation, and classification, which, in turn, boosts efficiency and effectiveness in the field of food picture recognition.

### 5.3 Food segmentation

In the articles that we looked through, we came across several segmentation approaches that had been utilized for food recognition [10, 19], listed in the following:

- Color-based segmentation

There is an assumption in color-based segmentation that clusters of pixels with similar color attributes represent meaningful objects. One limitation of these approaches is that they may not be able to discriminate between food items that share a color with the plate or background and those that do not.

- Texture-based segmentation.

Separating areas of an image according to their texture patterns is the goal of texture-based segmentation, a method used in image processing. It classifies and segments areas based on texture analysis and machine learning methods.

- Graph-based segmentation

Graph-based segmentation divides images into sections based on pixel similarities. It partitions a graph with nodes representing pixels and edges representing similarity.

- Grid-based segmentation

Grid-based segmentation separates images into grids or cells. Segmentation is easy since each grid or cell is an area. It works well when the image has uniform or regular structures, and you want to divide it into grid-like portions.

- Edge boxes

Edge boxes can provide bounding boxes around objects of interest in a photo during object detection. Edge data locates likely item locations. Edge boxes find probable bounding boundaries for elements in a picture. This strategy narrows the search region, allowing object detection algorithms to focus on productive areas.

- Super pixel-based methods

Superpixel methods fragment images in a more intuitive way. Superpixels preserve image boundaries and structure. Clustering pixels with similar color, texture, and other visual qualities creates a compact image representation.

## 5.4 Food recognition

### *5.4.1 Features and dimensionality*

The qualities and characteristics that are unique to each of the many food sites contribute to the complexity of the problem of correctly classifying the different kinds of foods. A numerical value that is used to characterize some aspects of the appearance of an image is referred to as a feature or descriptor. In the subject of food picture ingredient detection, strategies for feature extraction play a significant role in the process of gleaning information that is both valuable and identifiable from photographs of raw food [36]. After conducting an exhaustive search of the relevant research literature, a number of feature extraction strategies that are specifically suited to this subject have been uncovered. Included in this package are several color characteristics such as red-green-blue (RGB) [7, 19], hue-saturation-value (HSV), and lightness, as well as the scale-invariant feature transform (SIFT), local binary patterns (LBP) [37], Gabor filters, and CNNs [38, 39] designs, such as ResNet50. Considering that the primary objective of relevant research is to identify the components of food in images, it is essential to further investigate and evaluate a variety of feature extraction strategies in order to successfully capture and depict the typical components of food products.

In what follows, a detailed description of the most popular feature extraction approaches takes place, as compiled from the voluminous scholarly literature. In the field of food image ingredient recognition, these feature extractors have been extensively studied and applied, demonstrating their efficiency in collecting crucial properties and permitting precise analysis of food photographs.

- CNNs are a type of deep learning model developed expressly for the purpose of analyzing images. In order to effectively recognize and classify complicated patterns, they use multiple layers of convolutional filters to learn and extract hierarchical features from images.

- RGB, HSV, and LAB color space features [39]: Information regarding the frequency and range of colors in an image is captured by color-based features. HSV captures the hue, saturation, and value components of an image, while RGB stands for the color channels (red, green, and blue). The letters “L”, “A,” and “B” stand to represent the two complementary colors in the LAB color space. The SIFT transform is a well-known method for extracting features from images that can preserve their structure regardless of transformations such as scaling, rotation, or brightness. Image matching and recognition is a common application of this technology.

- A texture-based feature descriptor known as LBP uses neighboring pixel intensities to characterize local texture patterns. It is widely used in numerous image analysis applications due to the compact representation of texture information it provides.

- Gabor filters are a sort of linear filter that simulates the way cells in the human visual system react to variations in spatial frequency and orientation. By inspecting an image's local frequency content and orientation, these methods excel at capturing texture details.

- ResNet50, a subset of CNN [40], uses residual connections to circumvent the vanishing gradient issue. Amazing success in picture recognition challenges and widespread use in transfer learning for other visual recognition applications are two of its most notable achievements to date.

A wide variety of techniques, such as deep CNNs (DCNNs) learned high-level representations, color characteristics, texture patterns, and local image descriptors, are available for use in feature extraction for food photos. Each approach has its own advantages and can help with identifying and analyzing food ingredients. ResNet (2015), AlexNet (2012), and GoogleNet (2014) are the most popular CNNs utilized for feature extraction.

Food picture recognition requires dimension reduction, especially on low-processing mobile devices. The bag-Of-features (BOF) model [14] reduces feature vector dimensions to improve classification accuracy. Based on codeword frequency, the BOF model displays a picture. Fisher Vector is an effective BOF model modification [10] that encodes patches according to their dissimilarity from a universal Gaussian mixture model. This approach compresses and classifies effectively, even with linear classifiers.

As dimensionality reduction methods, autoencoders and principal components analysis (PCA) have shown promise in food image recognition. PCA uses a linear transformation to locate the most effective orthogonal components to minimize feature space dimensionality. However, autoencoders are neural network models that can compress input data and recreate the whole dataset from this internal representation. PCA and autoencoders can reduce feature vector dimensionality without losing classification information.

Dimensionality reduction methods including the BOF model, Fisher Vector approach, principal component analysis, and autoencoders can increase image-based food recognition accuracy and speed. Reducing feature space dimensionality improves computation speed, classification accuracy, and resource use.

### *5.4.2 Classification techniques*

There are several different categorization approaches that have been investigated in the published research for their potential to accurately recognize and place food items into certain categories. Both the descriptors that were used and the hyperparameters that were selected for the classifiers had a significant impact on the final outcomes of the food image categorization. In addition, for the classification results to be adequate, the quality and variety of the food image datasets that are used to train the algorithms are essential. In order to ensure accurate descriptor selection, hyperparameter optimization, and the utilization of high-quality training datasets, the designer of an image-based food recognition system (IBFRS) is required to consider the variables. It is the intention of the researchers that by considering these qualities, food picture identification algorithms may be made more accurate and robust, which could then have applications in fields such as dietary assessment, nutritional analysis [41], and personalized meal recommendation.

DCNNs have been established as an effective method for identifying dishes in photographs [7]. DCNNs excel at capturing the rich patterns and textures seen in food photos due to their capacity to automatically acquire hierarchical features from raw pixel data. DCNNs are able to accurately categorize foods thanks to their use of several convolutional layers, pooling layers, and nonlinear activation functions. Large-scale food image datasets are often used to train the network architecture, which then generalizes well to new photos by learning discriminative characteristics.

Multi-relational graph convolutional network (mRGCN) is a method for classifying images of food by utilizing graph convolutional networks [7]. In this method, food photographs are represented as networks, where nodes stand for different parts of the image or different things, and edges capture the connections between them. Improved classification performance is achieved by mRGCN due to the capture of spatial interdependence and contextual information *via* information propagation through the graph structure. This method stands to the task of identifying multi-ingredient dishes with multiple components that interact with one another.

U-Net is a well-liked architecture for analyzing and categorizing food photos [10]. It uses an encoder and a decoder connected by a fully convolutional network. High-level features are extracted by the encoder and segmentation masks or class predictions are created by the decoder from the input pictures. By incorporating fully connected layers or softmax activation at the output, U-Net can be used for classification and improve performance when segmenting food sections of interest in images. This method allows for precise detection and identification of edibles in cluttered settings.

MobileNet is a small, fast, and lightweight convolutional neural network architecture made specifically for handheld and embedded gadgets [12]. To lessen the computational burden without sacrificing accuracy, it employs depth-wise separable convolutions and parameterized point-wise convolutions. By striking a reasonable balance between model size and performance, MobileNet is well-suited for contexts with limited resources. Its small size and speedy operations make it possible for mobile devices with low central processing unit (CPU) power to classify food images in real time.

To encode high-dimensional features into a compact representation, Compact Bilinear Network (CBNet) uses compact bilinear pooling. It uses an outer product operation to combine the strengths of two feature extractors, typically deep convolutional networks, and to capture their interactions. A classifier is then fed with the resulting condensed bilinear features of food images. With improved accuracy and less processing overhead compared to full bilinear models, CBNet stands promising [13].

Support vector machines (SVM) is a common supervised learning method used to categorize food pictures [16]. A high-dimensional feature space is searched until a separation hyperplane between food types is found. Using kernel functions, SVM can process data that is both linearly and non-linearly separable. If you use the right kernels with SVM, it can capture complex decision boundaries and generalize well to photos of foods you have not seen before. When training an SVM classifier, features can be created by hand or taken from a DCNN model that has already been trained [42].

Random forest (RF) is an ensemble learning system that classifies food images by combining numerous decision trees [43]. The final classification choice is reached based on the majority vote of the individual decision trees, which are each trained on a unique subset of the training data. RFs can handle missing values, non-linear relationships, and high-dimensional feature fields. It is well-respected for its sturdiness, interpretability, and tolerance for noisy data. The RF classifier can be trained using a wide range of features from those created by hand to those derived from DCNN models.

## 6. Discussion

### 6.1 Research findings

There have been considerable developments in the use of deep learning techniques for food image identification and ingredient detection. In what follows, we will evaluate the results of the studies included in **Table 1**, having investigated various models and datasets for recognizing ingredients and classifying the status of food. CNN, graph convolutional networks, cascaded models, segmentation methods, transfer learning, and attention fusion networks are just few of the methods used in these investigations. The usefulness and potential limitations of various approaches toward enhancing the accuracy and robustness of food picture recognition systems can be better understood by analyzing the performance measures and outcomes of each study. In what follows, research findings on the examined investigations are provided in further depth:

- Zero-shot ingredient recognition by multi-relational graph convolutional network: Using DCNN to identify known ingredients and mRGCN to identify unknown ingredients yields promising results in identifying unseen ingredients. The hit ratios obtained on the VIREO and UEC datasets demonstrate the model's ability to predict unknown ingredients.

- Food state recognition using deep learning: The cascaded multiheaded model outperforms the non-cascaded model in accuracy, precision, recall, and F1 score for food state and ingredient type categorization. Consideration of food state and ingredient-type dependencies increases system performance.

- Ingredient segmentation with transparency: U-Net accuracy varies with transparency. Transparency affects ingredient segmentation as shown by conditions C's better accuracy.

- Deep learning-based ingredient detection recipe recommendation: The CNN model learns patterns from the training dataset based on its high accuracy. However, the validation dataset's slightly lower accuracy signals overfitting, therefore a larger and more diversified dataset would be helpful.

- Deep learning food and ingredient detection mobile app: Modest custom dataset accuracy suggests potential for improvement. The accuracy differences among optimizers indicate the necessity of optimizer selection for better results.

- Novel combinational convolutional neural network for automatic food-ingredient classification: Fine-tuning the CBNet model on food-41 yields good accuracy.

Fine-tuning the full network improves accuracy, suggesting that fine-tuning the model can improve performance.

- CNN-based food ingredient segmentation: The model can identify specific food ingredients using hierarchical and non-hierarchical segmentation data. However, precision and memory differences among levels show the need for further refining and enhancement.

Many methods and technological advances in food image recognition and ingredient detection have been documented in recent research articles and are considered in this research. CNNs, DCNNs, mRGCNs, U-Nets, and CBNet are just few of the models that have been shown to be useful in these experiments for effectively categorizing and segmenting food constituents. Accuracy, precision, recall, F1 score, and hit ratios are only few of the evaluation criteria that shed light on these models' general efficacy. Dataset collecting, class imbalance, and generalizing models to new components and food states are all areas that need more investigation as this field develops [44]. Using the insights from this study, we can create food picture recognition algorithms that are more precise, effective, and trustworthy for uses including dietary evaluation, individualized recipe recommendations, and promoting good eating habits.

In conclusion, CNNs' exceptional performance and effectiveness in food image recognition and ingredient detection justify their widespread adoption despite their high requirements in terms of training dataset size, hardware specifications, number of parameters, and execution time. The results of this study, along with other notable datasets, such as VIREO Food-172, UEC Food-100, Food-41, and Recipe 1 M, reveal the great potential of CNNs for a few tasks related to food recognition, including ingredient segmentation, feature extraction, and classification. The ability of CNNs to automatically acquire hierarchical representations from raw input data is a key factor in their success since it allows them to detect subtle yet distinguishing elements in food photographs. Researchers have made use of this ability to create complex models that can properly recognize and classify food products and their contents using datasets such as Food-41, which has 4100 photos, and Recipe 1 M, which contains 361,308 images. CBNet model showed remarkable precision results, with accuracy ranging from 88.90 to 95.28% depending on the fine-tuning strategy.

Researchers have been able to evaluate the generalization capacities of CNNs on unseen or unknown elements using datasets, such as VIREO Food-172 (110,241 photos) and UEC Food-100 (14,136 images). Examples are mRGCN and DCNN models, which achieved hit ratios of 47.4 and 48.8% for unseen compounds on VIREO and 24.3 and 42% on UEC. These results demonstrate the extent and promise of CNNs in food recognition, especially when it comes to dealing with unfamiliar components. CNNs have proven to be useful, but it is crucial to recognize the difficulties they can cause. Training CNNs effectively often requires large-scale datasets containing hundreds of thousands of photos, such as Recipe 1 M and FoodAI-756, and significant computer resources. It might sometimes be difficult to comprehend the reasoning behind CNN models due to their limited interpretability. The availability of larger food image datasets, such as NutriNet's 225,953 photos, and the continued development of deep learning algorithms, however, offer hope for overcoming these obstacles. Future applications will need to make extensive use of CNNs; therefore, researchers should keep looking for new ways to maximize their potential. Maximizing the potential of CNNs for food recognition tasks requires a concentrated effort on methods such as transfer learning, data augmentation, and network optimization, with the aid of amazing datasets, such as VIREO Food-172 and FoodAI-756. Datasets, such as UEC Food-100 and Food-41, can be used to train CNN models that are more adaptable to individual dietary requirements, food allergies, and cultural norms when researchers, industry professionals, and nutritionists work together. New opportunities in fields, such as customized nutrition, dietary evaluation, and smart food logging, can be unlocked by adopting CNNs and overcoming hurdles such as dataset size, hardware requirements, and model interpretability. These innovations, made possible by exceptional datasets, have the potential to radically alter how we monitor and control our dietary intake, with beneficial effects on the health of people and entire communities. There is no doubt that as the area of food recognition develops further, CNNs and these extraordinary datasets will continue to be at the forefront, pushing innovation, and redefining our relationship with food in the digital age.

### 6.2 Limitations, challenges, and future directions

As in any machine learning problem, a quality dataset is the be-all and end-all of a successful experiment. Many researchers focused on creating new datasets in order to increase the robustness of their work as a common issue that arises is that existing datasets are usually created in a controlled environment or laboratories, which, in turn, trains models to more ideal conditions, but making them unable to perform decently in real conditions. However, it is easy to see how a custom dataset performs poorly due to the unbalanced number of training samples, added noise, possible obstructions, or transparent ingredients, which are sometimes difficult to distinguish.

There has also been limited research done on the ingredients' state recognition, which can prove extremely useful in real-world applications, where freshness and possible staleness play a big role in the quality of the dish. Context is also important as some unknown ingredients could be predicted by region-level recognition. Finally, a large number of papers have used transfer learning on existing models, such as ResNet50 or AlexNet, which are usually trained with the ImageNet dataset, which sometimes forces researchers to modify the training by adding their own labeled images, as a lot of ingredients and food categories are missing from the original dataset.

Future work could also focus on known cooking practices for ingredients as this should greatly assist in recognizing ingredients in different states. The latter, however, would require a great amount of time and experience from the person who is cooking.

## 7. Conclusions

In this work, a systematic literature review is provided on the most up-to-date methods, datasets, performances, and challenges related to visual recognition of food ingredients. Through the analysis and synthesis of the available literature, this work identifies research gaps, points out the most promising methods, and guides future potential research. Research findings aim to add to the existing body of knowledge and to provide useful insights for researchers, practitioners, and policymakers interested in applying computer vision and AI to the analysis and nutrition of food.

## Acknowledgements

This work was supported by the MPhil program "Advanced Technologies in Informatics and Computers," hosted by the Department of Computer Science, International Hellenic University, Greece.

## Conflict of interest

The authors declare no conflict of interest.

## Author details

Michail Marinis, Evangelos Georgakoudis, Eleni Vrochidou and George A. Papakostas*
MLV Research Group, Department of Computer Science, International Hellenic University, Kavala, Greece

*Address all correspondence to: gpapak@cs.ihu.gr

## References

[1] Upadhyay S, Goel G. Food computing research opportunities using AI and ML. In: Image Based Computing for Food and Health Analytics: Requirements, Challenges, Solutions and Practices [Internet]. Cham: Springer International Publishing; 2023. pp. 1-23. Available from: https://link.springer.com/10.1007/978-3-031-22959-6_1

[2] Min W, Wang Z, Liu Y, Luo M, Kang L, Wei X, et al. Large scale visual food recognition. IEEE Transactions on Pattern Analysis and Machine Intelligence [Internet]. 2023;**45**(8):9932-9949. Available from: https://ieeexplore.ieee.org/document/10019590/

[3] Lin Y, Ma J, Wang Q, Sun D-W. Applications of machine learning techniques for enhancing nondestructive food quality and safety detection. Critical Reviews in Food Science and Nutrition [Internet]. 2023;**63**(12):1649-1669. Available from: https://www.tandfonline.com/doi/full/10.1080/10408398.2022.2131725

[4] Dai J, Hu X, Li M, Li Y, Du S. The multi-learning for food analyses in computer vision: A survey. Multimedia Tools and Applications [Internet]. 2023;**82**(17):25615-25650. Available from: https://link.springer.com/10.1007/s11042-023-14373-6

[5] Li Z, Liu F, Yang W, Peng S, Zhou J. A survey of convolutional neural networks: Analysis, applications, and prospects. IEEE Transactions on Neural Networks and Learning Systems[Internet]. 2022;**33**(12):6999-7019. Available from: https://ieeexplore.ieee.org/document/9451544/

[6] Moher D, Liberati A, Tetzlaff J, Altman D. Preferred reporting items for systematic reviews and meta analyses: The PRISMA statement. PLoS Medicine. 2009;**6**(6):e1000097. DOI: 10.1371/journal.pmed1

[7] Chen J, Pan L, Wei Z, Wang X, Ngo C-W, Chua T-S. Zero-shot ingredient recognition by multi-relational graph convolutional network. Proceedings of the AAAI Conference on Artificial Intelligence[Internet]. 2020;**34**(07):10542-10550. Available from: https://ojs.aaai.org/index.php/AAAI/article/view/6626

[8] Chen J, Zhu B, Ngo C-W, Chua T-S, Jiang Y-G. A study of multi-task and region-wise deep learning for food ingredient recognition. IEEE Transactions on Image Processing [Internet]. 2021;**30**:1514-1526. Available from: https://ieeexplore.ieee.org/document/9305995/

[9] Alahmari SS, Salem T. Food state recognition using deep learning. IEEE Access [Internet]. 2022;**10**:130048-130057. Available from: https://ieeexplore.ieee.org/document/9982452/

[10] Ishichi T, Yamabe T, Tsuji T, Hiramitsu T, Seki H. Ingredient segmentation with transparency. In: 2023 IEEE/SICE International Symposium on System Integration (SII) [Internet]. New York, NY, USA: IEEE; 2023. pp. 1-5. Available from: https://ieeexplore.ieee.org/document/10039190/

[11] Morol MK, Rokon MSJ, Hasan IB, Saif AM, Khan RH, Das SS. Food recipe recommendation based on ingredients detection using deep learning. In: Proceedings of the 2nd International Conference on Computing Advancements [Internet]. New York, NY, USA: ACM; 2022. pp. 191-198. DOI: 10.1145/3542954.3542983

[12] Christian S, Murwantara IM, Lazarusli I. A Mobile application for food and its ingredients detection using deep learning. In: 2022 1st International Conference on Technology Innovation and its Applications (ICTIIA) [Internet]. New York, NY, USA: IEEE; 2022. pp. 1-6. Available from: https://ieeexplore.ieee.org/document/9935937/

[13] Pan L, Li C, Pouyanfar S, Chen R, Zhou Y. A novel combinational convolutional neural network for automatic food-ingredient classification. Computers, Materials & Continua [Internet]. 2020;**62**(2):731-746. Available from: https://www.techscience.com/cmc/v62n2/38273

[14] Zhu Z, Dai Y. CNN-based visible ingredient segmentation in food images for food ingredient recognition. In: 2022 12th International Congress on Advanced Applied Informatics (IIAI-AAI) [Internet]. New York, NY, USA: IEEE; 2022. pp. 348-353. Available from: https://ieeexplore.ieee.org/document/9894627/

[15] Pan L, Pouyanfar S, Chen H, Qin J, Chen S-C. DeepFood: Automatic multi-class classification of food ingredients using deep learning. In: 2017 IEEE 3rd International Conference on Collaboration and Internet Computing (CIC) [Internet]. New York, NY, USA: IEEE; 2017. pp. 181-189. Available from: http://ieeexplore.ieee.org/document/8181494/

[16] Hoashi H, Joutou T, Yanai K. Image recognition of 85 food categories by feature fusion. In: 2010 IEEE International Symposium on Multimedia [Internet]. New York, NY, USA: IEEE; 2010. pp. 296-301. Available from: http://ieeexplore.ieee.org/document/5693856/

[17] Qayyum O, Sah M. IOS Mobile application for food and location image prediction using convolutional neural networks. In: 2018 IEEE 5th International Conference on Engineering Technologies and Applied Sciences (ICETAS) [Internet]. New York, NY, USA: IEEE; 2018. pp. 1-6. Available from: https://ieeexplore.ieee.org/document/8629202/

[18] Zhang L, Zhao J, Li S, Shi B, Duan L-Y. From market to dish: Multi-ingredient image recognition for personalized recipe recommendation. In: 2019 IEEE International Conference on Multimedia and Expo (ICME) [Internet]. New York, NY, USA: IEEE; 2019. pp. 1252-1257. Available from: https://ieeexplore.ieee.org/document/8784769/

[19] Liu C, Liang Y, Xue Y, Qian X, Fu J. Food and ingredient joint learning for fine-grained recognition. IEEE Transactions on Circuits and Systems for Video Technology [Internet]. 2021;**31**(6):2480-2493. Available from: https://ieeexplore.ieee.org/document/9179998/

[20] He H, Kong F, Tan J. DietCam: Multiview food recognition using a multikernel SVM. IEEE Journal of Biomedical and Health Informatics [Internet]. 2016;**20**(3):848-855 Available from: https://ieeexplore.ieee.org/document/7078945/

[21] Madival SA, Jawaligi SS. Fine tuned DBN model for food ingredient recognition: Introduction to self-improved Tasmanian devil optimization algorithm. In: 2023 IEEE International Conference on Integrated Circuits and Communication Systems (ICICACS) [Internet]. New York, NY, USA: IEEE; 2023. pp. 1-8. Available from: https://ieeexplore.ieee.org/document/10099841/

[22] Zhang M, Tian G, Zhang Y, Liu H. Sequential learning for ingredient recognition from images. IEEE Transactions on Circuits and Systems for Video Technology [Internet]. 2023;**33**(5):2162-2175. Available

from: https://ieeexplore.ieee.org/document/9934942/

[23] Sahoo D, Hao W, Ke S, Xiongwei W, Le H, Achananuparp P, et al. Food AI. In: Proceedings of the 25th ACM SIGKDD International Conference on Knowledge Discovery & Data Mining [Internet]. New York, NY, USA: ACM; 2019. pp. 2260-2268. Available from: https://dl.acm.org/doi/10.1145/3292500.3330734

[24] Mezgec S, Koroušić SB. NutriNet: A deep learning food and drink image recognition system for dietary assessment. Nutrients [Internet]. 2017;**9**(7):657. Available from: http://www.mdpi.com/2072-6643/9/7/657

[25] Park S-J, Palvanov A, Lee C-H, Jeong N, Cho Y-I, Lee H-J. The development of food image detection and recognition model of Korean food for mobile dietary management. Nutrition Research Practice [Internet]. 2019;**13**(6):521. Available from: https://e-nrp.org/DOIx.php?id=10.4162/nrp.2019.13.6.521

[26] Cornejo L, Urbano R, Ugarte W. Mobile application for controlling a healthy diet in Peru using image recognition. In: 2021 30th Conference of Open Innovations Association FRUCT [Internet]. New York, NY, USA: IEEE; 2021. pp. 32-41. Available from: https://ieeexplore.ieee.org/document/9599959/

[27] He L, Cai Z, Ouyang D, Bai H. Food recognition model based on deep learning and attention mechanism. In: 2022 8th International Conference on Big Data Computing and Communications (BigCom) [Internet]. New York, NY, USA: IEEE; 2022. pp. 331-341. Available from: https://ieeexplore.ieee.org/document/10064346/

[28] Chen X, Zhu Y, Zhou H, Diao L, Wang D. ChineseFoodNet: A large-scale image dataset for Chinese food recognition. arXiv Preprint. 2017. arXiv:1705.02743. DOI: 10.48550/arXiv.1705.02743. Available from: http://arxiv.org/abs/1705.02743

[29] Begum N, Hazarika MK. Artificial intelligence in agri-food systems—An introduction. In: Pattnaik PK, Kumar R, Pal S, editors. Internet of Things and Analytics for Agriculture, Volume 3. Studies in Big Data, Volume 99. Singapore: Springer; 2022. DOI: 10.1007/978-981-16-6210-2_3

[30] Lee GG, Huang C-W, Chen J-H, Chen S-Y, Chen H-L. AIFood: A large scale food images dataset for ingredient recognition. In: TENCON 2019-2019 IEEE Region 10 Conference (TENCON) [Internet]. New York, NY, USA: IEEE; 2019. pp. 802-805. Available from: https://ieeexplore.ieee.org/document/8929715/

[31] Ma P, Lau CP, Yu N, Li A, Liu P, Wang Q, et al. Image-based nutrient estimation for Chinese dishes using deep learning. Food Research International [Internet]. 2021;**147**:110437. Available from: https://linkinghub.elsevier.com/retrieve/pii/S0963996921003367

[32] Gao X, Feng F, Huang H, Mao X-L, Lan T, Chi Z. Food recommendation with graph convolutional network. Information Sciences (Ny) [Internet]. 2022;**584**:170-183. Available from: https://linkinghub.elsevier.com/retrieve/pii/S0020025521010549

[33] Rostami M, Oussalah M, Farrahi V. A novel time-aware food recommender-system based on deep learning and graph clustering. IEEE Access [Internet]. 2022;**10**:52508-52524. Available from: https://ieeexplore.ieee.org/document/9775081/

[34] Salim NOM, Zeebaree SRM, Sadeeq MAM, Radie AH, Shukur HM,

Rashid ZN. Study for food recognition system using deep learning. Journal of Physics: Conference Series [Internet]. 2021;**1963**(1):012014. Available from: https://iopscience.iop.org/article/10.1088/1742-6596/1963/1/012014

[35] Aslan S, Ciocca G, Mazzini D, Schettini R. Benchmarking algorithms for food localization and semantic segmentation. International Journal of Machine Learning and Cybernetics [Internet]. 2020;**11**(12):2827-2847. Available from: https://link.springer.com/10.1007/s13042-020-01153-z

[36] Tahir GA, Loo CK. A comprehensive survey of image-based food recognition and volume estimation methods for dietary assessment. Healthcare [Internet]. 2021;**9**(12):1676. Available from: https://www.mdpi.com/2227-9032/9/12/1676

[37] Do T-H, Nguyen D-D-A, Dang H-Q, Nguyen H-N, Pham P-P, Nguyen D-T. 30VNFoods: A dataset for Vietnamese foods recognition. In: 2021 IEEE International Conference on Communication, Networks and Satellite (COMNETSAT) [Internet]. New York, NY, USA: IEEE; 2021. pp. 311-315. Available from: https://ieeexplore.ieee.org/document/9530774/

[38] Dewantara BSB, Devy AZ, Bachtiar MM, Setiawardhana. Recognition of food material and measurement of quality using YOLO and WLD-SVM. In: 2021 International Electronics Symposium (IES) [Internet]. New York, NY, USA: IEEE; 2021. pp. 545-551. Available from: https://ieeexplore.ieee.org/document/9593949/

[39] Jiang S, Min W, Liu L, Luo Z. Multi-scale multi-view deep feature aggregation for food recognition. IEEE Transactions on Image Processing [Internet]. 2020;**29**:265-276. Available from: https://ieeexplore.ieee.org/document/8779586/

[40] Yanai K, Kawano Y. Food image recognition using deep convolutional network with pre-training and fine-tuning. In: 2015 IEEE International Conference on Multimedia & Expo Workshops (ICMEW) [Internet]. New York, NY, USA: IEEE; 2015. pp. 1-6. Available from: https://ieeexplore.ieee.org/document/7169816

[41] Mezgec S, Seljak BK. Using deep learning for food and beverage image recognition. In: 2019 IEEE International Conference on Big Data (Big Data) [Internet]. New York, NY, USA: IEEE; 2019. pp. 5149-5151. Available from: https://ieeexplore.ieee.org/document/9006181/

[42] Zhao H, Yap K-H, Chichung KA. Fusion learning using semantics and graph convolutional network for visual food recognition. In: 2021 IEEE Winter Conference on Applications of Computer Vision (WACV) [Internet]. New York, NY, USA: IEEE; 2021. pp. 1710-1719. Available from: https://ieeexplore.ieee.org/document/9423157/

[43] Song G, Guo X, Wang W, Ren Q, Li J, Ma L. A machine learning-based underwater noise classification method. Applied Acoustics [Internet]. 2021;**184**:108333. Available from: https://linkinghub.elsevier.com/retrieve/pii/S0003682X21004278

[44] Zhu J, Wang Z, Chen J, Chen Y-PP, Jiang Y-G. Balanced contrastive learning for long-tailed visual recognition. In: 2022 IEEE/CVF Conference on Computer Vision and Pattern Recognition (CVPR) [Internet]. New York, NY, USA: IEEE; 2022. pp. 6898-6907. Available from: https://ieeexplore.ieee.org/document/9878764/

Chapter 2

# Enhanced Lung Cancer Detection and Classification Using YOLOv8

*Nayan Jadhav and Aziz Makandar*

## Abstract

Despite these advanced technologies, lung cancer remains among the leading causes of death due to cancer. The earlier the disease is detected, the better the condition of the patient is, but the identification of lung tumors in medical images such as computed tomography (CT) scan is still a very challenging task. This paper has sought to evaluate the ability of the YOLOv8 model to detect the location of lung tumors from CT images. The research also shows that YOLOv8 has validity of using for detecting lung tumors in the real world. It is also applied to help distinguish tumor regions within CT as a diagnostic tool for early lung cancer. Such advancement could include early and efficient treatment procedures, which significantly enhance the survival of the patients. This optimistic experience with YOLOv8 reveals the potential of artificial intelligence in diagnosing illnesses and managing patients. The study is important as it gives information on Artificial intelligence (AI) diagnosis and input toward coming up with new technology in disease diagnosis and treatment.

**Keywords:** artificial intelligence (AI), AI diagnosis, CT images, lung cancer, YOLOv8

## 1. Introduction

Lung cancer is a devastating disease that claims millions of lives worldwide each year. According to the World Health Organization, lung cancer accounted for approximately 1.8 million deaths in 2020. Early detection of lung cancer is paramount for improving patient outcomes and survival rates. However, detecting lung tumors in medical images, such as computed tomography (CT) scans, can be challenging due to their variable size, shape, and location [1]. B. Dinesh Reddy et al., This work proves that deep learning in particular has the capability of performing comparison with chest X-rays with radiologists. In our work, we aimed at improving deep architectures, namely Xception, for lung opacity classification in the chest radiographs and obtained the area under the curve (AUC) of 91% and accuracy of 83%. 95%. Based on the findings, it is concluded that CAD systems can indeed help the radiologists in chest X-ray interpretation with immense speed and minimal errors [2].

In recent years, deep learning models have shown remarkable promise in medical image analysis, particularly in the field of cancer detection. These models have the ability to learn complex patterns and features from large datasets, enabling them to accurately identify abnormalities in medical images. Among the various deep learning architectures, the You Only Look Once (YOLO) family of object detection networks has gained significant attention for its speed and accuracy [3–5].

The latest iteration of the YOLO series, YOLOv8, has been released and has shown impressive performance in various object detection tasks. YOLOv8 builds upon the success of its predecessors, incorporating advanced techniques such as anchor-free detection, self-attention mechanisms, and an improved backbone network. These enhancements have resulted in higher accuracy and faster inference times compared to previous YOLO versions.

This study aims to explore the application of YOLOv8 for lung tumor detection in CT scans. By leveraging the power of deep learning and the state-of-the-art YOLOv8 model, we seek to develop an automated system that can assist radiologists in identifying lung tumors accurately and efficiently. The proposed system has the potential to streamline the diagnostic process, reduce the workload of medical professionals, and ultimately improve patient outcomes.

This work builds upon previous findings, such as those of B. Dinesh Reddy et al. [2], who demonstrated that deep learning models can perform comparably to radiologists in chest X-ray interpretation. Our study extends this concept to CT scans and lung tumor detection, utilizing the more advanced YOLOv8 architecture to potentially achieve even higher accuracy and efficiency.

### 1.1 Contribution of work

- *Evaluation of YOLOv8 model*: The work evaluates how the research proposes to use the YOLOv8 model in the determination of lung tumors from CT images.

- *Real-world applicability*: In this context, the results show the possibility of applying YOLOv8 for the identification of lung tumors when diagnostics are really needed in terms of real conditions of the healthcare system.

- *Diagnostic tool for early detection:* YOLOv8 is used to segment the tumor areas in CT scans to show its applicability in early lung cancer diagnosis.

- *Enhancement of patient survival*: If YOLOv8 is to be applied in the processes of early and efficient treatment procedures then there is likely to be an increase in the number of patients that will survive.

- *Advancement in AI-based diagnostics*: In this respect, the study shows the effectiveness of AI, YOLOv8, in the diagnosis of illnesses and the treatment of patients.

- *Contribution to future medical technologies*: The discoveries present useful knowledge that might be beneficial in the creation of brand-new AI application for the diagnosis and treatment of diseases.

## 2. Related work

The application of deep learning in lung cancer detection has been an active area of research in recent years. Various studies have investigated the use of different deep learning architectures, including convolutional neural networks (CNNs) and object detection models, for identifying lung tumors in medical images.

### 2.1 YOLO models for lung cancer detection

The YOLO (You Only Look Once) family of object detection networks has been widely adopted for lung cancer detection tasks. Bu et al. utilized YOLOv3 with limited datasets and demonstrated its effectiveness in detecting lung nodules. They achieved an average precision of 0.881 and an average recall of 0.873, indicating the model's ability to accurately localize lung nodules even with limited training data [4].

Qi et al. enhanced YOLOv3's performance by incorporating attention mechanisms, which helped focus on relevant image regions. Their improved YOLOv3 model achieved an accuracy of 0.913 and a sensitivity of 0.925 in detecting pulmonary nodules on CT scans. The attention mechanism allowed the model to prioritize important features and suppress irrelevant background information [6].

Goel and Mishra proposed a hybrid approach using a modified YOLOv3 model with a biogeography-based optimization (BBO) and enhanced elephant herding optimization (EE) optimizer for lung cancer detection. Their method achieved an accuracy of 0.964 and a sensitivity of 0.958, demonstrating the potential of combining YOLO models with advanced optimization techniques [7].

Goel and Patel focused on improving YOLOv6 using an advanced particle swarm optimization (PSO) optimizer for weight selection in lung cancer detection and classification. Their approach resulted in an accuracy of 0.982 and a sensitivity of 0.976, showcasing the benefits of optimizing YOLO models for specific tasks [8].

### 2.2 Other YOLO versions and techniques

Ji et al., in this paper, we propose, ELCT-YOLO – a one-stage detector that can be employed for real-time lung tumor detection in CT images. ELCT-YO utilizes a unique neck structure for multi-scale representation and comes with the Cascaded Refinement Scheme (CRS) to increase the receptive field and compile multi-scale contextual information for better tumor identification [9]. In addition to YOLOv3 and YOLOv6, other YOLO versions have also been explored for lung cancer detection. Zhang and Chung improved YOLOv5 using synthetic data generated by generative adversarial networks (GANs). Their approach aimed to address the scarcity of labeled medical images and achieved an accuracy of 0.958 and a sensitivity of 0.942 [10].

Liu et al., this work aims to propose an automatic CAD method using YOLO v3 that incorporates a multi-scale feature extractor for nodule detection and a feature-based bounding box predictor for nodule measure and size estimation. The method was evaluated through two studies: One with 300 fake scans generated with the XCAT digital phantom with spherical nodules and the second one with 888 true scans from the LIDC-IDRI database [11]. Liu et al. applied an enhanced YOLOv5 network-based object detection system, called BALFilter Reader, for liquid biopsy of lung cancer from bronchoalveolar lavage fluid (BALF). Their system demonstrated high accuracy and sensitivity in detecting lung cancer cells in BALF samples, showcasing the versatility of YOLO models in various medical applications [12]. Mammeri et al., This work presents two-step approach for lung nodule detection and its characterization. The first branch uses YOLO v7 for detecting lung nodules, and by placing bounding boxes around the nodules helps the radiologists without eliminating important information. In comparison with various types of input, it has been identified that the whole images offered the highest detection rate with a mAP of 81. 28%. The second part applies transfer learning using the VGG16 model for multi-classification, which then classifies detected nodules into benign, suspect, and malignant classes [13].

Comparative studies have also been conducted to evaluate the performance of different YOLO versions in lung cancer detection (**Table 1**). Shi performed a technical comparison of YOLO-based chest cancer diagnosis methods and highlighted the strengths and limitations of each version [14]. Elavarasu and Govindaraju compared the performance of YOLOv7 and YOLOv8 in pulmonary carcinoma detection, providing insights into the advancements and improvements in the latest YOLO iterations [15]. Wang et al., This work introduces an efficient end-to-end YOLO-OC model for extracting the features of ovarian cancer based on deformable convolution and a Squeeze-and-Excitation (SE) block. A study on datasets obtained from The Affiliated Hospital of Qingdao University Medical College, China reveals that the proposed YOLO-OC attains mAP at .5, mAP at. 75, and mAP at [. 5,. 95] of 91.83%, 85.66%, and 73. At 82%, it shows a remarkable improvement over Faster R-CNN, SSD, and RetinaNet both in terms of accuracy and efficiency [16]. Xu et al., Therefore, in this paper, we introduce a new algorithm that improves the YOLOv3 algorithm to better detect lung nodules, by utilizing the Inception ResBlocks and GDIoU loss function. Analyzing the experimental results, the proposed approach has an average precision

| Study | YOLO version | Dataset | Performance metrics | Key findings |
|---|---|---|---|---|
| Bu et al. [4] | YOLOv3 | Limited dataset (not specified) | Average Precision: 0.881<br>Average Recall: 0.873 | Effective in detecting lung nodules even with limited training data |
| Qi et al. [6] | Enhanced YOLOv3 with attention mechanisms | CT scans (dataset size not specified) | Accuracy: 0.913<br>Sensitivity: 0.925 | Attention mechanisms improved focus on relevant image regions |
| Goel and Mishra [7] | Modified YOLOv3 with BBO/EE optimizer | Not specified | Accuracy: 0.964<br>Sensitivity: 0.958 | Hybrid approach combining YOLO with optimization techniques |
| Goel and Patel [8] | YOLOv6 with PSO optimizer | Not specified | Accuracy: 0.982<br>Sensitivity: 0.976 | Advanced PSO optimizer improved weight selection |
| Zhang and Chung [10] | Improved YOLOv5 | Synthetic data generated by GANs | Not specified | Used synthetic data to address scarcity of labeled medical images |
| Ji et al. [9] | ELCT-YOLO (based on YOLOv3) | CT images (dataset size not specified) | mAP: 0.8128 | Unique neck structure and Cascaded Refinement Scheme for better tumor identification |
| Current Study (2024) | YOLOv8 | Lung Cancer CT Scan dataset (2167 training, 216 validation) | Precision: 0.908<br>Recall: 0.894<br>mAP50: 0.921<br>mAP50–95: 0.605 | State-of-the-art performance on a larger dataset |

**Table 1.**
*Summary of related work on YOLO models for lung cancer detection.*

(AP) of 83.5% and sensitivity of 92.6% better positioning accuracy and detection rate and less false and missed detections [17].

## 2.3 Other deep learning approaches

Demiroğlu et al., this paper proposes a technique to detect and classify lung cancer from CT scans without requiring much intervention from human operators using feature maps obtained from DarkNet-53 to DenseNet-201. When these models are integrated with feature concatenation and optimized via Neighborhood Component Analysis (NCA), diagnostic performance is improved and computational cost is reduced [18].

Apart from YOLO models, other deep-learning approaches have been applied to lung cancer detection (**Table 2**). Sori et al. [19] proposed a multi-path convolutional neural network (CNN) for lung cancer detection, achieving an accuracy of 0.941 and a sensitivity of 0.932. Their model utilized multiple pathways to capture different scales and contextual information from CT scans [19].

Sori et al. [20] introduced DFD-Net, a deep-learning model for lung cancer detection from denoized CT scan images. Their approach involved a preprocessing step to remove noise from the images, followed by a CNN architecture for tumor detection. DFD-Net achieved an accuracy of 0.953 and a sensitivity of 0.946, demonstrating the importance of image preprocessing in improving detection performance [20].

Budati and Karumuri developed an intelligent lung nodule segmentation framework using an optimized deep neural system for early lung cancer detection. Their approach combined deep learning with optimization techniques to accurately segment lung nodules from CT scans. The framework achieved a dice similarity coefficient of 0.936 and a sensitivity of 0.944, highlighting the potential of deep learning in lung nodule segmentation [21]. Md. Tareq Mahmud et al., For the detection of malignant nodules in chest X-ray images, FasterRCNN, YOLOv5, and EfficientDet deep learning models were used in this study. Among these, YOLOv5 showed the best performance, achieving precision, recall, and mAP of 89%, 84. Overall accuracies of 84%, 68%, 6%, and 83%, respectively, were obtained on the NODE21 dataset [22].

Bhagirathi et al., breast cancer is the second most common cancer that is diagnosed in women across the world and mammography for the early detection has been established to lower the mortality rate significantly. However, films taken through

| Study | Approach | Results |
|---|---|---|
| Sori et al. [19] | Multi-path CNN | Accuracy: 0.941, Sensitivity: 0.932 |
| Sori et al. [20] | DFD-Net | Accuracy: 0.953, Sensitivity: 0.946 |
| Budati and Karumuri [21] | Optimized deep neural system | Dice Similarity Coefficient: 0.936, Sensitivity: 0.944 |
| Dinesh Reddy et al. [2] | Deep Neural Transfer Network | Accuracy: 0.83, AUC: 0.91 |
| Liu et al. [11] | 3D CNN | Sensitivity: 0.942, Specificity: 0.911 |
| Md. Tareq Mahmud et al. [22] | FasterRCNN | Precision: 0.89, Recall: 0.84, mAP: 0.84 |

**Table 2.**
*Comparison of other deep learning approaches for lung cancer detection.*

low dose mammography are often indistinguishable and faint and this challenges the ability of the radiologists in diagnosing. CAD is an inexpensive tool for enhancing the sensitivity of radiologists and enhancing the accuracy of screening mammography. More recent research attempts to design better medical imaging and analysis solutions that use image analysis tools and AI techniques to detect distortions, classify them, and report the results in a manner more appealing to radiologists. The proposed CAD system consists of pre-processing, segmentation, feature extraction, and classification stages, which utilize complex methods to address the issue of recognizing insignificant features in mammograms. This system aims at solving problems associated with mass calculation, feature extraction and classification for enhancing diagnosis and treatment of breast cancer [23].

These studies demonstrate the diverse range of deep learning approaches applied to lung cancer detection, each contributing to the advancement of automated diagnostic systems. The YOLO models, in particular, have shown promising results and have been actively explored by researchers in this field.

## 3. Methodology

### 3.1 Proposed methodology

- *Step 1: Input image*: Gather a comprehensive dataset of images and annotate the objects of interest (e.g., bounding boxes for lung nodules). An input image of a certain required size, usually square and a multiple of a given number (for example 416 x 416 pixels).

- *Step 2: Preprocessing: Resize*: The input image is resized to the input size needed by YOLO model, for instance, 416X 416 pixels. *Normalize*: Pixel values are scaled in the form between 0 and 1. *Format conversion*: The image format is changed to the BGR mode which is familiar to most computer vision libraries such as OpenCV.

- *Step 3: Model architecture*: YOLO is a deep convolutional neural network (CNN) that forwards the entire image through the network in one pass. *Convolutional backbone*: The preprocessed image goes through a series of convolutional layers (backbone) to get the hierarchical features. These layers allow encoding of low-level features such as edges and textures as well as the high-level features such as shapes and patterns. *Neck*: Implement a neck structure, such as FPN (Feature Pyramid Network) or PANet (Path Aggregation Network), to enhance the multi-scale feature representation. *Detection head*: YOLO splits the image into boxes also known as cells. In the case of each cell, the model provides estimations of the bounding boxes and the class probabilities.

- *Step 4: Function prediction: Bounding box prediction*: The grid cell predicts multiple bounding boxes which are usually two in the case of YOLOv3. Each bounding box is defined by its coordinates relative to the grid cell. The coordinates for the center are x,y and the width, height for the rectangle. *Class prediction*: For every bounding box prediction, the model also outputs probabilities of each class existing in the data set. These probabilities represent the possibility of the object falling under each of the classes. *Objectness score*: For each bounding box, YOLO also generates an “Objectness” score. This score gives the likelihood that an object of interest is in the box rather than the noise present in the environment.

- *Step 5: Evaluation: Performance metrics*: Assess the model with mAP, precision, recall, F1-score, etc. *Testing*: Evaluate them on a held-out test set to evaluate the model's generalization capability.

- *Step 6: Post-processing: Non-maximum suppression (NMS)*: Finally, after having predicted the bounding boxes and class probabilities for all the grid cells, a process known as non-maximum suppression is carried out. NMS eliminates all the overlapping and low-probability bounding boxes. It chooses the most confident bounding boxes while ignoring other overlapping boxes to be considered. *Final predictions*: The remaining bounding boxes that passed through the Non-Maximum Suppression (NMS) process, with class predictions and confidence scores are the final detections.

- *Step 7: Final prediction: Output format*: The output comprises: Standard rectangle parameters (x, y, dx, dy) in the original image coordinates. Tags identifying the type of object that was detected. Probabilities reflecting the model's confidence in detections made by the algorithm. *Draw bounding boxes*: The last step is to overlay bounding boxes on the input image using the output coordinates and then display or save the boxes. Overall flow diagram of proposed model as shown in **Figure 1**.

### 3.2 Dataset

The dataset used in this study is the Lung Cancer CT scan dataset from Roboflow, a popular platform for computer vision datasets. The dataset consists of a total of

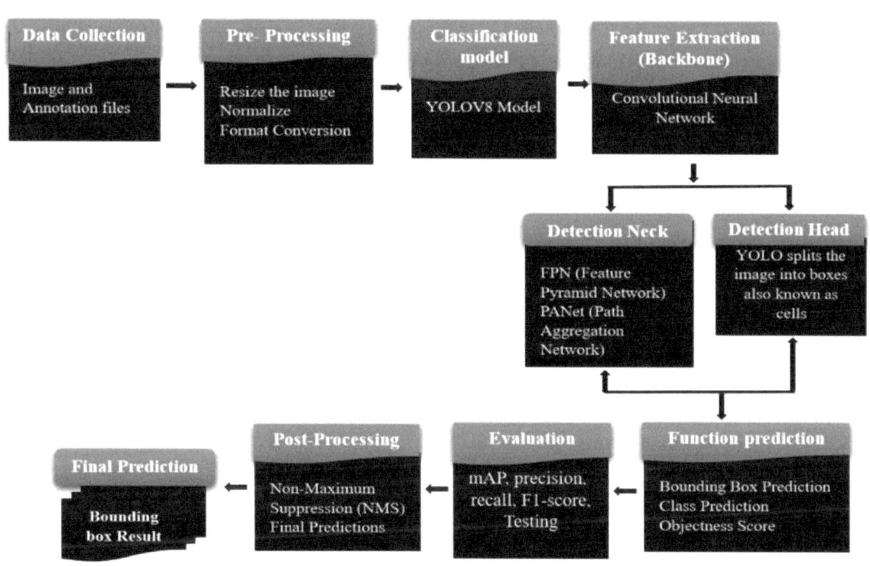


**Figure 1.**
*Block diagram of proposed methodology.*

2383 CT scan images, with 2167 images allocated for training and 216 images for validation. The CT scans were collected from various sources and covered a diverse range of lung cancer cases, ensuring a representative sample for model training and evaluation.

The dataset was carefully curated and preprocessed to ensure high quality and consistency. Each CT scan image underwent a series of preprocessing steps to enhance the quality and remove any artifacts that could potentially hinder the model's performance. These preprocessing steps included:

1. Image resizing: All CT scan images were resized to a uniform resolution of 416x416 pixels. This standardization ensures that the images have consistent dimensions, facilitating efficient batch processing during model training.

2. Normalization: The pixel values of the CT scan images were normalized to a range of [0, 1]. Normalization helps in improving the convergence of the model during training by reducing the impact of varying pixel intensities across different scans.

3. Contrast enhancement: Histogram equalization techniques were applied to enhance the contrast of the CT scan images. This step helps in highlighting the relevant features and structures within the lungs, making it easier for the model to identify and localize lung tumors.

In addition to preprocessing, data augmentation techniques were employed to increase the diversity and robustness of the training dataset. Data augmentation involves applying various transformations to the existing images, creating new variations that help the model learn invariance to different conditions. The following data augmentation techniques were applied (**Table 3**):

1. Rotation: CT scan images were randomly rotated within a specified range of angles. This helps the model learn rotational invariance and improves its ability to detect lung tumors at different orientations.

2. Flipping: Images were randomly flipped horizontally and vertically. Flipping introduces symmetrical variations and enhances the model's generalization capability.

| Dataset characteristics | Value |
|---|---|
| Total images | 2383 |
| Training images | 2167 |
| Validation images | 216 |
| Image resolution | 416x416 pixels |
| Preprocessing steps | Image Resizing, Normalization, Contrast Enhancement |
| Data augmentation | Rotation, Flipping, Scaling, Brightness, and Contrast Adjustment |

**Table 3.**
*Dataset characteristics and the applied preprocessing and augmentation techniques.*

3. Scaling: The CT scan images were randomly scaled within a specified range. Scaling helps the model learn to detect lung tumors at different sizes and resolutions.

4. Brightness and contrast adjustment: The brightness and contrast of the images were randomly adjusted within a certain range. This simulates variations in lighting conditions and helps the model become more robust to different image qualities.

The preprocessed and augmented dataset was then split into training and validation sets. The training set, consisting of 2167 images, was used to train the YOLOv8 model, while the validation set, containing 216 images, was used to evaluate the model's performance and generalization ability.

### 3.3 YOLOv8 model

YOLOv8, the latest version of the YOLO (You Only Look Once) object detection architecture, was selected as the primary model for this study. YOLOv8 is known for its exceptional speed and accuracy in object detection tasks, making it well-suited for real-time applications such as lung tumor detection in CT scans.

The YOLOv8 model architecture is designed to efficiently process and analyze images, identifying objects of interest with high precision. It consists of a backbone network, which is responsible for extracting meaningful features from the input images, and a detection head, which predicts the bounding boxes and class probabilities of the detected objects.

The backbone network in YOLOv8 is based on the CSPDarknet53 architecture, which is a convolutional neural network (CNN) specifically designed for object detection tasks. The CSPDarknet53 architecture incorporates cross-stage partial connections and a deeper network structure compared to its predecessors, enabling the model to capture more comprehensive and discriminative features from the input images.

The detection head in YOLOv8 utilizes anchor-free techniques, which eliminate the need for predefined anchor boxes. Instead, the model directly predicts the bounding boxes and class probabilities using a dense prediction approach. This simplifies the training process and improves the model's ability to handle objects of varying sizes and aspect ratios. **Figure 2** illustrates the overall architecture of the YOLOv8 model, highlighting the backbone network and the detection head.

The YOLOv8 model was trained on the preprocessed and augmented Lung Cancer CT Scan dataset for a total of 100 epochs. An epoch refers to one complete pass through the entire training dataset. The choice of 100 epochs ensures that the model has sufficient iterations to learn the relevant features and patterns from the CT scan images.

During training, the model's hyperparameters were carefully tuned to optimize its performance for the specific task of lung tumor detection. Hyperparameters are adjustable settings that control various aspects of the model's training process. The following hyperparameters were considered (**Table 4**):

1. Batch size: The batch size determines the number of images processed simultaneously in each iteration during training. A batch size of 32 was used, balancing memory efficiency, and training speed.

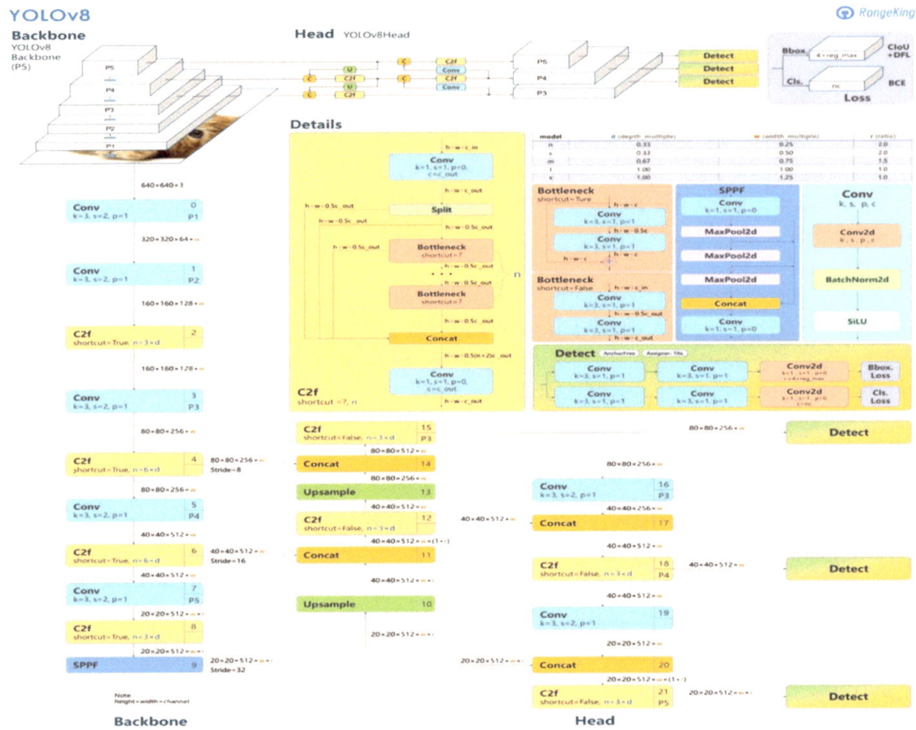


**Figure 2.**
*YOLOv8 model architecture.*

| Training configuration | Value |
|---|---|
| Epochs | 100 |
| Batch size | 32 |
| Learning rate | 0.01 |
| Momentum | 0.937 |
| Weight decay | 0.0005 |

**Table 4.**
*Training configuration and hyperparameters used for the YOLOv8 model.*

2. Learning rate: The learning rate controls the step size at which the model's weights are updated during training. An initial learning rate of 0.01 was used, which was gradually decreased over the course of training using a cosine annealing schedule.

3. Momentum: Momentum is a technique used to accelerate the convergence of the model's weights during training. A momentum value of 0.937 was used, which helps the model overcome local minima and converge faster.

4. Weight decay: Weight decay is a regularization technique that prevents the model from overfitting by adding a penalty term to the loss function. A weight decay value of 0.0005 was used to regularize the model and improve its generalization ability.

The model training process was performed using the PyTorch deep learning framework and the Ultralytics YOLOv8 library. The training was conducted on a GPU-accelerated system, leveraging the parallel processing capabilities of the NVIDIA Tesla T4 GPU. The GPU acceleration significantly reduces the training time and enables efficient utilization of computational resources.

## 4. Evaluation metrics

To assess the performance of the trained YOLOv8 model in detecting lung tumors from CT scan images, a comprehensive set of evaluation metrics was employed. These metrics provide a quantitative measure of the model's accuracy, precision, and overall effectiveness in identifying lung tumors. The following evaluation metrics were used:

- Precision: Precision measures the proportion of true positive detections among all the positive detections made by the model. It quantifies the model's ability to correctly identify lung tumors while minimizing false positives. Precision is calculated using the formula: Precision = True Positives/ (True Positives + False Positives). A higher precision indicates that the model has a lower rate of false positive detections, meaning it is less likely to incorrectly identify non-tumor regions as tumors.

- Recall (Sensitivity): Recall, also known as sensitivity, measures the proportion of true positive detections among all the actual positive instances in the dataset. It quantifies the model's ability to identify as many lung tumors as possible, minimizing false negatives. Recall is calculated using the formula: Recall = True Positives/ (True Positives + False Negatives). A higher recall indicates that the model is able to detect a higher percentage of the actual lung tumors present in the CT scan images.

- F1-score: The F1-score is the harmonic mean of precision and recall, providing a balanced measure of the model's overall performance. It takes into account both the model's ability to accurately identify lung tumors and its ability to minimize false positives and false negatives. The F1-score is calculated using the formula: F1-score = 2 * (Precision * Recall) / (Precision + Recall). A higher F1-score indicates a better balance between precision and recall, suggesting that the model performs well in both aspects.

- Mean Average Precision (mAP): Mean Average Precision is a widely used metric in object detection tasks. It provides a single value that summarizes the model's performance across different confidence thresholds. mAP is calculated by taking the mean of the average precision (AP) values at different intersection over union (IoU) thresholds. The IoU threshold determines the minimum overlap required between the predicted bounding box and the ground truth bounding box for a detection to be considered a true positive. The AP is calculated by plotting the precision-recall curve at different confidence thresholds and computing the area under the curve (AUC). mAP is reported at two common IoU thresholds: mAP at 0.5 and mAP at 0.5:0.95. mAP at 0.5 considers detections with an IoU threshold of 0.5, while mAP at 0.5:0.95 averages the AP values across IoU

| Metric | Value |
|---|---|
| Precision | 0.908 |
| Recall | 0.894 |
| F1-score | 0.901 |
| mAP at 0.5 | 0.921 |
| mAP at 0.5:0.95 | 0.615 |

**Table 5.**
*Evaluation metrics achieved by the trained YOLOv8 model on the validation set.*

thresholds from 0.5 to 0.95 with a step size of 0.05. A higher mAP value indicates better overall performance, considering both the accuracy and completeness of the lung tumor detections (**Table 5**).

The evaluation metrics demonstrate the YOLOv8 model's strong performance in detecting lung tumors from CT scan images. The high precision value of 0.908 indicates that the model has a low rate of false positive detections, minimizing the chances of incorrectly identifying non-tumor regions as tumors. The recall value of 0.894 suggests that the model is able to detect a significant proportion of the actual lung tumors present in the validation set. The F1-score of 0.901 reflects a good balance between precision and recall, indicating that the model performs well in both aspects. The mAP at 0.5 value of 0.921 and mAP at 0.5:0.95 value of 0.615 further validate the model's overall effectiveness in detecting lung tumors across different confidence thresholds and IoU thresholds.

**Figure 3** shows the precision-recall curve of the YOLOv8 model on the validation set. The precision-recall curve visualizes the trade-off between precision and recall at different confidence thresholds. The area under the curve (AUC) represents the overall performance of the model. A higher AUC indicates better performance, with an ideal curve reaching the top-right corner of the plot.

**Figure 4** presents the F1-score curve of the YOLOv8 model across different epochs during training. The F1-score curve provides insight into the model's learning progress and convergence. As the training progresses, the F1-score typically improves, indicating that the model is learning to detect lung tumors more accurately.

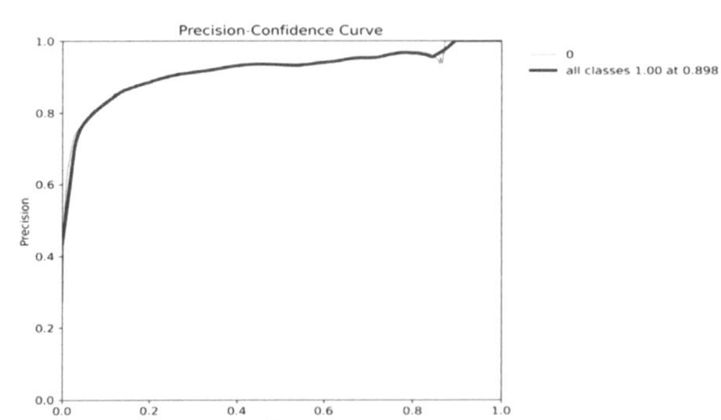


**Figure 3.**
*Precision-recall curve.*

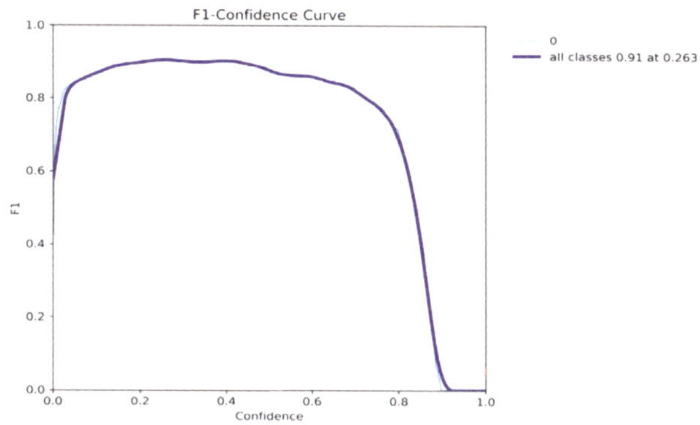


**Figure 4.**
*F1-score curve.*

The evaluation metrics and visualizations demonstrate the effectiveness of the YOLOv8 model in detecting lung tumors from CT scan images. The high precision, recall, and F1-score values, along with the impressive mAP scores, highlight the model's ability to accurately identify lung tumors while minimizing false positives and false negatives. The robustness and generalization capability of the YOLOv8 model can be attributed to several factors, including the careful preprocessing and augmentation of the dataset, the selection of appropriate hyperparameters, and the use of advanced techniques such as anchor-free detection and a deep backbone network. Furthermore, the visualization of the model's performance across different epochs provides valuable insights into the training process. The F1-score curve shows a steady improvement over the course of training, indicating that the model is learning to detect lung tumors more effectively as it processes more data.

## 5. Results

The trained YOLOv8 model demonstrated remarkable performance in detecting lung tumors from CT scan images. The model's effectiveness was evaluated using a comprehensive set of metrics, including precision, recall, F1-score, and mean average precision (mAP), on the validation set. The validation set, consisting of 216 CT scan images, served as an independent dataset to assess the model's performance on unseen data. This allows for a fair evaluation of the model's generalization capability and its ability to detect lung tumors accurately in real-world scenarios (**Table 6**).

The precision value of 0.908 indicates that the model has a high level of accuracy in identifying lung tumors. It means that 90.8% of the positive detections made by the

| Metric | Value |
|---|---|
| Precision | 0.908 |
| Recall | 0.894 |
| mAP50 | 0.921 |
| mAP50–95 | 0.605 |

**Table 6.**
*Evaluation metrics achieved by the YOLOv8 model on the validation set.*

model are indeed true lung tumors. This high precision is crucial in a medical context, as it minimizes the risk of false positives, which could lead to unnecessary further investigations or interventions. The recall value of 0.894 suggests that the model is able to detect a significant proportion of the actual lung tumors present in the validation set. This means that 89.4% of the lung tumors in the CT scan images are successfully identified by the model. A high recall is important to ensure that the model does not miss any potential tumors, reducing the risk of false negatives and delayed diagnosis.

The mean average precision (mAP) metrics provide a comprehensive evaluation of the model's performance across different confidence thresholds and intersection over union (IoU) thresholds. The mAP50 value of 0.921 indicates that the model achieves an average precision of 92.1% when considering detections with an IoU threshold of 0.5. This means that the model is highly accurate in localizing the lung tumors within the CT scan images. The mAP50–95 value of 0.605 represents the average precision across IoU thresholds ranging from 0.5 to 0.95, with a step size of 0.05. This metric provides a more stringent evaluation of the model's performance, considering the accuracy of the detected bounding boxes at different levels of overlap with the ground truth annotations. The mAP50–95 value of 0.605 demonstrates that the model maintains a strong performance even at higher IoU thresholds, indicating its ability to precisely localize the lung tumors.

**Figure 5** illustrates the precision-recall curve of the YOLOv8 model on the validation set. The precision-recall curve showcases the trade-off between precision and recall at different confidence thresholds. The curve provides insights into the model's

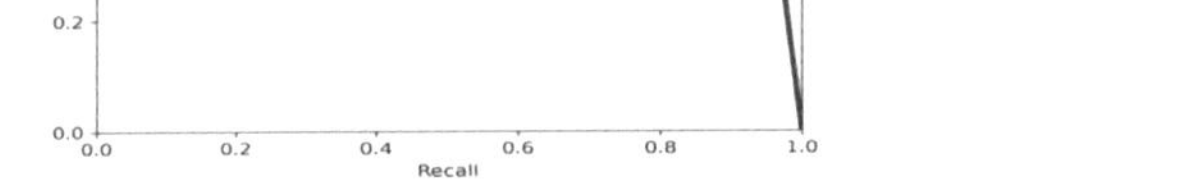


**Figure 5.**
*Precision-recall curve on validation set.*

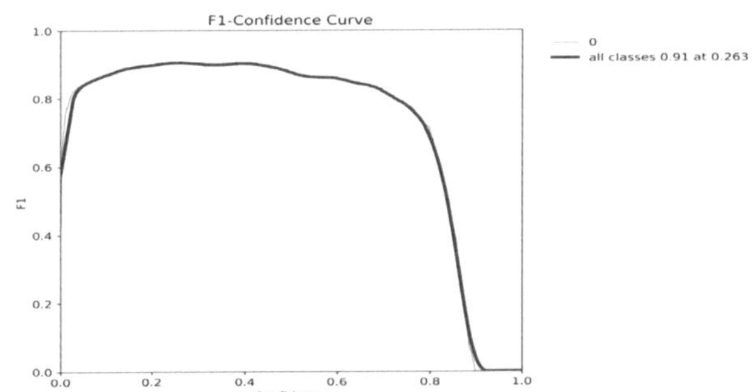


**Figure 6.**
*F1-score curve on validation set.*

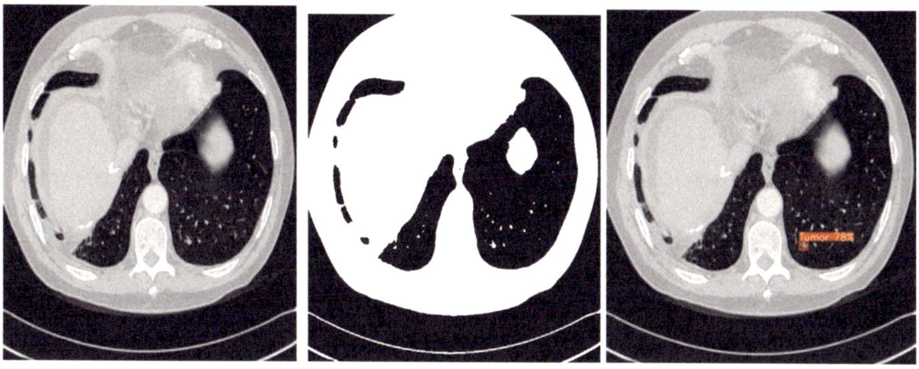


a) b) c)

**Figure 7.**
*Yolo model output. (a) Original Image, (b) Preprocessed Image and (c) Resultant image.*

performance across a range of operating points, allowing for the selection of an appropriate threshold based on the desired balance between precision and recall.

The precision-recall curve demonstrates the model's strong performance, with a high area under the curve (AUC). The curve remains close to the top-right corner of the plot, indicating that the model maintains high precision while achieving high recall. This suggests that the model is capable of accurately detecting lung tumors while minimizing both false positives and false negatives. **Figure 6** presents the F1-score curve of the YOLOv8 model across different epochs during training. The F1-score is the harmonic mean of precision and recall, providing a single metric that balances both aspects. The F1-score curve allows for monitoring the model's learning progress and convergence over the course of training.

The F1-score curve shows a steady improvement in the model's performance as the training progresses. The curve rises quickly in the early epochs, indicating that the model is rapidly learning to detect lung tumors. As the training continues, the F1-score stabilizes and reaches a high value, demonstrating the model's ability to generalize well to unseen data. The precision, recall, and F1-score curves collectively showcase the model's learning progress and its high performance in detecting lung tumors. The curves provide visual evidence of the model's effectiveness and its ability to achieve a good balance between precision and recall. **Figure 7** provides the overall result of the YOLOv8 model with preprocessed image and tumor detected with caused percentage using model.

## 6. Discussion

The results obtained from the YOLOv8 model in detecting lung tumors from CT scan images demonstrate the strong capabilities of deep learning in the domain of medical image analysis. The high precision and recall values achieved by the model indicate its potential to assist radiologists and healthcare professionals in the early detection and diagnosis of lung cancer. The precision value of 0.908 suggests that the model has a low false positive rate, meaning that the majority of the detections made by the model are indeed true lung tumors. This is particularly important in a medical context, as false positive detections can lead to unnecessary further investigations, patient anxiety, and increased healthcare costs. The high precision of the YOLOv8 model can help reduce the burden on healthcare systems by minimizing the need for additional confirmatory tests.

On the other hand, the recall value of 0.894 indicates that the model is able to detect a significant proportion of the actual lung tumors present in the CT scan images. A high recall is crucial in the early detection of lung cancer, as missing even a single tumor can have severe consequences for the patient's prognosis and treatment options. The YOLOv8 model's ability to identify a large percentage of lung tumors highlights its potential to aid in the timely diagnosis and initiation of appropriate treatment plans.

The mean average precision (mAP) scores further validate the model's performance across different confidence thresholds and IoU thresholds. The mAP50 value of 0.921 and mAP50–95 value of 0.605 demonstrate the model's robustness in accurately localizing the lung tumors within the CT scan images. These scores indicate that the model is not only able to detect the presence of lung tumors but also precisely determine their location and extent. The precision-recall curve and F1-score curve provide visual representations of the model's learning progress and its ability to balance precision and recall. The curves showcase the model's convergence toward high performance and its capability to generalize well to unseen data. These visualizations offer valuable insights into the model's behavior and can guide further refinements and optimizations.

However, it is important to acknowledge the limitations and challenges associated with the application of deep learning models in medical image analysis. One of the primary concerns is the interpretability and explainability of the model's predictions. While the YOLOv8 model demonstrates strong performance in detecting lung tumors, understanding the underlying reasoning behind its decisions is crucial for building trust and acceptance among healthcare professionals. Future research should focus on developing techniques to enhance the interpretability of deep learning models, allowing for more transparent and explainable predictions (**Table 7**).

Another challenge is the integration of deep learning models into clinical workflows. The successful deployment of the YOLOv8 model in real-world settings requires collaboration between computer scientists, radiologists, and healthcare institutions. Establishing standardized protocols for data acquisition, preprocessing, and model evaluation is essential to ensure the reliability and reproducibility of the results.

| Model | Results |
|---|---|
| YOLOv8 (Current Study, 2024) | Precision: 0.908<br>Recall: 0.894<br>mAP50: 0.921<br>mAP50–95: 0.605 |
| YOLOv7 [13] | AP: 0.835<br>Sensitivity: 0.926 |
| YOLOv6 with PSO optimizer [8] | Accuracy: 0.982<br>Sensitivity: 0.976 |
| YOLOv5 [10] | Not specified (used synthetic data) |
| YOLOv3 with attention [6] | Accuracy: 0.913<br>Sensitivity: 0.925 |
| YOLOv3 [4] | Average Precision: 0.881<br>Average Recall: 0.873 |

**Table 7.**
*Comparison of YOLO versions for lung cancer detection.*

Furthermore, regulatory considerations and ethical implications must be addressed to ensure the responsible and safe use of deep learning models in patient care.

## 7. Conclusion and future work

This study presents a lung cancer detection approach using the state-of-the-art YOLOv8 deep learning model. The YOLOv8 model was trained on the Lung Cancer CT Scan dataset, consisting of 2167 training images and 216 validation images, to detect lung tumors from CT scan images. The trained model achieved remarkable performance on the validation set, with a precision of 0.908, recall of 0.894, mAP50 of 0.921, and mAP50–95 of 0.605. These results demonstrate the model's strong capability in accurately detecting lung tumors while minimizing false positives and false negatives. The precision-recall curve and F1-score curve further validate the model's learning progress and its ability to balance precision and recall. The promising results obtained in this study highlight the potential of deep learning, specifically the YOLOv8 model, in aiding the early diagnosis of lung cancer. The model's high performance suggests that it can serve as a valuable tool for radiologists and healthcare professionals, assisting them in the detection and localization of lung tumors from CT scan images. However, it is important to acknowledge the limitations and challenges associated with the application of deep learning models in medical image analysis. Further validation on larger and more diverse datasets is necessary to assess the model's generalization ability and performance across different patient populations and imaging protocols. Additionally, efforts should be made to enhance the interpretability and explainability of the model's predictions, ensuring transparency, and building trust among healthcare professionals.

Future work should focus on several key areas to support the real-world deployment of the YOLOv8 model in clinical settings. Firstly, model refinement and optimization techniques can be explored to further improve the model's performance and robustness. This may involve investigating alternative network architectures, incorporating additional data augmentation strategies, and fine-tuning the hyperparameters.

## Acknowledgements

Corresponding author Nayan Jadhav contributed to the conceptualization, methodology, data collection, and analysis. Nayan Jadhav was responsible for writing the original draft, with contributions from first author Dr. Aziz Makandar; they also provided supervision and paper administration, contributed to the review and editing of the manuscript, and provided critical feedback and revision of the manuscript.

All authors have read and approved the final manuscript.

## Declarations

The authors declare that informed consent was obtained from all individual participants included in the study. Participants were informed about the study's objectives, procedures, potential risks, and benefits. Their participation was voluntary, and they had the right to withdraw at any time without any repercussions. All procedures were conducted in accordance with the ethical standards of the institutional research, declaration, and later amendments or comparable ethical standards.

## Author details

Nayan Jadhav* and Aziz Makandar
Department of Computer Science, Karnataka State Akkamahadevi Women University, Vijayapura, India

*Address all correspondence to: jadhavnayan321@gmail.com

## References

[1] Garg P, Poddar N, Khan SA. A literature review on lung cancer detection approaches using medical images. International Research Journal of Modernization in Engineering Technology and Science. 2023;**5**(4): 123-130. DOI: 10.56726/irjmets44569

[2] Reddy BD, Rao NT, Bhattacharyya D. Deep neural transfer network technique for lung cancer detection. Lecture Notes in Electrical Engineering (Springer). 2023;**997**:237-247. DOI: 10.1007/978-981-99-0085-5_20

[3] Biserinska H. YOLO Models for Automatic Lung Nodules Detection from CT Scans. 2020. Available from: http://arno.uvt.nl/show.cgi?fid=156394

[4] Bu Z, Zhang X, Lu J, Lao H, Liang C, Xu X, et al. Lung nodule detection based on YOLOv3 deep learning with limited datasets. Molecular & Cellular Biomechanics. 2022;**19**(1):17-28. DOI. 10.32604/mcb.2022.018318

[5] Deng W, Wang Z, Ren X, Zhang X, Wang B, Yang T. YOLO_v3-based pulmonary nodules recognition system. Adv. Intell. Syst. Comput. 2020:11-19. DOI: 10.1007/978-981-15-8462-6_2

[6] Qi H, Jia J, Zhang R. Detection of CT Pulmonary Nodule Based on Improved Yolo Using Attention Mechanism. 2022. doi:10.1145/3577530.3577533

[7] Goel L, Mishra S. A hybrid of modified YOLOv3 with BBO/EE optimizer for lung cancer detection. Multimedia Tools and Applications. 2023;**82**(5):17454-17470. DOI: 10.1007/s11042-023-17454-8

[8] Goel L, Patel P. Improving YOLOv6 using advanced PSO optimizer for weight selection in lung cancer detection and classification. Multimedia Tools and Applications. 2024;**83**(1):18441-18460. DOI: 10.1007/s11042-024-18441-3

[9] Ji Z, Zhao J, Liu J, Zeng X, Zhang H, Zhang X, et al. ELCT-YOLO: An efficient one-stage model for automatic lung tumor detection based on CT images. Mathematics. 2023;**11**(10):2344-2344. DOI: 10.3390/math11102344

[10] Zhang J, Chung T-M. An improved YOLO V5 model for pulmonary nodule detection with synthetic data generated by GAN. In: Proceedings of the 2022 IEEE International Conference on Big Data. IEEE; 2022. pp. 1018-1025. Available from: https://ieeexplore.ieee.org/abstract/document/10189535

[11] Liu C, Hu S-C, Wang C, Lafata K, Yin F-F. Automatic detection of pulmonary nodules on CT images with YOLOv3: Development and evaluation using simulated and patient data. Quantitative Imaging in Medicine and Surgery. 2020;**10**(10):1917-1929. DOI: 10.21037/qims-19-883

[12] Liu Z, Zhang J, Wang N, Feng Y, Tang F, Li T, et al. Enhanced YOLOv5 network-based object detection (BALFilter reader) promotes PERFECT filter-enabled liquid biopsy of lung cancer from bronchoalveolar lavage fluid (BALF). Microsystems & Nanoengineering. 2023;**9**(1):1-13. DOI: 10.1038/s41378-023-00580-6

[13] Mammeri S, Amroune M, Haouam M-Y, Bendib I, Silva AC. Early detection and diagnosis of lung cancer using YOLO v7, and transfer learning. Multimedia Tools and Applications.

2023;**82**(4):16864-16880. DOI: 10.1007/s11042-023-16864-y

[14] Shi J. A technical comparison of YOLO-based chest cancer diagnosis methods. Highlights in Science, Engineering and Technology. 2023;**41**: 35-42. DOI: 10.54097/hset.v41i.6740

[15] Elavarasu M, Govindaraju K. Unveiling the advancements: YOLOv7 vs YOLOv8 in pulmonary carcinoma detection. Journal of Robotics and Control (JRC). 2024;**5**(2):459-470. DOI: 10.18196/jrc.v5i2.20900

[16] Wang X, Li H, Wang L, Yu Y, Zhou H, Wang L, et al. An improved YOLOv3 model for detecting location information of ovarian cancer from CT images. Intelligent Data Analysis. 2021;**25**(6):1565-1578. DOI: 10.3233/ida-205542

[17] Xu K, Jiang H, Tang W. A New Object Detection Algorithm Based on YOLOv3 for Lung Nodules. 2020. doi:10.1145/3404555.3404609

[18] Demiroğlu U, Şenol B, Yildirim M, Eroğlu Y. Classification of computerized tomography images to diagnose non-small cell lung cancer using a hybrid model. Multimedia Tools and Applications. 2023;**82**(3):14943-14960. DOI: 10.1007/s11042-023-14943-8

[19] Sori WJ, Feng J, Liu S. Multi-path convolutional neural network for lung cancer detection. Multidimensional Systems and Signal Processing. 2018;**30**(4):1749-1768. DOI: 10.1007/s11045-018-0626-9

[20] Sori WJ, Feng J, Godana AW, Liu S, Gelmecha DJ. DFD-net: Lung cancer detection from denoised CT scan image using deep learning. Frontiers of Computer. 2021;**15**:152701. DOI: 10.1007/s11704-020-9050-z

[21] Budati M, Karumuri R. An intelligent lung nodule segmentation framework for early detection of lung cancer using an optimized deep neural system. Multimedia Tools and Applications. 2023;**82**(6):17791-17810. DOI: 10.1007/s11042-023-17791-8

[22] Tareq Mahmud M, Shuvo SI, Iqbal N, Momen S. Leveraging deep object detection models for early detection of cancerous lung nodules in chest X-rays. Data Analytics in System Engineering Lecture Notes in Networks and Systems. 2024:79-98. DOI: 10.1007/978-3-031-54820-8_9

[23] Halalli B, Makandar A. Computer aided diagnosis-medical image analysis techniques. Breast Imaging. 2018;**85**(85):109, 113-125. DOI: 10.5772/intechopen.69792. Available from: https://www.intechopen.com/chapters/56615

Section 2

# Machine Learning and Data Mining

Chapter 3

# Friction and Wear in Journal Bearings: Accurate Testing and Simulation with an Outlook on Predictive Maintenance with Machine Learning

*Sophia Bastidas and Hannes Allmaier*

## Abstract

Oil-lubricated journal bearings have been used extensively in combustion engines and other applications requiring high reliability under high mechanical loads. Friction and wear of journal bearings have been researched for decades; however, the authors were the first to demonstrate a simulation method that can predict reliably and accurately the friction of journal bearings under very high, dynamic loads as they occur in combustion engines. Building on this foundation, a novel journal bearing test-rig has been developed to measure the amount of generated wear debris in real-time during the test and can directly measure the friction of one journal bearing only. With this data, novel insights into journal bearings' friction and wear processes under high loads become possible and provide the basis for predictive maintenance using machine learning algorithms.

**Keywords:** journal bearings, friction, wear, bearing test-rig, predictive maintenance, machine learning

## 1. Introduction

Journal bearings, like the ones used in internal combustion engines and turbines, are relatively simple mechanical components consisting of a rotating shaft and a bearing shell with the lubricant that separates the contacting surfaces of both components. Journal bearings have been traditionally designed to work under hydrodynamic lubrication conditions, where there is no contact between the surfaces, thus reducing wear and extending their useful lifetime. However, continuous operation under hydrodynamic lubrication conditions implies an increase in the total friction losses due to the lubricant shear, which translates to fuel consumption increase and reduction of the system efficiency. In this way, to reduce the friction losses, the bearing should be operated in the transition between hydrodynamic and mixed lubrication conditions, where the friction coefficient is minimum, determined by both the lubricant viscosity and the surface roughness due to the existence of metal–metal contact.

However, the drawback of operating under mixed lubrication is the wear increase and reduced bearing useful lifetime.

With the aim to understand better the lubrication of the bearing, the wear phenomena under mixed lubrication, and the different conditions and factors involved, experimental and simulation tools have been developed with highly accurate results. The authors' research group has worked on these two approaches for many years, and in this chapter, a new journal-bearing test-rig is presented especially aimed at research under mixed lubrication conditions. Furthermore, it was designed to measure the friction force in the test journal bearing directly and not as a total friction force, including the support bearings, as is common in standard bearing test-rigs. To complement the experimental research, an elastohydrodynamic simulation model was developed adapted to the design characteristics of the test-rig, including the elastic deformation of the components, the rheological properties of the lubricant, varying with temperature, pressure, and shear rate, and the surface roughness properties of the contacting surfaces.

In parallel and taking advantage of the significant amount of data available from simulation, it was decided to use machine learning (ML) tools in a simple application to predict the lubrication regime in the test bearing from different operating conditions and simulation parameters. This application is only an overview example of the different capabilities of ML in tribology. It is expected to be expanded using experimental data from the journal bearing test-rig in future works. A brief literature review of ML for bearings' research is presented in the following Section 1.1. Finally, a conclusions and outlook section was included at the end of this chapter to summarize the main results and present some proposals for future work.

### 1.1 ML for journal bearings' research

ML algorithms have been used extensively in many different science and industry applications, including tribology [1], to find hidden trends and relations between parameters, operating conditions, and processes that could explain and predict the performance of a system and, ultimately, give the foundations for decision-making. The application of ML in bearings' research is, therefore, a valuable tool, not only for understanding complex tribological processes occurring in the bearing contact but also for performance prediction. This predicting capability could be applied, for example, to predictive maintenance, calculation of remaining useful lifetime, and even help to reduce the amount of required experimental tests as highlighted in the research work developed by Ünlü et al. [2]; in this work, the friction coefficient and wear loss of journal bearings were investigated under both dry and lubricated conditions using experimental tests on a journal bearing wear test-rig and predicted with an artificial neural network (ANN) model. The input data included time, applied load, and speed. The ANN results demonstrated the accurate predicting capabilities of the ML model compared to experimental results, which ultimately reduces the need for experimental data and the time involved. Another application of neural networks was shown by Moder et al. [3] to predict the lubrication regime of journal bearings using experimental torque data in the frequency domain. This data used for training was obtained from different testing combinations of bearing-shaft materials, applied load, and shaft speed conditions and was labeled manually into four classifications: boundary, mixed, fluid thin, and fluid thick lubrication. A simpler logistic regression algorithm was also tested, yielding highly accurate results similar to those obtained using the neural network model.

A semi-supervised ML algorithm using Random Forest (RF) classification was used by Prost et al. [4] to predict the operating conditions of a self-lubricating journal bearing. To this end, experimental data from a lateral force sensor was used to classify the operation of the bearing into four states ranging from steady to critical conditions. In this work, semi-supervised refers to the combination of manual labeling made by an expert user and the use of clustering tools such as k-means. Furthermore, noise removal was performed during data pre-processing and resampling to balance the amount of data in each classification label. The trained RF model was able to classify the bearing operation states for unseen data with high accuracy and, as pointed out by the authors, it could be the basis for the prediction of the remaining useful lifetime. In this way, in a following work by Prost et al. [5], an ANN model and five supervised classification algorithms were proposed to predict the operating state of a porous journal bearing. Experimental results from multiple sensors, such as torque, wear, and acceleration, collected under operating conditions promoting mixed lubrication and accelerated wear, were used to improve the predicting capabilities of the ML models. Results showed that an ensemble classifier based on aggregated decision trees yielded the highest accuracy, and the onset of the critical stage was predicted reliably, which could be especially useful in real applications for maintenance planning.

## 2. Journal bearing test-rig

Journal bearing test-rigs provide the experimental data required to develop accurate simulation and machine learning models. The authors operate a novel kind of bearing test-rig that provides high-resolution data that is invaluable for research. As shown in **Figure 1**, the main components of the test-rig are the test journal bearing, two support bearings, the connecting rod to transmit the applied load to the test

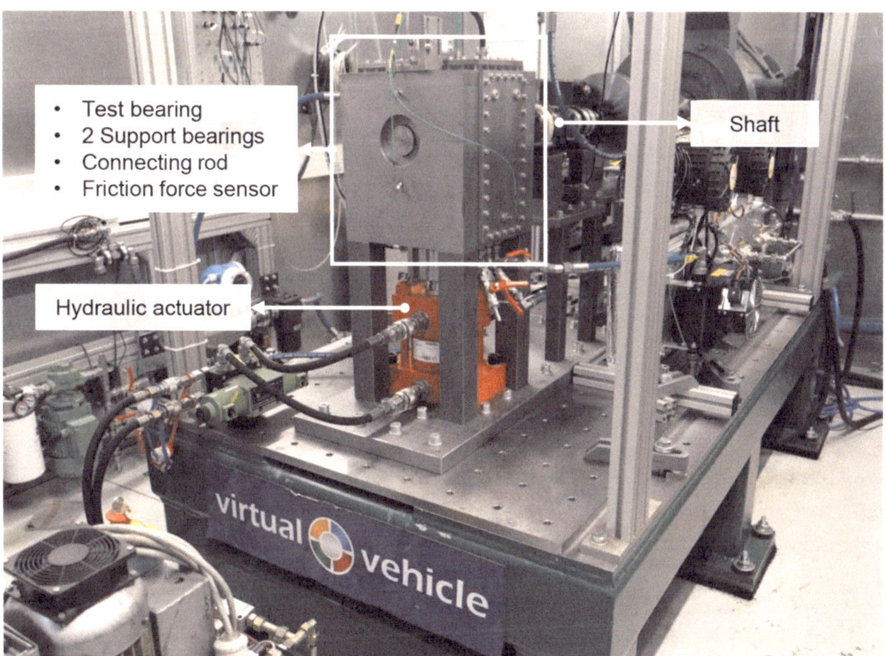


**Figure 1.**
*Journal bearing test-rig.*

bearing, the shaft, the hydraulic actuator for the load application, and the friction force sensor. However, as the used simulation methodology was shown to be very accurate for uncritical operating conditions in past publications [6–10], it will be used for the following investigations for the simple reason that simulation is much more convenient to generate results with arbitrary resolution. This allows more flexibility for developing a machine learning method and removes the complexity of unwanted noise and inaccuracies that are naturally part of experimental data. At the same time, simulation can generate (almost) any amount of data required for machine learning, while experimental data are (almost) always limited in quantity. Future work will, however, utilize this experimental data as well.

## 3. Journal-bearing test-rig simulation model

To complement the development of the journal bearing test-rig presented in Section 2, an isothermal elasto-hydrodynamic simulation model was developed considering the mechanical components' elastic deformation, the lubricant oil's rheological properties, and the contact between the surfaces. The model is based on the Reynolds equation for non-Newtonian fluids, including the Patir and Cheng flow factors to account for rough surfaces [11, 12], the Greenwood and Tripp contact model [13], and the Jakobsson-Floberg-Olsson approach [14] to account for cavitation and mass conservation. An oil model, described in Section 3.3, considering the oil's piezo-viscous effect and non-Newtonian behavior, was implemented using the measured oil properties. Furthermore, surface roughness properties and a constant boundary friction coefficient were included to accurately simulate severe mixed lubrication conditions. This simulation approach is based on models developed by the research group, previously documented in the publications [7–10]. In this way, only the main characteristics of the current simulation model are described here.

The simulation model was implemented in the flexible multi-body solver AVL Excite Power Unit (version 2022R1),[1] it includes the test connecting rod and test bearing, modeled as finite element structures, and the shaft, modeled as a simplified beam body. The model was solved in time domain, applying numerical time integration and backward differentiation. At each time step, equations of motion were calculated for all the bodies as well as contact equations using the Newton–Raphson method. The elastic deformation of the test bearing and shaft was also considered and calculated for each time step. A schematic diagram of the simulation model is presented in **Figure 2**.

### 3.1 Model components

The components of the simulation model consist of flexible and rigid bodies and joints. The first group includes the test connecting rod and the shaft. The connecting rod was modeled as a finite element condensed body, for which a pre-process was performed with the ANSA pre-processor (version 22.0.0)[2] to mesh the body and reduce the degrees of freedom. This last process allowed to obtain a condensed body that retains only the nodes in contact with other simulation model components. For the

---

[1] AVL List GmbH, Hans-List-Platz 1, 8020 Graz Austria, www.avl.com

[2] BETA CAE Systems International AG, Platz 4 CH-6039 Root D4, Switzerland, www.beta-cae.com

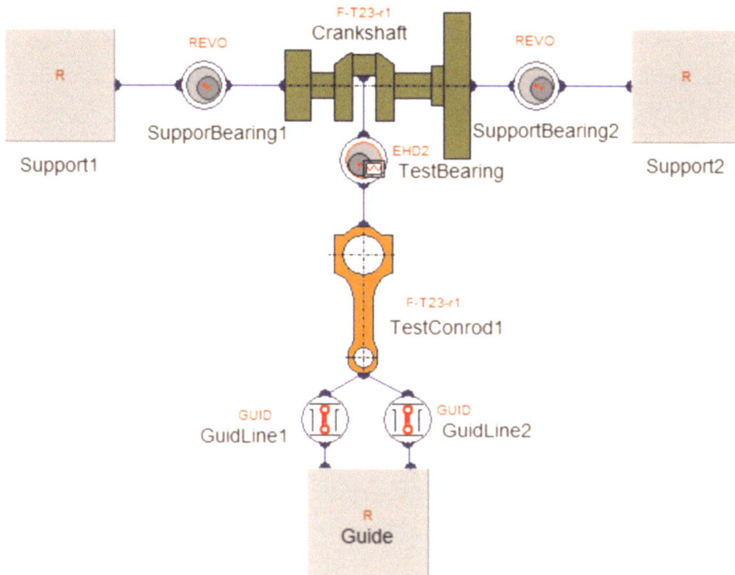


**Figure 2.**
*Schematic diagram of the simulation model.*

connecting rod, the retained nodes are those on the bearing surface and two nodes at the bottom to guide the rod and for load application. A simplified beam body was defined for the shaft with point masses distributed along the rotational axis. The second group consists of three rigid bodies, two located at each side of the shaft acting as support brackets for the support bearings and a third body at the bottom to guide the connecting rod in the vertical direction. Finally, the joints include an elasto-hydrodynamic joint (EHD2) to model the contact between the test bearing and the shaft and two revolute (REVO) joints for the contact between the support bearings and the shaft. For the EHD joint, a hydrodynamic (HD) mesh was defined, with 201 nodes in the circumferential direction and 21 nodes in the axial direction, for the discretization of the bearing surface. The Reynolds equation was evaluated at each HD node along with the oil properties dependent on temperature, pressure, and shear rate.

### 3.2 Test bearing geometry and surface roughness

The test bearing corresponds to a big-end bearing with a diameter of 51.5 mm, width of 17.2 mm, and radial clearance of 17 mm; it has two oil supply holes in the shell at 90° and 270°. The journal bearing is considered run-in, and since wear occurs at the bearing edges due to the shaft elastic bending, a wear profile was added to the bearing shell geometry. This profile consists of a spline contour in the bearing axial direction with a flat area at the center and a parabolic profile at the bearing edges with a maximum deviation of $5\mu m$.

For these first simulations, and given that no experimental results from the bearing test-rig are still available, it was decided to use surface roughness parameters obtained by the research group in previous projects. The selected parameters are summarized in **Table 1**. They include the asperity summit roughness ($\sigma$), mean summit height ($\delta$), the combined Young's module ($E^*$), and the elastic factor $K$, necessary for the asperity contact model. Additionally, the asperities' orientation ($\Gamma$) was set to 2 for the Patir

<table>
<tr><th>Parameter</th><th>Bearing shell</th><th>Shaft</th></tr>
<tr><td>$\sigma$ ($\mu m$)</td><td>0.2</td><td>0.2</td></tr>
<tr><td>$\delta$ ($\mu m$)</td><td>0.4</td><td>0.1</td></tr>
<tr><td>$\Gamma$ (−)</td><td>2</td><td>2</td></tr>
<tr><td>$E^*$ (GPa)</td><td colspan="2">57.7</td></tr>
<tr><td>$K$ (−)</td><td colspan="2">0.003</td></tr>
<tr><td>$\mu_{Bound}$ (−)</td><td colspan="2">0.02</td></tr>
</table>

**Table 1.**
*Surface roughness parameters for the test bearing and shaft.*

and Cheng model, and a boundary friction coefficient ($\mu_{Bound}$) equal to 0.02. See [7], for a more detailed description of the measurement and determination of these surface roughness parameters.

## 3.3 Lubricant oil rheology

The lubricant oil used in the simulation model is a standard multigrade 0W20 oil for automotive applications. Its main properties are presented in **Table 2**. Given that the simulation model assumes isothermal conditions, the bearing temperature is considered constant with a value representative of the complete bearing contact (see more details in Section 3.4) and varies with the applied load and speed.

To model the oil viscosity variation with temperature, pressure, and shear rate, the Vogel [15], Barus [16], and Cross [17] equations were included in the model. The rheological properties of the investigated oil were employed to obtain the parameters used in the Vogel-Barus-Cross equations. These parameters are summarized in **Table 3**; a complete description of their derivation is presented in a previous publication [7].

## 3.4 Journal bearing temperatures

For the isothermal elasto-hydrodynamic model, which assumes that the temperature of the bearing and oil in the lubrication gap is constant in the entire contact, an equivalent global oil temperature was defined, representative of the temperature values found in the highly loaded zone of the bearing and the lower temperatures at the zone without applied load.

Given that there is currently no available data from experimental tests in the bearing test-rig, the temperature values used in this simulation are derived from previous results presented in [7] for different experimental conditions. In this way,

| Property | Value |
|---|---|
| Density at 40°C ($kg/m^3$) | 832.5 |
| Dynamic viscosity at 40°C ($mPa.s$) | 37.5 |
| Dynamic viscosity at 100°C ($mPa.s$) | 6.8 |
| HTHS viscosity at 150°C and $10^6 s^{-1}$ shear rate ($mPa.s$) | 2.7 |

**Table 2.**
*0W20 oil rheological properties.*

| Property | Value |
|---|---|
| A ($mPa.s$) | 0.0516 |
| B (°C) | 1127.6 |
| C (°C) | 130.7 |
| $\alpha$ ($1/Pa$) | 9.5e-9 |
| r (−) | 0.53 |
| m (−) | 0.79 |
| K (s) | 7.9e-8 |

**Table 3.**
*Parameters for the Vogel-Barus-Cross equations.*

| Shaft speed (rpm) | Temperature (°C) | Shaft speed (rpm) | Temperature (°C) |
|---|---|---|---|
| 100 | 103.05 | 900 | 108.20 |
| 200 | 103.70 | 1000 | 109.98 |
| 300 | 104.34 | 1500 | 112.06 |
| 400 | 104.98 | 2000 | 115.17 |
| 500 | 105.63 | 3000 | 120.72 |
| 600 | 106.27 | 4000 | 127.55 |
| 700 | 106.91 | 5000 | 134.47 |
| 800 | 107.56 | | |

**Table 4.**
*Test bearing temperature.*

the temperature values defined for the test bearing in the simulation model are summarized in **Table 4** with a supply oil temperature of 110°C.

### 3.5 Stribeck tests

The first experimental test planned to be performed in the journal bearing test-rig is the so-called Stribeck test, where a constant static load is applied to the test bearing while the engine speed is varied. This approach will allow to evaluate further and improve the understanding of mixed lubrication; additionally, for the simulation model, these Stribeck tests will serve to verify the mixed lubrication approach adopted in the simulation based on the Greenwood and Tripp contact model and the constant dry friction coefficient. The results obtained from these tests are represented in Stribeck curves, where the different lubrication regimes can be identified similarly as in **Figure 3**. In this plot, the lubrication regimes are defined by the friction coefficient and the Sommerfeld number (S), which relates the oil viscosity ($\eta$), the relative velocity of the surfaces (U), and the load applied to the contact (W).

In this way, the test-rig simulation model was set up with testing conditions expected to promote the appearance of all the lubrication regimes in the bearing, especially mixed lubrication, and therefore, get an overview of the expected results

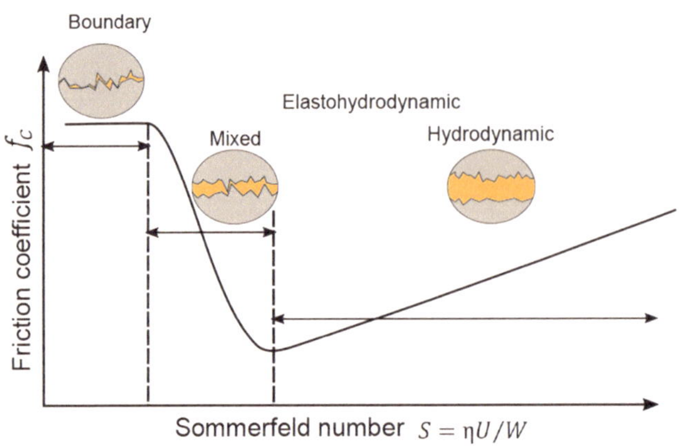


**Figure 3.**
*Identification of the lubrication regimes in the Stribeck curve.*

from the experimental tests. The selected simulating conditions consist of two static loads of 20 and 40 kN (22.6 and 45.2 MPa specific load, respectively), shaft speeds from 100 to 5000 rpm, and oil supply temperature of 110°C.

The sampling period for each simulation run was set for four shaft revolutions; the results were extracted from the last two revolutions to account for the time needed for the applied load to reach the desired value and stabilize.

**Figure 4** shows the results as Stribeck-like curves of the simulations ran for the two load cases; the $x$ axis presents the shaft speed variation, and the $y$ axis contains the resultant friction torque acting on the test bearing surface due to hydrodynamic and asperity contact losses.

The obtained Stribeck curves show that the test bearing experiences all the lubrication regimes, from boundary-mixed lubrication to hydrodynamic lubrication, for the two load cases by varying the shaft speed. Nonetheless, given that the main focus of the test-rig is to improve the understanding of mixed lubrication, the experimental tests would better focus on the plot's left side with speeds up to 3000 rpm. An

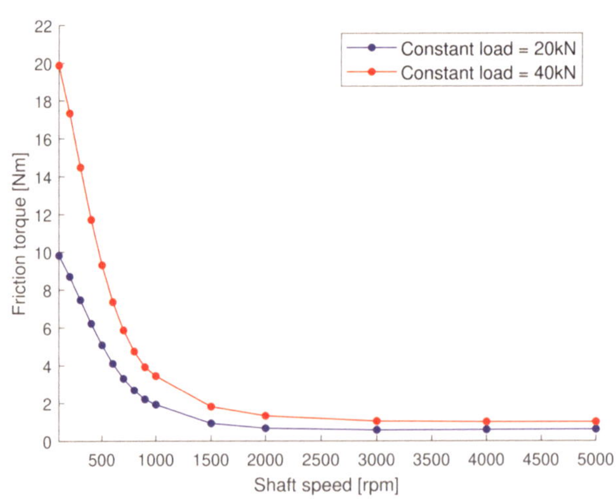


**Figure 4.**
*Stribeck-like curves obtained with the bearing test-rig simulation model for 20 and 40 kN applied constant load.*

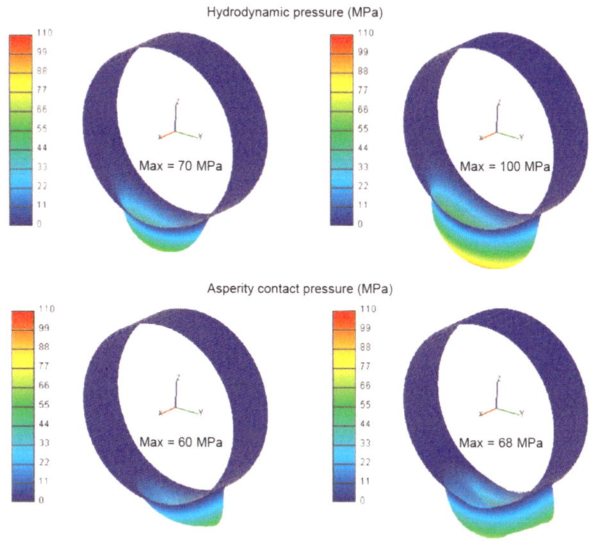


**Figure 5.**
*Hydrodynamic and asperity contact pressure distribution in the test bearing with 20 kN (left) and 40 kN (right) applied load.*

example of the expected lubricating conditions at 500 rpm can be seen in **Figure 5**, where the hydrodynamic and asperity contact pressure distributions have been plotted on the bearing surface for the two load cases, and once the load reaches stable conditions. Under these load and low shaft speed conditions, it can be seen that the contact between the bearing and the shaft is dominated by mixed lubrication with a significant contribution of asperity contact, as observed previously in the Stribeck curves of **Figure 4**.

Once experimental tests are available, the simulation model will be updated with actual data from the test-rig, such as temperatures measured at the bearing, which will allow to verify the simulation approach, focused on mixed lubrication.

## 4. Identification of journal bearing lubrication regime using ML

This section aims to provide an example of the capabilities of ML in bearings' research through a simple application, using data from simulation and a RF classification algorithm, to identify the lubrication regime existent in the bearing contact throughout a working cycle. Especial attention was given to the mixed lubrication regime, which is the leading research focus of the journal bearing test-rig presented in Section 2, and the simulation model discussed in Section 3. This section includes a description of the data used for training and testing the ML model, the pre-process to label the data, and results analysis of the ML model application with two and three classification labels and using a complete and reduced training data set.

### 4.1 Data used in the ML model and pre-process

The data used to train and test the ML model correspond to the results obtained with the bearing test-rig simulation model presented in [7]; the simulation comprises three EHD bearings, two acting as support bearings and one as test bearing, and a periodic dynamic load with a frequency of 80 Hz applied in a downward directing to the test bearing. Three load conditions were simulated with a maximum value of 40, 80, and 105 kN, corresponding to 50, 100, and 130 MPa specific loads, respectively. Two lubricant oils were investigated: an SAE 0W20 and an SAE 5W30 oil. The shaft speed was varied from 1000 to 7000 rpm in a stepwise run-up in intervals of 1000 rpm, followed by a run-down to 1000 rpm again. This configuration gives 13 simulation runs for each applied load and oil combination. Each simulation was run for 37.5 ms with a step size of 0.1 ms, corresponding to 376 data points per simulation run.

For the ML model, three simulation parameters were selected to predict the lubrication regime: the friction torque acting on the test bearing, the oil film parameter ($\lambda$), and the Sommerfeld number ($S$). These parameters have been plotted in **Figure 6** for one simulation run; it also includes the asperity contact area in percentage (dashed line) used to label the training data as explained further in Section 4.2.

$\lambda$ is the minimum oil film thickness ratio to the root mean square of the combined surface roughness, as presented in Eq. (1) [18]. The asperity roughness values $\sigma_{s,S}$ and $\sigma_{s,J}$ can be found in [7]. $S$ was obtained from Eq. (2) [18], where $r$ is the shaft radius, $c$ the radial clearance, $U$ is the shaft speed, and $L$ and $D$ are the bearing's width and diameter, respectively.

$$\lambda = \frac{h}{\sqrt{\sigma_{s,S}^2 + \sigma_{s,J}^2}} \tag{1}$$

$$S = \left(\frac{r}{c}\right)^2 \frac{\eta U}{W/LD} \tag{2}$$

With these simulation parameters, the training data set ($mxn$ matrix) was built using the results for 100 MPa and 0W20 oil; the resultant data set has dimensions of $m = 4888$ data points and $n = 3$ features; the rest of the simulation data were used to test the ML model.

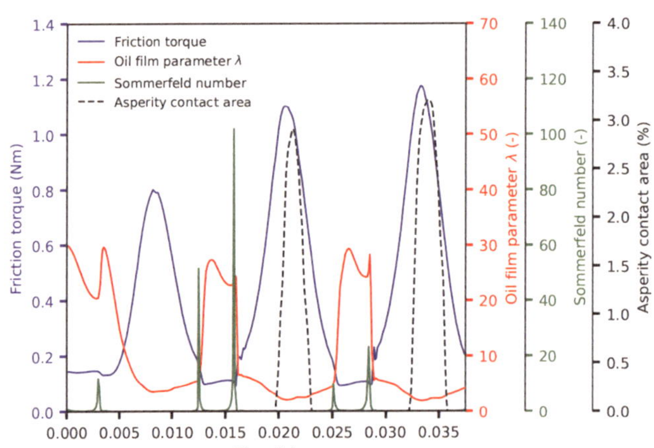


**Figure 6.**
*Simulation parameters used as predictors in the ML model; the asperity contact area in dashed line was used to label the training data set. Example for one simulation run at 1000 rpm, 100 MPa applied load, and 0W20 oil.*

### 4.2 Data labeling

Given that RF is a supervised algorithm, it needs labeled data to learn the relationship between the predictors or features and the labels and, therefore, be able to predict the label of new data using only the features. The percentage of asperity contact area was selected to determine the lubrication regime found in the test bearing contact at each data point and assign the corresponding label. This parameter, presented previously in **Figure 6**, is defined as the bearing area ratio, where contact between the surfaces is present, to the total area of the test bearing. Pressure in this area is greater than zero due to the asperities' interaction.

For the first approximation, two labels were used to classify the lubrication regime: 0 for no mixed lubrication where the percentage of asperity contact area is equal to zero, and 1 for mixed lubrication with values of percentage asperity contact area greater than zero. For the second approximation, three labels were defined: no mixed lubrication, weak lubrication, and significant mixed lubrication. **Table 5** summarizes these labels' definitions.

The number of data points in each classification label for the training data set is presented in **Table 6**. About 70% of the data correspond to label 0 for both approximations, as expected for journal bearings primarily working under hydrodynamic lubrication conditions. These can also be seen in **Figure 6**, where the asperity contact area (%) only takes values greater than zero at short periods during the simulation run.

### 4.3 Random Forest ML model and metrics

The RF model was developed with the ML library scikit-learn [19], and the following hyperparameters were used: n estimators = 5 for the number of individual decision trees, max depth = 3 for the maximum number of levels in each decision tree, and criterion = "entropy". To check the overall accuracy of the RF model, first, it was

| | | Conditional | | Label |
|---|---|---|---|---|
| 2 labels | | % Asperity contact | = 0 | 0 = No mixed lubrication |
| | 0 < | % Asperity contact | | 1 = Mixed lubrication |
| 3 labels | | % Asperity contact | ≤ 0.5 | 0 = No mixed lubrication |
| | 0.5 < | % Asperity contact | ≤ 3 | 1 = Weak mixed lubrication |
| | 3 < | % Asperity contact | | 2 = Significant mixed lubrication |

**Table 5.**
*Conditionals to label the data into two or three classifications.*

| | Number of data points in each label (%) | |
|---|---|---|
| Labels | For 2 labels | For 3 labels |
| 0 | 66.51 | 68.94 |
| 1 | 33.49 | 11.25 |
| 2 | — | 19.80 |

**Table 6.**
*Number of data points of the training data set in each classification label for the approximations with 2 and 3 labels.*

trained with a randomized selection of 70% of the training data set and tested with the remaining 30%, giving a result of 0.9921 for the RF trained with the data set for 2 labels and 0.9252 for the RF with 3 labels. For the successive tests, the RF model was trained again using the complete training data set, for 2 or 3 labels as needed.

The RF model performance was evaluated with the metrics: accuracy, precision, and recall calculated with the scikit-learn function classification report, and confusion matrices were used for visual representation. The accuracy gives an overall view of the model performance as the percentage of correct predictions; however, this score may not reflect the actual predicting performance of the RF for each classification label when the data is imbalanced. A confusion matrix can be calculated to account for this issue; it offers a visual representation of the true labels, shown in the rows, and predicted labels, shown in the columns, for all the tested data points. In this way, the values in the diagonal of the matrix are the number of times the RF model predicted the corresponding label correctly, while the values in the other cells are mislabeled. The precision metric is the ratio of correctly predicted members of a label to the total number of times the model predicted that specific label. Conversely, the recall metric is defined as the ratio of correctly predicted members of a label to the total number of true members of that specific label [19].

### *4.3.1 ML model for two and three labels*

To test the predicting performance of the RF models and compare the results, they were tested with three test data sets: 50 MPa and 0W20 oil, 100 MPa and 5W30 oil, and 130 MPa and 0W20 oil, which include two load levels, greater and lower, than the one used for training, and a different lubricant oil. Here it should be noted that given that the test data comes from simulation, information on the true labels is available to compare with the predicted results.

An example of the results obtained with the two RF models is presented in the following **Figure 7a** for the classification with 2 labels, and **Figure 7b** for the classification with 3 labels, for the test data set 50 MPa and 0W20 oil, and shaft speed of 1000 rpm. The plots show the percentage of asperity contact area in the bearing ($y$ axis) throughout the complete simulation run (37.5 ms) ($x$ axis). Since this parameter was used to label the training data set, identifying if the RF predictions are correct is straightforward. This way, the true values of the percentage of asperity contact area are shown with opaque colors, and the predicted values are shown in corresponding semi-transparent colors.

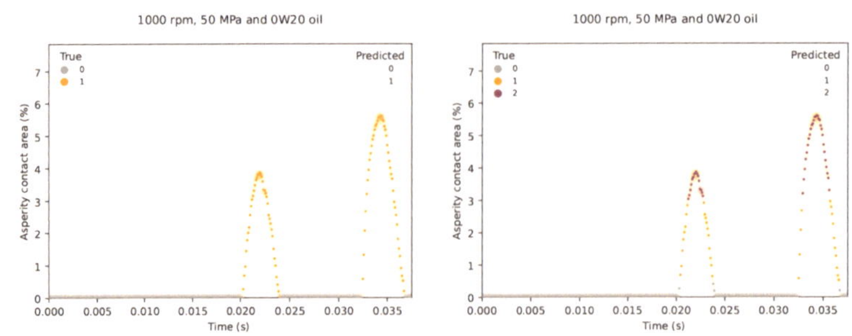


(a) (b)

**Figure 7.**
*True and predicted lubrication regimes using (a) two and (b) three labels.*

From **Figure 7a**, it can be observed that the RF model for two labels predicted the lubrication regime of new unseen data with high accuracy, even when testing a lower load than the one used for training. However, the results were not as accurate for the RF model with three labels, especially for the prediction of significant mixed lubrication (label 2). In **Figure 7b**, the true values corresponding to label 2 can be observed as opaque magenta dots for asperity contact area values greater than 3%. Nonetheless, the RF model classified most of these data points as label 1 (semi-transparent orange circles).

To complete this analysis, the confusion matrix for this test data set (50 MPa and 0W20 oil) is shown in **Figure 8**, and a summary of the metrics, precision, and recall, are presented in **Table 7** for the three test data sets evaluated in this section.

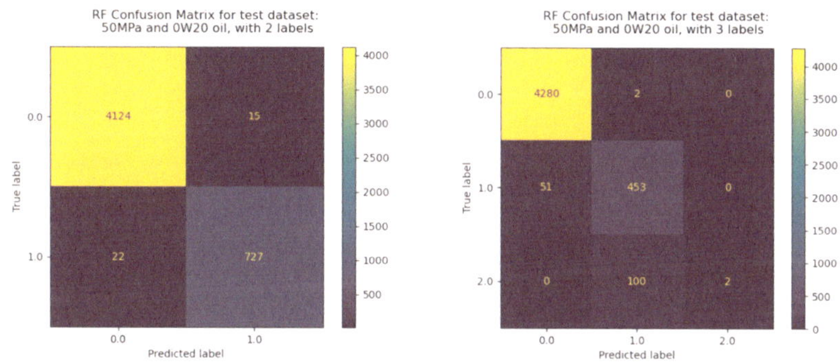


**Figure 8.**
*Confusion matrix for the test data set 50 MPa and 0W20 oil with 2 and 3 labels.*

| | For 2 labels | | For 3 labels | |
|---|---|---|---|---|
| **Labels** | **Precision** | **Recall** | **Precision** | **Recall** |
| | | 50 MPa and 0W20 oil | | |
| 0 | 0.99 | 1 | 0.99 | 1 |
| 1 | 0.98 | 0.97 | 0.82 | 0.9 |
| 2 | — | — | 1 | 0.02 |
| Accuracy | 0.9924 | | 0.9687 | |
| | | 100 MPa and 5W30 oil | | |
| 0 | 0.99 | 1 | 0.99 | 0.99 |
| 1 | 0.99 | 0.98 | 0.87 | 0.42 |
| 2 | — | — | 0.65 | 0.98 |
| Accuracy | 0.9932 | | 0.9343 | |
| | | 130 MPa and 0W20 oil | | |
| 0 | 0.99 | 1 | 0.99 | 0.99 |
| 1 | 1 | 0.99 | 0.80 | 0.50 |
| 2 | — | — | 0.83 | 0.97 |
| Accuracy | 0.9934 | | 0.9313 | |

**Table 7.**
*Precision and recall metrics for the RF model evaluate on the test data sets for the approximations with 2 and 3 labels.*

From **Table 7**, it can be seen that the overall accuracy of both RF models evaluated for all the test data sets is very good, especially for the classification into 2 labels with precision and recall metrics close to 1. Nonetheless, looking at the results for the classification into 3 labels, although the accuracy is very good, the recall metrics are low for labels 1 and 2 in some cases. It is especially noticeable the recall result of 0.02 for label 2 in the test data set 50 MPa and 0W20 oil, which can be observed in more detail in the confusion matrix of **Figure 8**; here, the trained RF model is not able to correctly learn how to discern between the classification labels 1 and 2, predicting almost all the significant mixed lubrication data (label 2) as weak mixed lubrication (label 1). This issue may arise due to the imbalanced training data set shown in **Table 6**. Therefore, since classification into label 1 is determined by a closed small range (0.5–3% asperity contact area), the RF model may not have sufficient training data to learn how to delimit the classification of this label.

#### *4.3.2 Using a reduced training data set*

Given the results of previous Section 4.3.1, it was decided to balance the training data set with the aim of improving the prediction performance of the RF model, especially to be able to predict weak and significant mixed lubrication conditions, labels 1 and 2. For that, the number of data points classified as label 0 was reduced to represent a maximum of 50% of the total training data, in contrast to the 63% in the original training data set. The results of the reduced training data set are summarized in the following **Table 8**.

The three previous test data sets were used again to evaluate the RF model trained with the reduced data. **Table 9** summarizes the accuracy, precision, and recall metrics.

| Labels | Number of data points in each label (%) |
|---|---|
| 0 | 48.33 |
| 1 | 18.72 |
| 2 | 32.95 |

**Table 8.**
*Number of data points of the reduced training data set in each classification label.*

| Labels | Precision | Recall |
|---|---|---|
| | 50 MPa and 0W20 oil | |
| 0 | 0.99 | 1 |
| 1 | 0.95 | 0.92 |
| 2 | 0.82 | 0.85 |
| Accuracy | 0.9863 | |
| | 100 MPa and 5W30 oil | |
| 0 | 1 | 0.98 |
| 1 | 0.85 | 0.78 |
| 2 | 0.77 | 0.95 |
| Accuracy | 0.9581 | |

| Labels | Precision | Recall |
|---|---|---|
| | 130 MPa and 0W20 oil | |
| 0 | 1 | 0.98 |
| 1 | 0.80 | 0.45 |
| 2 | 0.80 | 0.98 |
| Accuracy | 0.9233 | |

**Table 9.**
*Precision and recall metrics for the RF model using the reduced training data set evaluated on the test data sets.*

Comparing the results from this table and **Table 7**, it can be concluded that using the reduced data for training improved the prediction performance of the RF, especially looking at the recall metric of label 2 for the test data set 50 MPa and 0W20 oil, which increased from 0.02 to 0.85.

An example of the predicted lubrication regimes is shown in the following **Figure 9** in terms of the percentage of asperity contact pressure found in the bearing for the testing conditions 50 MPa, 0W20 oil, and shaft speed of 1000 rpm, the same as in **Figure 7b** (RF with the complete training data set) for comparison purposes. As can be seen, using the reduced training data set significantly improved the predicting performance of the RF, especially for severe mixed lubrication conditions (label 2), which are now correctly predicted for most of the data points.

A second example of these results is shown in **Figure 10** corresponding to the testing conditions 130 MPa, 0W20 oil, and shaft speed of 4000 rpm. As seen in this figure and **Table 9**, the overall RF model predicting performance is lower than for the other test data sets but still very good. Nonetheless, the recall metric for label 1 is low, which may result from testing a higher load than the one used for training. This situation is observed in **Figure 10**, as many weak mixed lubrication points (label 1) were predicted as significant mixed lubrication, although mainly on the left side of the curves.

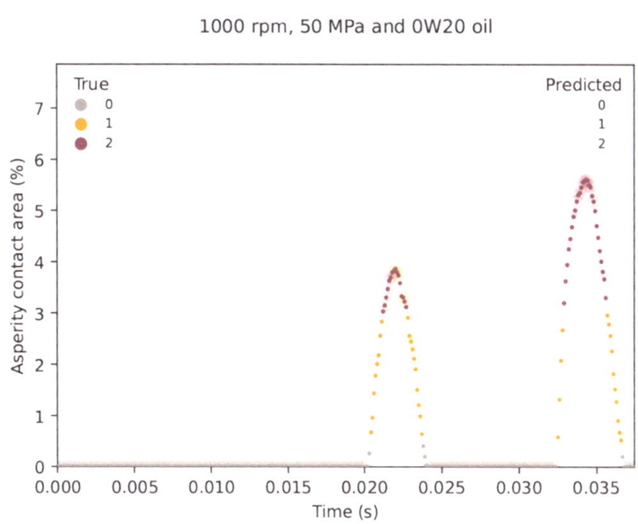


**Figure 9.**
*True and predicted lubrication regimes with the reduced training data set for the testing conditions 50 MPa, 0W20 oil, and 1000 rpm.*

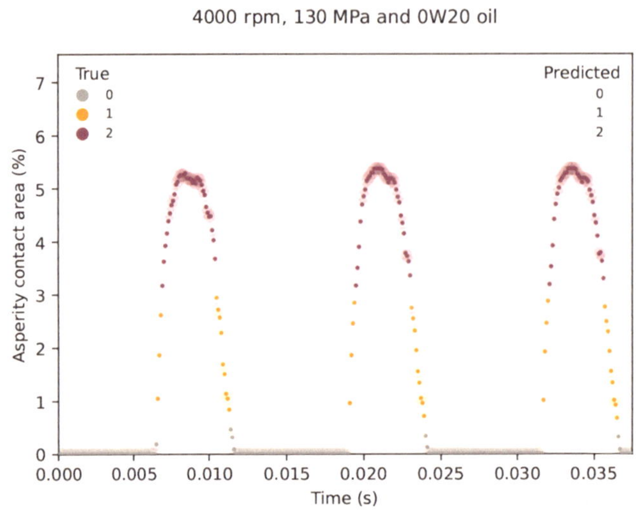


**Figure 10.**
*True and predicted lubrication regimes with the reduced training data set for the testing conditions 130 MPa, 0W20 oil, and 4000 rpm.*

## 5. Conclusions and outlook

This chapter presents three approaches for research on journal bearings with particular attention to mixed lubrication conditions; this includes experimental testing, simulation, and performance prediction using machine learning tools. A new journal bearing test-rig developed by the research group was presented for the experimental approach, able to directly measure the friction losses generated in the bearing contact and quantify the generated wear particles. To complement this experimental approach, a simulation model was also implemented considering the elastic deformation of the components, the rheological properties of the oil and the viscosity dependence on temperature, pressure, and shear rate, and the roughness parameters of the contacting surfaces for the asperities' interaction under mixed lubrication. Future works in the test-rig include the development of Stribeck tests to investigate further mixed lubrication and wear phenomena under these conditions; these measurements will also serve to validate the simulation approach.

For the journal bearing's performance prediction, a brief literature review was presented first, highlighting recent works aimed to predict the performance state of the bearing and lubrication regime under certain operating conditions and with the use of different measured parameters as predictors. A simple application using a Random Forest algorithm was presented in this chapter to predict the lubrication regime in the bearing using data from simulation and three predictors with highly accurate results. From this literature review and the application presented here, the great potential demonstrated by these ML algorithms for understanding the complex tribological process occurring in the bearing contact and predicting its performance can be highlighted. Equally important is the wide diversity of data that can be used for training, both from experimental and simulation results, which, adequately selected and pre-processed, can provide a robust foundation for the ML models. Future works include testing the RF model with experimental results from the bearing test-rig and improving the ML model to predict the bearing's remaining useful lifetime using ANN and physics-informed neural networks.

## Acknowledgements

Research leading to these results has received funding from the EU KDT Joint Undertaking under grant agreement n° 101096387 (project PowerizeD) and from the partners national programs/funding authorities.

The publication was written within the framework of the project PowerizeD which is Co-funded by the European Union. Views and opinions expressed are however those of the author(s) only and do not necessarily reflect those of the European Union Key Digital Technologies Joint Undertaking. Neither the European Union nor the granting authority can be held responsible for them. The project is supported by the Key Digital Technologies Joint Undertaking and its members (including top-up funding by the Austrian Federal Ministry for Climate Action (BMK)). The publication was written at Virtual Vehicle Research GmbH in Graz and partially funded by the COMET K2 Competence Centers for Excellent Technologies from the Austrian Federal Ministry for Climate Action (BMK), the Austrian Federal Ministry for Labour and Economy (BMAW), the Province of Styria (Dept. 12) and the Styrian Business Promotion Agency (SFG). The Austrian Research Promotion Agency (FFG) has been authorized for the programme management.

Additionally, author Sophia Bastidas acknowledges the Margarita Salas grant from the Universitat Politècnica de València, Ministerio de Universidades of Spain, and the Plan de Recuperación, Transformación y Resiliencia funded by the European Union-NextGenerationEU.

## Conflict of interest

The authors declare no conflict of interest.

## Nomenclature

| | |
|---|---|
| c | radial clearance |
| D | bearing diameter |
| $E$ | combined Young's module |
| $K$ | elastic factor |
| L | bearing width |
| r | shaft radius |
| S | sommerfeld number |
| U | velocity |
| W | applied load |
| $\delta$ | mean summit height |
| $\eta$ | oil viscosity |
| $\lambda$ | oil film parameter |
| $\mu_{Bound}$ | boundary friction coefficient |
| $\sigma$ | asperity summit roughness |
| $\Gamma$ | asperities' orientation |

## Abbreviations

| | |
|---|---|
| ANN | artificial neural network |
| EHD | elastohydrodynamic |

| | |
|---|---|
| HD | hydrodynamic |
| ML | machine learning |
| REVO | revolute joint |
| RF | random forest |
| SAE | Society of Automotive Engineers |

## Author details

Sophia Bastidas[1,2*†] and Hannes Allmaier[1†]

1 Virtual Vehicle Research Center GmbH, Graz, Austria

2 Universitat Politècnica de València, Valencia, Spain

*Address all correspondence to: sophia.bastidas@v2c2.at

† These authors contributed equally.

## References

[1] Marian M, Tremmel S. Current trends and applications of machine mearning in tribology – A review. Lubricants. 2021;**9**(9). DOI: 10.3390/lubricants 9090086

[2] Sadik Ünlü B, Durmuş H, Meriç C. Determination of tribological properties at CuSn10 alloy journal bearings by experimental and means of artificial neural networks method. Industrial Lubrication and Tribology. 2012;**64**(5): 258-264. DOI: 10.1108/ 00368791211249647

[3] Moder J, Bergmann P, Grün F. Lubrication regime classification of hydrodynamic journal bearings by machine learning using torque data. Lubricants. 2018;**6**(4):1-15. DOI: 10.3390/lubricants6040108

[4] Prost J, Cihak-Bayr U, Neacşu IA, Grundtner R, Pirker F, Vorlaufer G. Semi-supervised classification of the state of operation in self-lubricating journal bearings using a random forest classifier. Lubricants. 2021;**9**(5):27-44. DOI: 10.3390/lubricants9050050

[5] Prost J, Boidi G, Puhwein AM, Varga M, Vorlaufer G. Classification of operational states in porous journal bearings using a semi-supervised multi-sensor machine learning approach. Tribology International. 2023;**184**: 108464. DOI: 10.1016/j. triboint.2023.108464

[6] Allmaier H, Priestner C, Six C, Priebsch HH, Forstner C, Novotny-Farkas F. Predicting friction reliably and accurately in journal bearings – A systematic validation of simulation results with experimental measurements. Tribology International. 2011;**44**(10):1151-1160. DOI: 10.1016/ j.triboint.2011.05.010

[7] Sander DE, Allmaier H, Priebsch HH, Reich FM, Witt M, Füllenbach T, et al. Impact of high pressure and shear thinning on journal bearing friction. Tribology International. 2015;**81**:29-37. DOI: 10.1016/j.triboint.2014.07.021

[8] Sander DE, Allmaier H, Priebsch HH, Reich FM, Witt M, Skiadas A, et al. Edge loading and running-in wear in dynamically loaded journal bearings. Tribology International. 2015;**92**: 395-403. DOI: 10.1016/j. triboint.2015.07.022

[9] Allmaier H, Sander D, Priebsch H, Witt M, Füllenbach T, Skiadas A. Non-Newtonian and running-in wear effects in journal bearings operating under mixed lubrication. Proceedings of the Institution of Mechanical Engineers, Part J: Journal of Engineering Tribology. 2016;**230**(2):135-142. DOI: 10.1177/ 1350650115594191

[10] Sander DE, Allmaier H, Priebsch HH, Witt M, Skiadas A. Simulation of journal bearing friction in severe mixed lubrication-validation and effect of surface smoothing due to running-in. Tribology International. 2016;**96**:173-183. DOI: 10.1016/j. triboint.2015.12.024

[11] Patir N, Cheng HS. An average flow model for determining effects of three-dimensional roughness on partial hydrodynamic lubrication. ASME Journal of Lubrication Technology. 1978; **100**:12-17. DOI: 10.1115/1.3453103

[12] Patir N, Cheng HS. Application of average flow model to lubrication between rough sliding surfaces. ASME. Journal of Lubrication Technology. 1979;**101**:220-229. DOI: 10.1115/ 1.3453329

[13] Greenwood JA, Tripp JH. The contact of two nominally flat rough surfaces. Proceedings of the Institution of Mechanical Engineers. 1970;**185**(1): 625-633. DOI: 10.1243/PIME_PROC_1970_185_069_02

[14] Jakobsson B, Floberg L. The Finite Journal Bearing, Considering Vaporization. Gothenburg, Sweden: Gumperts Förlag; 1957

[15] Vogel H. The law of the relation between the viscosity of liquids and the temperature. Physikalishce Zeitschrift. 1921;**22**(1):645-646

[16] Isothermals BC. Isopiestics and isometrics relative to viscosity. American Journal of Science (1880-1910). 1893; **45**(266):87-96

[17] Cross MM. Rheology of non-Newtonian fluids: A new flow equation for pseudoplastic systems. Journal of Colloid Science. 1965;**20**(5):417-437. DOI: 10.1016/0095-8522(65)90022-X

[18] Rahnejat H. Tribology and Dynamics of Engine and Powertrain: Fundamentals, Applications and Future Trends. Oxford: Woodhead Publishing; 2010

[19] Pedregosa F, Varoquaux G, Gramfort A, Michel V, Thirion B, Grisel O, et al. Scikit-learn: Machine learning in Python. Journal of Machine Learning Research. 2011;**12**:2825-2830

Chapter 4

# Predicting Student Performance in Flipped Learning through Machine Learning Techniques: A Bibliometric Analysis with R

*Ragazou Vasiliki and Antonis Konstantinos*


## Abstract

Machine learning (ML) is an emerging field of study that utilizes data to enhance the learning process and optimize the learning environment. The primary goals of ML are to observe students' activities and provide early predictions about their academic performance, with the aim of enhancing student retention. Furthermore, ML aims to provide personalized feedback and streamline the provision of support to pupils. A flipped classroom is an educational approach that integrates both physical and digital spaces, known as blended learning environments. Flipped classes often use learning management systems that provide access to recorded lectures and digital resources. This facilitates the collection of statistics on students' interaction with these services. The present chapter used bibliometric analysis to examine the effect of ML in predicting students' performance in flipped classes. Information was extracted from the Scopus database for the period of 2014–2024. The data were examined using the R statistical programming language and the Biblioshiny software. Through the use of this strategy, we are presented with possibilities to enhance our skills and expertise in the respective domain. The investigation reveals that ML systems provide automated data-driven formative feedback, which supports students' self-regulation and enables instructors to identify areas and tactics for intervention and assistance.


**Keywords:** flipped learning, machine learning, student performance, prediction, bibliometric analysis

## 1. Introduction

Data mining methods have recently gained considerable attention in the education industry [1–3]. Data mining (DM) is a systematic process used to discover important insights and patterns from large datasets [4]. Data mining is a field that focuses on discovering new and potentially useful insights or important results from large databases. Furthermore, its primary goal is to reveal innovative trends and patterns from extensive datasets via the use of various classification methodologies.

Educational data mining (EDM) is the use of conventional data mining techniques to examine and address educational issues [5, 6]. EDM is the process of examining educational data via the use of data mining techniques. This includes the assessment of student data, academic transcripts, examination outcomes, student participation in classroom activities, and the frequency of student inquiries. EDM is an effective method used to uncover concealed patterns in educational data with the aim of forecasting academic advancement and enhancing the educational environment. EDM has expanded the scope of learning analytics (LA) [7]. LA is the systematic collection and analysis of student data to assess and evaluate the learning environment, with the goal of determining the highest level of achievement attained by either the student or the instructor [8]. LA is a methodical process of gathering, assessing, and displaying data on students and their educational environment, with the main goal of enhancing understanding and optimizing educational settings and the learning process. Moreover, it sheds light on the institutions that are promoting inventive approaches [8, 9].

Another aspect of LA includes the forecasting of student academic achievement [2, 10–14], the detection of patterns in system use and navigation, and the identification of students who may be prone to academic underperformance. Educational technology platforms, such as Massive Open Online Courses (MOOC), learning management systems (LMS), student information systems (SIS), and intelligent teaching systems (ITS), provide digital data that may be used to assess students' future behaviors. The EDM approach may use this information to examine the behaviors of high-achieving and at-risk children in connection to academic underperformance. Therefore, this research might be used to develop strategies based on student academic performance, with the goal of assisting educators in improving their teaching methods.

The gathered data on educational processes offer novel prospects for enhancing the learning experience and optimizing user involvement with digital platforms. Analyzing educational data facilitates advancements in several domains, including predicting student behavior, developing innovative pedagogical approaches, and establishing educational policies. By meticulously gathering and analyzing data, school administrators would be able to formulate policies grounded on actual evidence. Furthermore, this will provide a foundation for developing artificial intelligence (AI) software aimed at improving the educational process. EDM allows instructors to predict outcomes such as decreased course enrollment or school attrition rates, analyze internal variables that impact students' academic performance, and anticipate future academic achievements using statistical methods. Diverse data mining approaches are used to forecast student performance, detect students with subpar learning rates, and anticipate student attrition. Early prediction is a novel approach that uses evaluation tools to provide students with suggestions on suitable treatments and strategies in this domain.

Given the gravity of the pandemic, LMS has rapidly become indispensable in higher education. With the increasing usage of smart devices by students, the generated log data have become more readily available. Universities should emphasize enhancing their proficiency in using these data to forecast academic achievement and monitor student advancement. EDM enables educators to get novel insights by uncovering latent patterns in data pertaining to education. Through the use of this methodology, certain facets of the educational system may be assessed and enhanced in order to guarantee the excellence of education.

## 2. Literature review

EDM researchers have thoroughly investigated e-learning systems in several research studies. Numerous studies have sought to categorize educational data, while others have tried to forecast student achievement. Ref. [15] used data mining techniques to examine two separate attributes while studying the academic achievement of undergraduate students. The first phase is predicting the scholastic achievement of pupils upon completion of a 4-year educational curriculum. The second approach involves integrating student progress evaluations into the result forecast procedure. He classified the pupils into two clearly defined categories based on their level of achievement: high and low. The individual acknowledges the importance of teachers prioritizing a limited number of courses that exhibit exceptional quality or inadequacy. This enables them to promptly identify and assist youngsters who are not doing well while also offering guidance and opportunities to those who have exceptional abilities. In their study, the authors in Ref. [16] predicted students' academic success by considering 16 demographic characteristics, such as age, gender, class attendance, computer ownership, internet access, and the number of completed courses. ML algorithms, including random forest, logistic regression, k-nearest neighbors, and support vector machines, effectively forecasted the academic performance of the pupils with an accuracy ranging from 50 to 81%.

The students' academic performance marks, obtained from in-term activities, were integrated into a model created by the authors in Ref. [17]. The research used classification models that leveraged the Gradient Boosting Machine (GBM) to predict the academic development of individuals. The findings indicate that the most reliable predictors of performance scores were the number of absences and the achievement scores from the previous year. The researchers have found potential indicators of success or failure, such as demographic factors including age, educational institution, and geographic region. Furthermore, he postulated that this framework may function as a blueprint for the creation of novel policies that are specifically tailored to avert failures. The authors in Ref. [18] conducted a comprehensive data analysis to identify students who were most susceptible to academic failure while considering environmental variables. Empirical research confirms that the use of data mining approaches may lead to more accurate classification of problematic youngsters. Furthermore, their approach allows for the classification of pupils based on varying degrees of hypersensitivity. The authors in Ref. [19] devised an ML method to ascertain the crucial parameters influencing the curriculum of academic institutions and to establish the connections between these aspects. The study determined that the intensity of parental influence, the class size, the amount of competitiveness, and the gender distribution were the primary factors that influenced improved academic achievement. The aforementioned results were inferred by the examination of regression trees. Furthermore, the study revealed that the ratio of female students and the school's size had a substantial impact on the model's anticipated accuracy, as shown by the outcomes acquired via the implementation of the random forest approach.

Ref. [20] proposed using an ML methodology to ascertain the academic performance of kids who are vulnerable to certain dangers. The student's cognitive ability, study habits, and academic involvement were efficiently used to generate a forecast with an accuracy rate of 85% in categorization. The researchers found that it is feasible to identify academically underperforming students based on their methods. The authors in Ref. [21] presented a ML model that integrates several aspects such as health issues, academic accomplishment, motivation, education, and feelings of social support. By using this process, he successfully identified students who were likely to drop out of school and accurately predicted their academic performance. The presence of prior foundation knowledge had the most substantial influence on attrition rates, but the use of effective learning mechanisms emerged as the most notable predictor of GPA.

The authors in Ref. [7] created an artificial neural network (ANN) model to examine student data on their use of the LMS. The data indicate that demographic characteristics and clickstream patterns have a substantial impact on students' academic achievement. The students who successfully completed the courses demonstrated academic achievement. There was no correlation between the scholars' academic achievement and their level of participation in the learning environment. However, the study concluded that the deep learning model has the possibility to be an essential tool in predicting student performance at an early stage. The authors in Ref. [22] discovered a correlation between the internet use habits of university students and their academic achievement. In addition, ML techniques were used to produce predictions about the academic performance of the kids. The suggested approach significantly improved the accuracy of predicting students' academic achievement. A study revealed that there is a negative association between internet data use and academic performance, whereas the frequency of internet usage is positively linked to academic accomplishment. Moreover, he demonstrated that the integration of online features had a substantial impact on the academic performance of students. The authors in Ref. [23] examined if using data alone from the LMS is enough to predict academic performance. Based on his research, the behavior-based prediction model accurately forecasted the need for course repetition with a 75% level of accuracy. Furthermore, he said that this approach facilitates the identification and provision of assistance to students who may have challenges in future academic periods. The authors in Ref. [24] developed a specific tool to assist students who are in danger of failing in their next semesters of study. Unlike previous school years, he saw a 14% decrease in the percentage of students who failed.

Previous studies on predicting academic accomplishment have included several ML techniques, including logistic regression, probit regression, multiple regression, and neural networks, as well as C4.5 and J48 decision trees. The current study used random forests, genetic programming, and Naïve Bayes methods. The aforementioned algorithms have achieved remarkably high levels of predicted precision. In order to accurately predict a student's academic success, it is crucial to have a thorough understanding of the many aspects and traits that impact their achievements and results. The authors in Ref. [25] performed a comprehensive study of 357 papers to investigate student performance. Specifically, they evaluated the impacts of 29 essential components. The major emphasis was on psychomotor skills, which included factors such as academic accomplishment, self-regulation, course and pre-course involvement, and student demographics (e.g., gender). However, attrition rates were mostly influenced by variables such as student motivation, routines, social and financial worries, stasis in personal growth, and work changes.

To improve the quality of education, as indicated by the literature review, it is necessary to have the capability to predict students' academic development and provide support to those who are in danger of falling behind. A significant amount of scholarly study has been dedicated to predicting academic success by analyzing various qualities. Student digital footprints include a range of online activities, such as browsing habits, length of class attendance, and degree of active engagement. Researchers have investigated demographic factors, including socioeconomic position, number of courses completed, gender, age, and internet access. The analysis has also included other variables such as cognitive capacities, study methods, patterns of studying approaches for learning, sense of social support, drive, socio-demographic aspects, physical well-being, and traits related to academic accomplishment. Moreover, scholars have examined the influence of assignments, projects, and tests, along with other variables, on academic performance. The models used in these assessments typically have a prediction accuracy ranging from 70 to 95%. Nonetheless, the gathering and examination of such an extensive amount of data is a tedious endeavor that necessitates specific proficiency. The authors in Ref. [18] state that collecting a substantial quantity of data is a difficult task, and socioeconomic data are unnecessary. Moreover, it is crucial to acknowledge that demographic and socioeconomic data may not consistently function as a reliable indicator for preventing failure, as emphasized by the authors in Ref. [23].

## 3. Materials and methods

This study used a bibliometric strategy to methodically examine selected scholarly papers with the aim of identifying recurring themes, limitations, and developing areas.

| Step | Keyword search |
|---|---|
| 1 | (("flipped learning") AND "machine learning")) |
| 2 | (("flipped learning") AND ("machine learning") OR "artificial intelligence")) |
| 3 | (("flipped learning") AND ("machine learning") OR "artificial intelligence") AND "digital education")) |
| 4 | (("flipped learning") OR ("online learning") AND ("machine learning") OR "artificial intelligence") AND "digital education")) |
| 5 | (("flipped learning") OR ("flipped classroom") OR ("online learning") AND ("machine learning") OR "artificial intelligence") AND "digital education")) |
| 6 | (("flipped learning") OR ("flipped classroom") OR ("online learning") AND ("machine learning") OR "artificial intelligence" OR "augmented reality") AND ("digital education" OR "educational innovation")) |
| 7 | (("flipped learning") OR ("flipped classroom") OR ("online learning") AND ("machine learning") OR "artificial intelligence" OR "augmented reality") AND ("digital education" OR "educational innovation" OR "education data mining")) |
| 8 | (("flipped learning") OR ("flipped classroom") OR ("online learning") AND ("machine learning") OR "artificial intelligence" OR "augmented reality" OR "robotics") AND ("digital education" OR "educational innovation" OR "education data mining")) |
| 9 | (("flipped learning") OR (elearning") OR ("flipped classroom") OR ("online learning") AND ("machine learning") OR "artificial intelligence" OR "augmented reality" OR "robotics") AND ("digital education" OR "educational innovation" OR "education data mining")) |
| 10 | (("flipped learning") OR (elearning") OR ("flipped classroom") OR ("online learning") AND ("machine learning") OR "artificial intelligence" OR "augmented reality" OR "robotics") AND ("digital education" OR "educational innovation" OR "education data mining")) AND (LIMIT-TO (DOCTYPE, "ar")) AND (LIMIT-TO (PUBSTAGE, "final") OR LIMIT-TO (PUBSTAGE, "aip")) AND (LIMIT-TO (SRCTYPE, "j")) |

**Table 1.**
*Keyword search formula.*

Bibliometric analysis enables the assessment of current research status and identification of prestigious academic journals, publishing corporations, or authors within a certain field. Applying the bibliometric approach with machine learning techniques is appropriate for forecasting student achievement in flipped learning due to its ability to provide a comprehensive overview of the academic subject matter and enhance understanding. This research employs a systematic analysis of compiled literature data acquired from sources such as Scopus, Web of Science (WoS), and Google Scholar. Quantitative and bibliometric methodologies have shown substantial expansion in recent years as means of assessing research output. A thorough assessment should be conducted to evaluate the effectiveness, accuracy, and consistency of an evaluation process.

The data used in the current study were obtained from Scopus in December 2023. The process of doing keyword searches is thoroughly explained and shown in **Table 1**.

**Figure 1** depicts the essential steps involved in choosing a reliable set of articles for bibliometric analysis using the preferred reporting items for systematic reviews and meta-analyses (PRISMA) flow diagram [26]. The search query for the collection yielded 876 sources, which we narrowed down to 732 by only choosing documents. Subsequently, a thorough examination was conducted on a total of 569 papers to exclude any that seemed unrelated to the topic or covered too many subjects for this particular study, which focuses on exploring innovative approaches to using machine learning for predicting the achievement of students in flipped learning. Upon manual evaluation of the articles, it was found that the names and keywords of numerous chosen sources did not clearly indicate the scope and characteristics of the investigated field. Consequently, the search criteria were modified to only include articles that are relevant to the present study subject, so excluding any references that are irrelevant. Following the completion of this filtering process, a grand total of 387 scientific articles remained, which were then included in the bibliometric analysis.

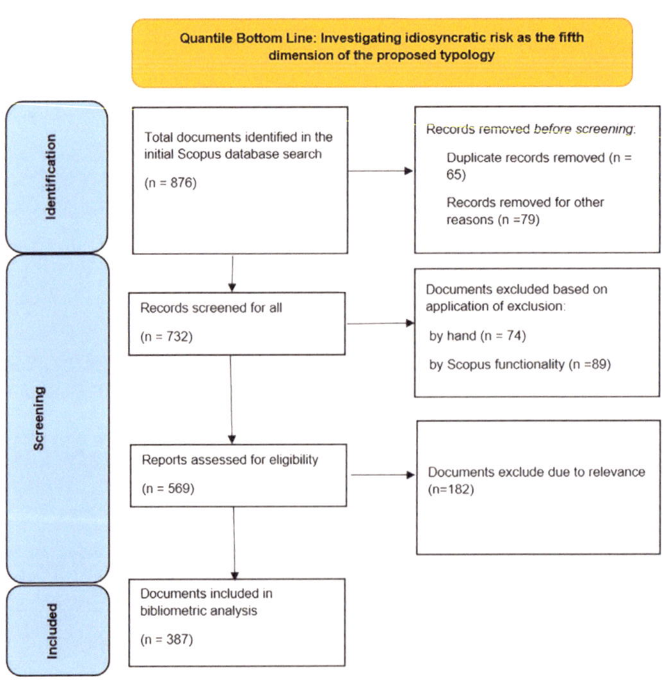


**Figure 1.**
*Selection process of the articles for bibliometric analysis using the PRISMA flow diagram method.*

## 4. ML and LA: the digitalization of the flipped classroom

The previous study conducted by the authors in Ref. [27] clearly showed the substantial impact that an instructional framework may have on a student's learning style. The authors in Ref. [27] propose that the instructional approach used by a teacher influences whether a student adopts a superficial or in-depth approach to learning. An educational strategy that excessively prioritizes the teacher's role and the transfer of information may often lead to students acquiring just a shallow understanding of the learning process. Adopting a student-centered strategy that enables learners to independently improve their understanding of the subjects being studied leads to a deeper educational experience. The educational style discussed here, known as active learning, has many parallels with the communicative language teaching method. The authors in Ref. [27] conducted a study on 48 science classes including first-year students. They discovered compelling evidence that active learning approaches effectively include students in a profound learning process, resulting in the attainment of higher-level learning objectives [28]. Foreign language (FL) presupposes that students engage in pre-class and/or post-class activities rather than passively observing classroom events. Consistently participating in academic activities throughout the term results in enhanced academic performance.

The authors in Ref. [29] conducted a meta-analysis where they analyzed 225 articles to compare the academic performance of undergraduate science, technology, engineering and mathematics (STEM) students who were enrolled in courses that used active learning approaches vs. standard lecturing. The researchers analyzed two outcome variables: the frequency of course failures and the academic proficiency of students on tests. Researchers noted a 1.5-fold increase in the likelihood of students failing traditional lecture-based courses compared to those that used an active learning strategy. The meta-analysis revealed that substituting conventional lectures with active learning techniques led to a significant average enhancement of 0.5 standard deviations in students' performance on tests that were either the same or comparable. Freeman et al.'s meta-analysis consistently showed that active learning yielded advantages across all STEM fields, including various course levels and experimental approaches. The primary research papers showed significant effects when active learning constituted the bulk of class time. Furthermore, the authors in Ref. [28] highlighted that there is evidence indicating that active learning has a greater influence on students' proficiency in advanced cognitive abilities than fundamental skills.

Despite its history of more than 15 years as an interactive learning method, foreign language (FL) has only just started to get recognition and become popular among educators. The assessment and analysis of formative learning as a method to improve student learning often demonstrate inadequacy [30]. Previous studies in the domain of FL teaching mostly collected data on students' viewpoints and comprehension of FL via the use of interviews and questionnaires. In addition, the researchers evaluated the extent of enhancement in the student's academic achievement by using both pre- and post-tests, along with course grades [31]. The bulk of the aforementioned research have confirmed the educational advantages linked to FL models, including higher attendance rates, enhanced academic achievement, and better student happiness. Although there are data supporting the benefits of FL for students, the authors in Ref. [31] caution educators against automatically believing that it is superior to conventional seminars. O'Flaherty and Phillips found a lack of research that provides convincing evidence supporting the effectiveness of the reversed learning approach compared to traditional teaching methods.

Undoubtedly, further efforts are necessary to enhance the methodological precision linked to this comparative analysis. The degree of learner autonomy within a FL curriculum is a complex and important matter that has a direct influence on students' progress in an FL environment [32]. Self-regulated learning is essential for students to actively participate in and effectively complete the preparation tasks specified in this particular active learning framework [33–35]. However, many students lack sufficient self-regulation skills and need support and guidance to successfully navigate their educational path in unexpected and challenging circumstances, which are often linked to the FL curriculum. The FL design examined in this research has a well-defined structure that stays consistent throughout the course.

Nevertheless, FL seems to have undergone digitalization with the use of ML. The integration of ML into teaching methods has been made possible by the widespread use of computers and information technology in education, driven by the progress of educational technologies in the near future. ML employs advanced data processing and analytics to replicate human cognition and functions. Ancestry has shown a significant inclination to explore blended learning and online education as areas of research. The authors in Ref. [36–38] have achieved notable advancements in the area of machine learning in education (MLEd), particularly in the development of educational features. Subsequently, the system has proposed educational pathways and enhanced training techniques. Presently, MLEd is used to forecast academic achievement. This approach has the capacity to improve the efficiency of education by identifying students who have a higher probability of failing their courses and subsequently improving and perfecting the courses to better cater to the individual needs of each student [36, 38].

ML performance prediction models may be classified into two distinct classes by analyzing two views inside a closed loop. The main objective of the first perspective, referred to as the ML model perspective, is to improve the precision of prediction models. Throughout this procedure, artificial intelligence models are generated and validated to precisely forecast students' academic achievement. The educational application viewpoint, which is seen as secondary, largely emphasizes the actual implementation and impact of ML prediction models. ML prediction models effectively aid educators and learners in improving the quality of education and knowledge acquisition. To get precise forecasts of academic achievement using ML models, it is essential to emphasize two key elements: the comprehensive integration of the model into educational institutions via significant research and the ongoing enhancement and refinement of the model itself. Although ML prediction models have been extensively examined in academia, the primary focus of research has been on their development and improvement. By using many algorithms, such as the one proposed by Jiao et al. in 2022, it is feasible to develop models that exhibit outstanding accuracy in predicting outcomes. Moreover, despite the present emphasis on creating artificial intelligence prediction models for educational purposes, there is a dearth of models that integrate real-time input and provide accurate feedback to both teachers and students, with the goal of improving the quality of students' learning. The combination of LA and ML has been acknowledged as an effective approach to address this issue (**Figure 2**). Most of the ongoing research on this topic is centered on this convergence.

**Figure 3** emphasizes the significance of ML in the process of digitizing the flipped classroom and its close correlation with LA. Artificial Intelligence is directly linked to the digitization of the flipped classroom. The use of artificial intelligence technology has the capacity to facilitate the implementation of individualized instruction within

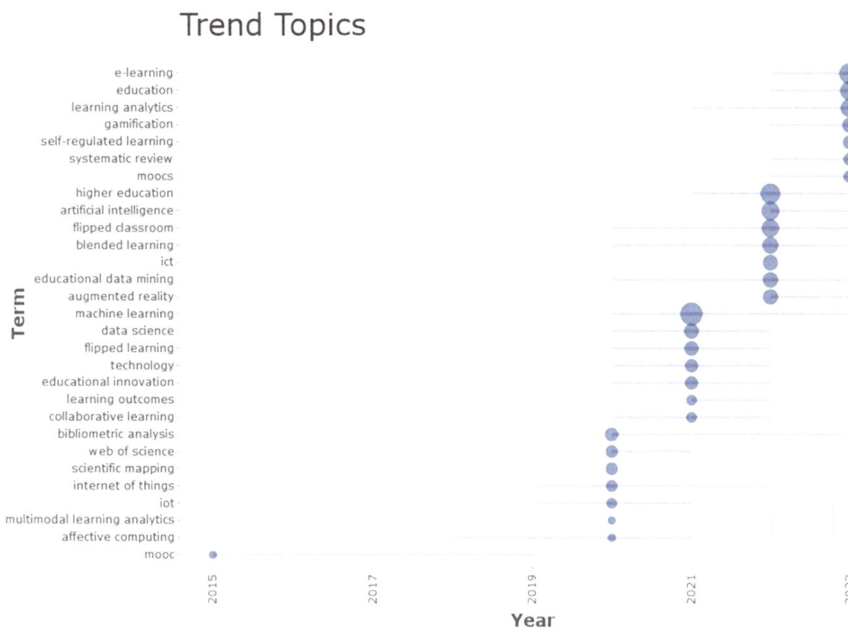


**Figure 2.**
*Research trends for the timeframe 2015–2023.*

the classroom environment. Artificial intelligence systems have the capability to fulfill four unique functions within the realm of education. These positions include acting as an astute mentor, a knowledgeable mentee, a sophisticated educational resource, or an advisor to politicians. Intelligent teaching methods include several facets. These manifestations include adaptive learning systems, personalized learning systems, and

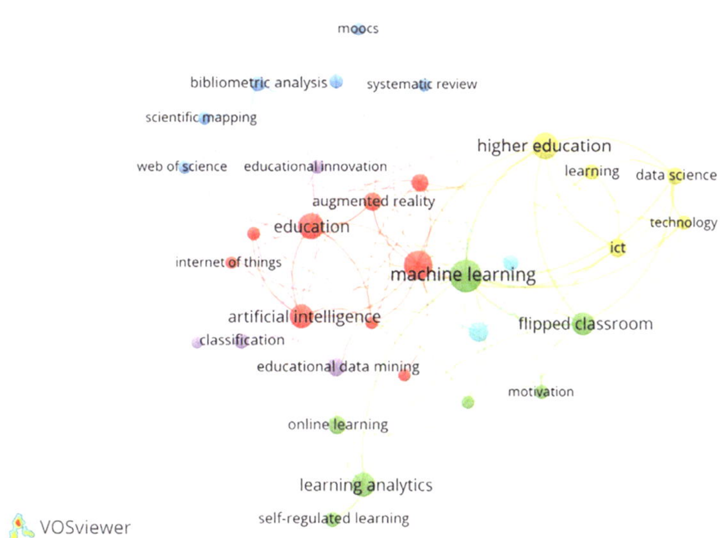


**Figure 3.**
*Co-citation analysis based on authors keywords.*

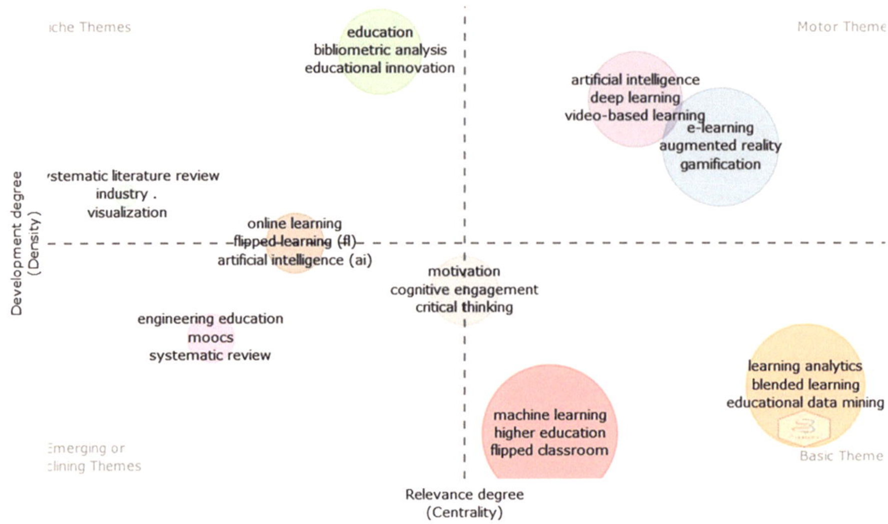


**Figure 4.**
*Thematic map.*

recommendation systems. Studies have shown that intelligent tutoring systems has the ability to augment the academic accomplishments of individual individuals.

The above is confirmed by **Figure 4** as well.

## 5. Massive open online courses (MOOCs) in machine learning: the future in the prediction of student performance

Multiple scholars have highlighted the need to include learning effectiveness in the instructional materials design process. Academic support pertains to the capacity of educational materials to aid students in efficiently remembering, recalling, and comprehending certain information.

The authors in Ref. [39] argue that successful implementation of a blended education paradigm requires the integration of inventive tactics that may be merged with traditional face-to-face instruction, such as MOOCs. The map of the Multiple Correspondence Analysis [39], shown in **Figure 5**, displays two distinct clusters: the red cluster and the blue cluster. The second outlines the difficulties that have not been thoroughly examined by the scholarly community so far. A concern highlighted in the blue cluster pertains to the significance of MOOCs. Furthermore, MOOCs are a modern educational innovation that may be used to improve distance learning. Moreover, they noted that it is a crucial element of the hybrid educational method, in which learning takes place via a blend of physical and digital settings. Several scholars have highlighted the significance of mutual comprehension and extended social, collaborative learning in education based on MOOCs.

According to the authors in Ref. [40], students' perception of MOOCs as being easy to use and beneficial significantly impacts their learning conduct. The authors in Ref. [40] identified several factors that contribute to the increasing attrition rate in MOOCs in their research. The factors include psychological, social, personal, course-related, time-related, and concealed financial duties. Furthermore, they emphasized the need to cultivate student excitement and encourage active participation to decrease the retention

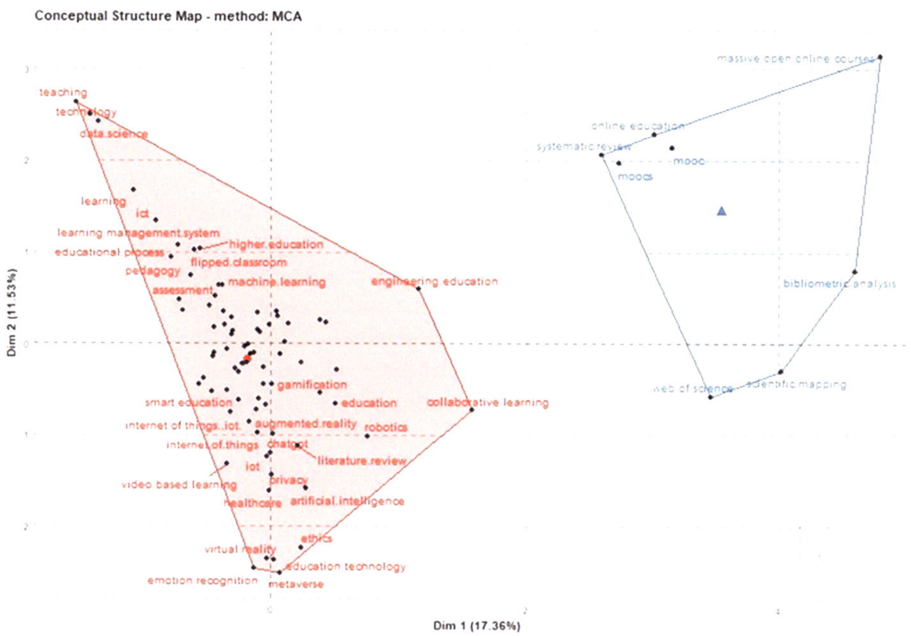


**Figure 5.**
*Multiple correspondence analysis (MCA).*

rates seen in MOOCs. Furthermore, well-crafted course frameworks are crucial for enhancing student involvement and fostering enthusiasm. In a further inquiry, the authors in Ref. [41] discovered that the level of cooperation in MOOCs, the efficiency of the system, and the quality of interface design all influence the quantity of knowledge obtained by students. Furthermore, it has been shown that the perspective of students about the utility, overall pleasure, and educational experience is significantly influenced by top-notch MOOCs, resulting in a persistent willingness to participate in MOOCs.

Additionally, MOOCs are crucial for universities and other organizations as they allow them to provide cost-effective, readily available, and top-notch educational materials to students and learners. Moreover, they provide an exceptional chance for educational institutions to expand their student population, since geographical or other obstacles may hinder some persons from enrolling in conventional on-campus classes. Open edX offers institutions a powerful platform to evaluate and improve the quality of their education by delivering material and tracking student progress. To summarize, Open edX enables academic institutions to make income by charging fees for access to certain courses and materials.

Furthermore, MOOCs enable the dissemination of top-notch education to a wide range of persons and promote the continuous education of various socioeconomic classes. MOOCs have the capacity to aid those who are currently not engaged in any pursuits in obtaining crucial skills necessary for employment. Moreover, they possess the capacity to facilitate the provision of complimentary staff training, and MOOCs are available to anybody worldwide who has internet connectivity. Social networking platforms and discussion forums enable the sharing of ideas and foster engagement among users. Similar to a traditional classroom setting, motivate students to acquire information by actively participating in group activities with their classmates, which may result in a more thorough comprehension.

## 6. Conclusions

While many acknowledge the effectiveness of multimodal teaching methods, most medical educators and theorists concur that a curriculum including LA tools goes beyond just hearing lectures passively. This is because the curriculum enhances the retention and application of newly learned information. LA utilizes several teaching tactics, including the flexible classroom, think-pair-share, turn and speak, and lecture with bullet point breaks. These techniques require students to actively develop, understand, and absorb knowledge gained over their educational journey, while also enhancing their ability to retain information and learn new skills. The flipped classroom educational style, which emerged in the late 1990s, has gained recognition due to its proven efficacy in academic environments. The reversed classroom utilizes defined teaching time to facilitate active learning. This system provides significant advantages by prioritizing the practical application of learned information, enhancing comprehension of the subject matter, and enhancing performance on standardized tests. Recently, there has been a growing realization that using a combination of different teaching approaches, known as a multimodal approach, is the most effective strategy for increasing the likelihood of success in academic pursuits. According to educational research, the most successful instructional strategy in the twenty-first century is integrating multiple pedagogical materials in a way that they complement one another. The combination or synergistic use of multimodal and system-based methodologies improves students' learning effectiveness.

ML applications, which were first established in 1955, have had a significant increase in utilization in recent years. This increase represents a fundamental change in technology, which is expected to provide useful resources for improving medical education. ML is mostly used in medical education to aid students in their learning, gauge their advancement, and, to a lesser extent, appraise the curriculum, as per educational research. Integrating ML technology into educational systems has the capacity to provide continuous feedback around the clock and a structured learning trajectory. Based on subgroup research, ML deployment is mostly focused on medical students. However, there is a limited amount of educational research evaluating the efficacy of this technology. The main objective of this academic inquiry was to evaluate the efficacy of voice-over-style lectures and artificial intelligence technologies in enhancing the learning experience. The hypothesis suggests that the adoption of ML in the flexible classroom would improve academic attainment and students' performance.

Moreover, the substantial collection of student behavioral data by many MOOC platforms has sparked scholarly curiosity in data mining methodologies. Hence, data mining methods are extensively used to analyze online learning behavior and determine the relationship between learning behavior and learning outcomes across the whole learning process. The authors in Ref. [42] analyzed two types of approaches used to develop prediction models utilizing behavioral data gathered from participants of MOOCs. The data included evaluations, completed assignments, and video lecture consumption. These models have the ability to provide precise and prompt forecasts of student performance. The research done by [43] analyzed the data pertaining to the online learning activities of 129 students using the Moodle platform. Research has shown that promoting active student engagement in course forums, consistent submission of assignments, and sharing of learning resources might potentially improve their learning results. The authors in Ref. [44] used the Naïve Bayes classifier to investigate student records and identified a direct association between learners' academic achievement and their engagement in activities such as completing online assessments and attending live virtual lectures. Therefore, it may be inferred that learning behavior has a substantial impact on the learning process, acting as a reliable indication of students' academic accomplishments and defining their level of learning competence. However, the present research lacks a comprehensive examination of the correlation between the evolving learning behavior patterns shown by students and their academic performance in MOOCs.

## Acknowledgements

The authors would like to thank Dr. Konstantina Ragazou for her assistance with methodologies and procedures during this research.

## Conflict of interest

The authors declare no conflict of interest.

## Author details

Ragazou Vasiliki* and Antonis Konstantinos
Department of Physics, University of Thessaly, Lamia, Greece

*Address all correspondence to: ragazou@uth.gr

## References

[1] Liao S-H, Chu P-H, Hsiao P-Y. Data mining techniques and applications—A decade review from 2000 to 2011. Expert Systems with Applications. 2012;**39**(12):11303-11311. DOI: 10.1016/j.eswa.2012.02.063

[2] Tomasevic N, Gvozdenovic N, Vranes S. An overview and comparison of supervised data mining techniques for student exam performance prediction. Computers in Education. 2020;**143**:103676. DOI: 10.1016/j.compedu.2019.103676

[3] Hasan R, Palaniappan S, Mahmood S, Abbas A, Sarker KU, Sattar MU. Predicting student performance in higher educational institutions using video learning analytics and data mining techniques. Applied Sciences. 2020;**10**(11):3894. DOI: 10.3390/app10113894

[4] Lakshmi BN, Raghunandhan GH. A conceptual overview of data mining. In: 2011 National Conference on Innovations in Emerging Technology, Erode, India. 2011. DOI: 10.1109/NCOIET.2011.5738828

[5] Romero C, Ventura S. Educational data mining: A review of the state of the art. IEEE Transactions on Systems, Man, and Cybernetics, Part C (Applications and Reviews). 2010;**40**(6):601-618. DOI: 10.1109/TSMCC.2010.2053532

[6] Romero C, Ventura S. Educational data mining and learning analytics: An updated survey. WIREs Data Mining and Knowledge Discovery. 2020;**10**(3):1-21. DOI: 10.1002/widm.1355

[7] Waheed H, Hassan S-U, Aljohani NR, Hardman J, Alelyani S, Nawaz R. Predicting academic performance of students from VLE big data using deep learning models. Computers in Human Behavior. 2020;**104**:106189. DOI: 10.1016/j.chb.2019.106189

[8] Siemens G, Baker RSJ d. Learning analytics and educational data mining. In: Proceedings of the 2nd International Conference on Learning Analytics and Knowledge—LAK'12. New York: ACM Press; 2012. p. 252. DOI: 10.1145/2330601.2330661

[9] Dawson S, Joksimovic S, Poquet O, Siemens G. Increasing the impact of learning analytics. In: Proceedings of the 9th International Conference on Learning Analytics & Knowledge. New York: ACM; 2019. pp. 446-455. DOI: 10.1145/3303772.3303784

[10] Abu Zohair LM. Prediction of student's performance by modelling small dataset size. International Journal of Educational Technology in Higher Education. 2019;**16**(1):27. DOI: 10.1186/s41239-019-0160-3

[11] Romero C, López M-I, Luna J-M, Ventura S. Predicting students' final performance from participation in on-line discussion forums. Computers in Education. 2013;**68**:458-472. DOI: 10.1016/j.compedu.2013.06.009

[12] Lerche T, Kiel E. Predicting student achievement in learning management systems by log data analysis. Computers in Human Behavior. 2018;**89**:367-372. DOI: 10.1016/j.chb.2018.06.015

[13] Ouyang F, Wu M, Zheng L, Zhang L, Jiao P. Integration of artificial intelligence performance prediction and learning analytics to improve student learning in online engineering course. International Journal of Educational Technology

in Higher Education. 2023;**20**(1):4. DOI: 10.1186/s41239-022-00372-4

[14] Xing W, Du D. Dropout prediction in MOOCs: Using deep learning for personalized intervention. Journal of Educational Computing Research. 2019;**57**(3):547-570. DOI: 10.1177/0735633118757015

[15] Asif R, Merceron A, Ali SA, Haider NG. Analyzing undergraduate students' performance using educational data mining. Computers in Education. 2017;**113**:177-194. DOI: 10.1016/j.compedu.2017.05.007

[16] Cruz-Jesus F et al. Using artificial intelligence methods to assess academic achievement in public high schools of a European Union country. Heliyon. 2020;**6**(6):e04081. DOI: 10.1016/j.heliyon.2020.e04081

[17] Fernandes E, Holanda M, Victorino M, Borges V, Carvalho R, Van Erven G. Educational data mining: Predictive analysis of academic performance of public school students in the capital of Brazil. Journal of Business Research. 2019;**94**:335-343. DOI: 10.1016/j.jbusres.2018.02.012

[18] Hoffait A-S, Schyns M. Early detection of university students with potential difficulties. Decision Support Systems. 2017;**101**:1-11. DOI: 10.1016/j.dss.2017.05.003

[19] Rebai S, Ben Yahia F, Essid H. A graphically based machine learning approach to predict secondary schools performance in Tunisia. Socio-Economic Planning Sciences. 2020;**70**:100724. DOI: 10.1016/j.seps.2019.06.009

[20] Shahzadi S et al. Machine learning empowered security management and quality of service provision in SDN-NFV environment. Computers, Materials & Continua. 2021;**66**(3):2723-2749. DOI: 10.32604/cmc.2021.014594

[21] Musso MF, Cascallar EC, Bostani N, Crawford M. Identifying reliable predictors of educational outcomes through machine-learning predictive modeling. Frontiers in Education (Lausanne). 2020;**5**:1-19. DOI: 10.3389/feduc.2020.00104

[22] Xu X, Wang J, Peng H, Wu R. Prediction of academic performance associated with internet usage behaviors using machine learning algorithms. Computers in Human Behavior. 2019;**98**:166-173. DOI: 10.1016/j.chb.2019.04.015

[23] Bernacki ML, Chavez MM, Uesbeck PM. Predicting achievement and providing support before STEM majors begin to fail. Computers in Education. 2020;**158**:103999. DOI: 10.1016/j.compedu.2020.103999

[24] Burgos C, Campanario ML, de la Peña D, Lara JA, Lizcano D, Martínez MA. Data mining for modeling students' performance: A tutoring action plan to prevent academic dropout. Computers and Electrical Engineering. 2018;**66**:541-556. DOI: 10.1016/j.compeleceng.2017.03.005

[25] Hellas A et al. Predicting academic performance: A systematic literature review. In: Proceedings Companion of the 23rd Annual ACM Conference on Innovation and Technology in Computer Science Education. New York: ACM; 2018. pp. 175-199. DOI: 10.1145/3293881.3295783

[26] Moher D. Preferred reporting items for systematic reviews and meta-analyses: The PRISMA statement. Annals of Internal Medicine. 2009;**151**(4):264. DOI: 10.7326/0003-4819-151-4-200908180-00135

[27] Trigwell K, Prosser M, Waterhouse F. Relations between teachers' approaches to teaching and students' approaches to learning. Higher Education (Dordr). 1999;**37**(1):57-70. DOI: 10.1023/A:1003548313194

[28] Trigwell K, Prosser M. Improving the quality of student learning: The influence of learning context and student approaches to learning on learning outcomes. Higher Education (Dordr). 1991;**22**(3):251-266. DOI: 10.1007/BF00132290

[29] Freeman S et al. Active learning increases student performance in science, engineering, and mathematics. Proceedings of the National Academy of Sciences. 2014;**111**(23):8410-8415. DOI: 10.1073/pnas.1319030111

[30] Abeysekera L, Dawson P. Motivation and cognitive load in the flipped classroom: Definition, rationale and a call for research. Higher Education Research and Development. 2015;**34**(1):1-14. DOI: 10.1080/07294360.2014.934336

[31] O'Flaherty J, Phillips C. The use of flipped classrooms in higher education: A scoping review. The Internet and Higher Education. 2015;**25**:85-95. DOI: 10.1016/j.iheduc.2015.02.002

[32] Kim MK, Kim SM, Khera O, Getman J. The experience of three flipped classrooms in an urban university: An exploration of design principles. The Internet and Higher Education. 2014;**22**:37-50. DOI: 10.1016/j.iheduc.2014.04.003

[33] Jovanovic J, Mirriahi N, Gašević D, Dawson S, Pardo A. Predictive power of regularity of pre-class activities in a flipped classroom. Computers in Education. 2019;**134**:156-168. DOI: 10.1016/j.compedu.2019.02.011

[34] Mason GS, Shuman TR, Cook KE. Comparing the effectiveness of an inverted classroom to a traditional classroom in an upper-division engineering course. IEEE Transactions on Education. 2013;**56**(4):430-435. DOI: 10.1109/TE.2013.2249066

[35] Lai C-L, Hwang G-J. A self-regulated flipped classroom approach to improving students' learning performance in a mathematics course. Computers in Education. 2016;**100**:126-140. DOI: 10.1016/j.compedu.2016.05.006

[36] Taheri H, Gonzalez Bocanegra M, Taheri M. Artificial intelligence, machine learning and smart technologies for nondestructive evaluation. Sensors. 2022;**22**(11):4055. DOI: 10.3390/s22114055

[37] Liao M, Zhu K, Wang G. Can human-machine feedback in a smart learning environment enhance learners' learning performance? A meta-analysis. Frontiers in Psychology. 2024;**14**:1-13. DOI: 10.3389/fpsyg.2023.1288503

[38] Nabizadeh AH, Leal JP, Rafsanjani HN, Shah RR. Learning path personalization and recommendation methods: A survey of the state-of-the-art. Expert Systems with Applications. 2020;**159**:113596. DOI: 10.1016/j.eswa.2020.113596

[39] Onah DFO, Pang ELL, Sinclair JE, Uhomoibhi J. An innovative MOOC platform: The implications of self-directed learning abilities to improve motivation in learning and to support self-regulation. The International Journal of Information and Learning Technology. 2021;**38**(3):283-298. DOI: 10.1108/IJILT-03-2020-0040

[40] Wang R, Cao J, Xu Y, Li Y. Learning engagement in massive open online courses: A systematic review. Frontiers

in Education (Lausanne). 2022;**7**:1-17. DOI: 10.3389/feduc.2022.1074435

[41] Cheng J, Yuen AHK, Chiu DKW. Systematic review of MOOC research in mainland China. Library Hi Tech. 2023;**41**(5):1476-1497. DOI: 10.1108/LHT-02-2022-0099

[42] Elbadrawy A, Polyzou A, Ren Z, Sweeney M, Karypis G, Rangwala H. Predicting student performance using personalized analytics. Computer (Long Beach California). 2016;**49**(4):61-69. DOI: 10.1109/MC.2016.119

[43] Chamizo-Gonzalez J, Cano-Montero EI, Urquia-Grande E, Muñoz-Colomina CI. Educational data mining for improving learning outcomes in teaching accounting within higher education. The International Journal of Information and Learning Technology. 2015;**32**(5):272-285. DOI: 10.1108/IJILT-08-2015-0020

[44] Al-Musharraf A, Alkhattabi M. An educational data mining approach to explore the effect of using interactive supporting features in an LMS for overall performance within an online learning environment. International Journal of Computer Science and Network Security. 2016;**16**(3):1-13

Chapter 5

# A Transformer-Based Architecture for Airborne Particles Forecasting: Case Study – PM2.5 in Mexico City

*Jose Luis Maciel-Jacobo, Marco Antonio Aceves-Fernández, Jesus Carlos Pedraza-Ortega and Efren Gorrostieta-Hurtado*

## Abstract

In this comprehensive research project, our goal is to predict the concentration levels of PM2.5, a critical air pollutant, in Mexico City. To address this challenge, we use an innovative approach based on the transformer model, specifically a modified version called the Informer. This project focuses on improving air quality prediction, a key step in tackling public health concerns and aiding decision-making in environmental management in one of the world's most densely populated cities. We trained the Informer model using a robust dataset of historical air quality records and evaluated its performance with standard metrics: mean absolute error (MAE) and mean squared error (MSE). The results showed MAE values of 4.6266 and 5.5844, and MSE values of 40.7972 and 55.4009 for each monitoring station, demonstrating the model's effectiveness in predicting PM2.5 levels. These results highlight the potential of the Informer in enhancing air quality management strategies. We also compared the Informer's performance with the LSTM model, showing that the Informer not only competes with but may outperform the LSTM in air quality prediction tasks. This underscores the promise of the Informer for future environmental monitoring.

**Keywords:** transformer, forecasting, particles, LSTM, informer

## 1. Introduction

Air quality, evaluated through the concentration of particulate matter with a diameter of 2.5 micrometers or smaller (PM2.5), stands as a crucial factor in evaluating environmental well-being. Precisely forecasting PM2.5 levels holds paramount importance for comprehending the dynamics of air quality and instituting efficient measures for pollution control. This research centers on the prediction of PM2.5 concentrations specifically in Mexico City (CDMX), a region known for its complex air quality dynamics.

However, the prediction task comes with inherent challenges, like the presence of missing data in the CDMX air quality dataset. The sporadic nature of data collection or technical issues can lead to gaps in the temporal records, posing challenges for modeling and forecasting. Addressing these data limitations with data imputation is crucial for developing a robust predictive model.

Furthermore, PM2.5 time series exhibit semi-chaotic behavior, characterized by intricate patterns, nonlinearities, and dependencies on various environmental factors such as wind direction, wind speed, and atmospheric stability. Understanding and modeling this semi-chaotic nature are pivotal for accurate predictions, as traditional linear models may fall short in capturing the complexity of the underlying processes.

In this context, we explore the application of a modified transformer, the Informer model, a powerful deep learning architecture, for predicting PM2.5 concentrations. The goal is to leverage the model's ability to capture complex temporal dependencies and handle missing data effectively. Through this research, we aim to contribute to the advancement of air quality prediction methodologies in urban environments with challenging data characteristics.

## 2. Background

### 2.1 Airborne pollution

Air pollution could be defined as atmospheric conditions wherein specific substances are present at concentrations that can lead to undesirable effects on both humans and the environment. These substances encompass gasses such as SOx, NOx, CO, and HCs, as well as particulate matter like smoke, dust, fumes, and aerosols, along with other elements, including radioactive materials. While many of these substances naturally exist in the atmosphere at low concentrations (background levels) and are typically considered harmless, a substance is deemed an air pollutant only when its concentration significantly exceeds the background value, resulting in adverse effects. Meaning, for a particular substance to be considered pollution, it should both surpass the background levels and cause adverse effects [1].

Urban air pollution is a global concern with significant implications. The increased utilization of fuels, rising electricity demand, and intensified mining activities since the Industrial Revolution have emerged as the primary contributors to atmospheric pollution, ultrafine particles are able to travel into the bloodstream and be deposited in organs such as the liver, spleen, or brain, with the possibility of penetration through trans-synaptic mechanisms [2].

#### *2.1.1 Particulate matter (PM)*

Particulate matter consists of particles from various origins, varying in size and composition. These particles are generally classified into three main groups based on size:

#### *2.1.2 Coarse particles*

These have a diameter ranging from 10 micrometers to less than 2.5 micrometers. Fine Particles: These are sized between 2.5 micrometers and 0.1 micrometers. Ultrafine Particles: These are smaller than 0.1 micrometers. Most monitoring systems measure particles by their mass concentration, focusing on those smaller than 2.5

micrometers (known as PM2.5) and those smaller than 10 micrometers (known as PM10). PM10 includes both fine and coarse particles, with PM2.5 often representing about 50–70% of the total mass of PM10. Ultrafine particles are also included in PM2.5 and PM10 measurements (**Figure 1**). The main sources of PM2.5 are motor vehicle traffic, power generation, and the industrial and domestic burning of oil, coal, or wood. These fine particles are made up of elemental carbon, transition metals, complex organic compounds, sulfates, and nitrates [3].

As mentioned before, PM2.5 particles consist of inhalable particles that are sufficiently small to enter the respiratory system as shown in **Figure 1**. Both short-term and long-term exposure can result in various health effects, including:

- Exacerbation of asthma
- Increased mortality from cardiovascular diseases
- Elevated mortality rates from respiratory diseases and lung cancer.

Exposure to PM2.5 is associated with an average reduction in life expectancy for the region's population by approximately 8.6 months. There is no evidence supporting a safe exposure level or a threshold below which no adverse health effects occur [4].

### 2.2 PM2.5 recommended values

There is no conclusive evidence indicating a specific threshold of health effects in humans, and the World Health Organization provides air quality guidelines. These guidelines outline the intended objectives for PM2.5 levels in the environment in comparison with the Mexican Norm (NOM-025), as illustrated in **Table 1**.

Regulations or standards for pollutants are established with the purpose of defining limits for their emissions from various sources or determining environmental concentrations indicative of good air quality. The Mexican Secretary of Health

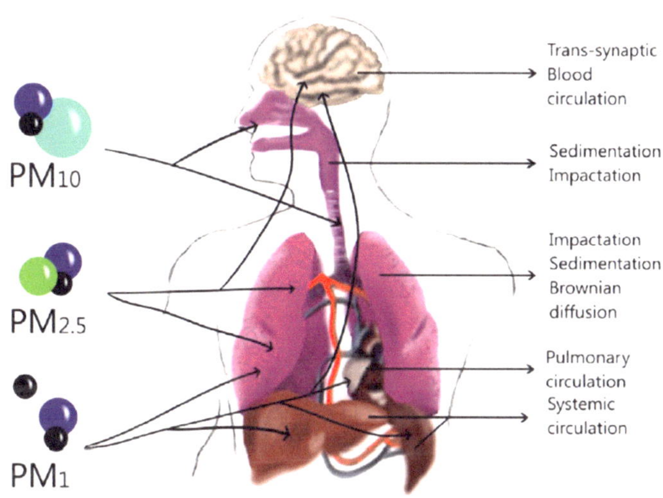


**Figure 1.**
*Particulate matter size comparison [2].*

| Type | WHO | NOM-025-SSA1–2021 |
|---|---|---|
| Short-term (24-hour) | $15\mu g/m^3$ | $25\mu g/m^3$ |
| Annual | $5\mu g/m^3$ | $10\mu g/m^3$ |

**Table 1.**
*World Health Organization and NOM-025-SSA1–2021 recommended values for PM2.5, adapted from [5, 6].*

(Secretaria de Salud) is responsible for setting these standards to ensure air quality in Mexico. Initially, in 1994, this agency issued the Official Mexican Standard NOM-024-SSA1–1993, outlining the permissible value for the concentration of total suspended particles in ambient air. Concurrently, NOM-025-SSA1–1993 was published for PM10 particles. Subsequently, these two standards were amalgamated, and the maximum permissible limit for PM2.5 was incorporated into NOM-025, published in the Official Gazette of the Federation in 2005. This updated standard set the 24-hour average concentration limit at 65 $\mu g/m^3$, and the annual average concentration limit at 15 $\mu g/m^3$ [7].

## 2.3 Time series

Time series are present across various domains, spanning meteorology, finance, econometrics, and marketing. Through data recording and analysis, we can delve into time series to analyze industrial processes or monitor business metrics like sales or engagement. Moreover, with the abundance of data, data scientists can leverage their knowledge in employing techniques for time-series forecasting. The initial step in comprehending and executing time-series forecasting involves understanding the nature of a time series. Basically a time series is data measured at regular time intervals, known as the sampling interval. Put simply, data could be recorded hourly, monthly, or annually. Examples of time series encompass the closing value of a specific stock, a household's electricity consumption, or the outdoor temperature. We can represent a time series of length n by

$$\{xt : t = 1,\ldots,n\} = \{x1, x2,\ldots,xn\} \tag{1}$$

Where n is the number of sampled values at discrete times.

X the measured values [8, 9].

A key characteristic of time-series data is that neighboring observations are often dependent on each other. Figuring out how these observations in a time series are related is really important for practical uses. Time-series analysis focuses on methods to analyze this interdependence. Doing this well means we need to develop and use stochastic and dynamic models for time-series data in areas where they really matter [10].

Data windowing Before dividing our time series in training, validation, and testing subsets, we have to perform data windowing, and data windowing as shown in **Figure 2**, is a procedure where we establish a series of data points within our time series, designating certain points as inputs (also named X) and others as labels (also named Y). This enables the deep learning model to be trained on the inputs, generate predictions, compare them against the labels, and iterate through this cycle until further improvement in prediction accuracy is not achievable, and it also allows us to shuffle our subsets without loosing the original order [8].

**Figure 2.**
*Data windowing with a sequence length of 5 and a prediction length of 1.*

## 2.4 Attention mechanisms

The concept of attention is particularly well-suited for natural language processing (NLP) scenarios where the information we seek is concealed within a long sequence. This challenge frequently arises in applications like machine translation and question–answering systems, where encoding the entire sentence into a fixed-length vector by a recurrent neural network is necessary. Consequently, the recurrent neural network often struggles to concentrate on the pertinent segments of the source sentence for accurate translation into the target sentence. In such instances, it becomes beneficial to align the target sentence with the relevant portions of the source sentence during translation. Attention mechanisms prove useful in isolating the pertinent parts of the source sentence while generating specific segments of the target sentence in these scenarios [11].

The fundamental concept of attention is to create a weighted distribution over the input sequence, giving greater weight to elements that are more important. In this way it allows us to determine the importance of the input elements and to merge these elements into a concise representation (known as the context vector) which encapsulates the features of the most significant elements, as shown in **Figure 3**. Since the context vector is smaller than the original input, it needs fewer computational resources for processing in subsequent stages, resulting in computational efficiency [13].

## 2.5 Transformer

The transformer has revolutionized AI in a wide range of natural processing tasks. This groundbreaking model was introduced in the 2017 influential paper "Attention

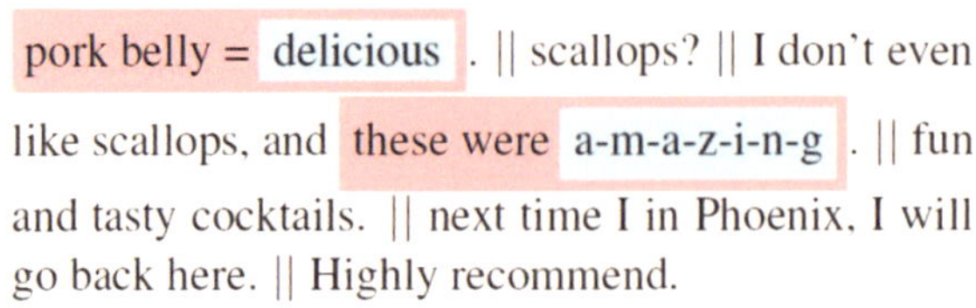


**Figure 3.**
*Example of attention in sentiment classification taken from [12].*

is All You Need" by Vaswani et al., and the essence of the paper aligns with its title. Surprisingly, a straightforward mechanism called "neural attention" proved capable of constructing robust sequence models without the need for recurrent layers or convolution layers. The concept of neural attention has rapidly evolved into one of the most influential ideas in the realm of deep learning [14].

Although transformers were initially designed for sequence-to-sequence learning in NLP, they have become pretty useful in various deep learning applications, like vision, speech, and reinforcement learning in general. Illustrated in **Figure 4**, the transformer consists of two main components, an encoder and a decoder. Prior to entering the encoder and decoder, the input (source) and output (target) sequence embeddings undergo addition with positional encoding. These embeddings then traverse modules based on self-attention. At a higher level, the

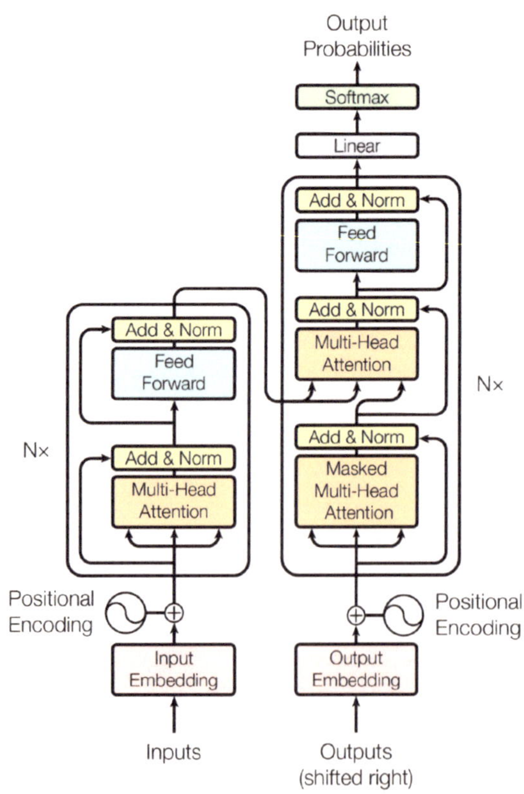


**Figure 4.**
*Transformer architecture [15].*

transformer encoder consists of a stack of multiple identical layers, each layer containing two sublayers (referred to as sublayers). The first sublayer is a multi-head self-attention pooling, and the second is a positionwise feed-forward network. In the encoder self-attention, queries, keys, and values are derived from the outputs of the preceding encoder layer. In the decoder self-attention, queries, keys, and values are sourced from the outputs of the previous decoder layer. Notably, each position in the decoder is restricted to attending only to positions in the decoder up to that specific position, to prevent the model to see the next part of the sequence, this special type of attention is called "masked attention", and it preserves the auto-regressive property, ensuring that predictions depend solely on the previously generated output tokens [16].

Since Google created the original transformer model, a multitude of models have emerged, drawing inspiration from it to tackle various tasks in diverse fields (such as NLP and time-series forecasting). While some of these models have adopted the standard transformer architecture in its entirety, others have selectively employed either its encoder or decoder component. Consequently, the specific architecture chosen influences the function and effectiveness of these transformer-based models. A frequently utilized element in transformer models is the self-attention mechanism, which is vital for their optimal operation and performance. All models based on the transformer framework incorporate self-attention and multi-head attention, often serving as the foundational learning layer within the architecture. Considering the importance of self-attention, the attention mechanism plays a pivotal role in the effectiveness of transformer models [17].

Transformer models can be utilized in three main ways:

- Encoder-Only: This configuration is typically applied for tasks like classification. In this setup, the model uses only the encoder part of the transformer architecture.
- Decoder-Only: This approach is used primarily for language modeling tasks. In this case, the model comprises only the decoder part of the transformer.
- Encoder–Decoder: Commonly used for machine translation, this mode incorporates both the encoder and decoder parts of the transformer. In this configuration, there are multiple instances of multi-headed self-attention modules. These include standard self-attention layers in both the encoder and decoder. Additionally, there is an encoder–decoder cross-attention module that enables the decoder to access and leverage information from the encoder [18].

### 2.6 Informer

The Informer architecture is a deep learning model based on the original transformer as developed by Vaswani et al. [15], where the primary modifications from the original include the ProbSparse self-attention mechanism. This mechanism aims to enhance computational efficiency and reduce memory consumption compared to the standard transformer architecture. Furthermore, Zhou et al. [19] also integrated a self-attention distilling process that significantly lowers the model's total space complexity [20].

The Informer algorithm model enhances the transformer architecture by using a similar multi-layered structure composed of Informer blocks. These modules feature

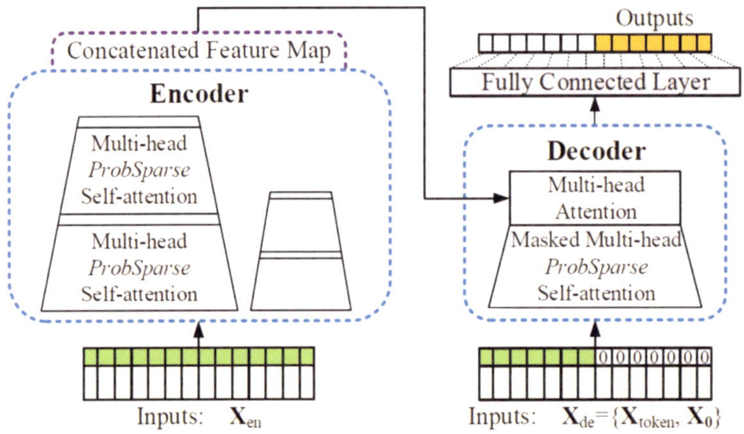


**Figure 5.**
*Informer architecture [19].*

a unique ProbSparse multi-head self-attention mechanism within an encoder–decoder setup. **Figure 5** illustrates the Informer model's fundamental design. On the left side of the figure, the encoder processes a substantial number of extended sequence inputs using the specialized ProbSparse self-attention, replacing the standard self-attention method. The robustness of the model is bolstered by the multiple layers of these blocks. On the right side of the figure, the decoder manages the long sequence input, zeroes out the target element, computes the feature map's weighted attentional blend, and then directly generates the output element. This model demonstrates an improvement in the predictive capabilities for long sequence time-series forecasting (LSTF) issues, underscoring the transformative model family's ability to capture the intricate long-range dependencies between the input and output in lengthy time-series data [21].

## 3. Methods

In **Figure 6**, we can see a diagram of our general methodology divided as follows:

- Data adquisition
- Station selection
- Data imputation
- Data standardization
- Informer training
- Informer testing.

### 3.1 Data acquisition

The automatic atmospheric monitoring network (RAMA) is a subsystem of the Mexico City Atmospheric Monitoring System (SIMAT) that performs continuous and

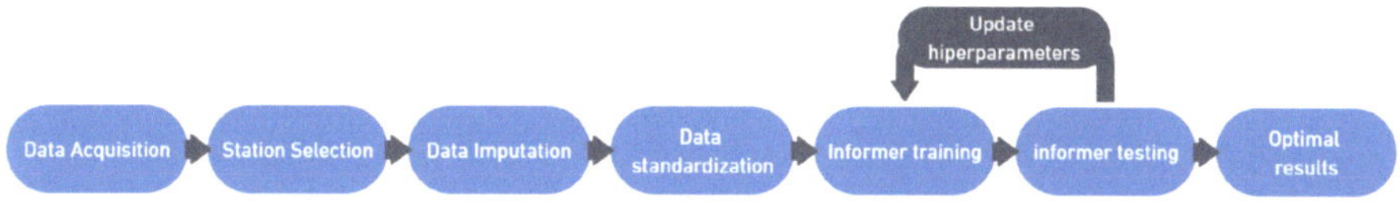


**Figure 6.**
*Proposed methodology.*

permanent minute-by-minute measurements in multiple strategic points (as shown in **Figure 7**) of various agents present in the air, including particles smaller than 2.5 micrometers (PM2.5) [22].

The data is divided by years and has three main columns, as shown in **Table 2**:

- Date
- Hour
- Stations.

The database comes directly from the RAMA Web site, where we can download different datasets from different years and pollutants (including PM2.5); this particular air pollutant has been monitored since 2003.

### 3.2 Data preparation

The model requires the data to adhere to a specific structure, requiring the inclusion of both date and time entries within the initial column labeled "date". Consequently, the subsequent dataset is arranged accordingly. Essential modifications to our database were necessary to conform to this prescribed format. In **Tables 3** and **4**, we can

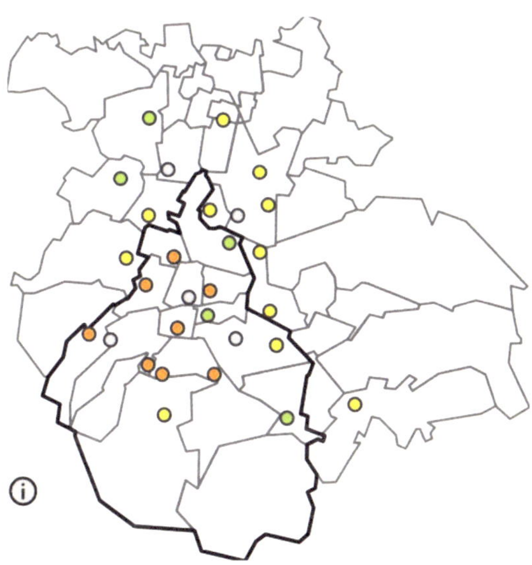

**Figure 7.**
*Monitored strategic points of CDMX [22].*

| Day | Hour | BJU |
|---|---|---|
| 2022-2101-01 | 0 | 55 |
| 2022-2101-01 | 1 | 71 |

**Table 2.**
*Original dataset sample.*

| Day | Hour | PM2.5 concentration |
|---|---|---|
| 2022-2101-01 | 0 | 55 |
| 2022-2101-01 | 1 | 71 |

**Table 3.**
*Original dataset sample.*

| date | PM2.5 concentration |
|---|---|
| 2022-2101-01 0:00:00 | 55 |
| 2022-2101-01 1:00:00 | 71 |

**Table 4.**
*Correct structure.*

visualize the original versus the final version resulting from these adjustments, which will be utilized to feed our model.

## 3.3 Station selection

In our database, instances of missing values are inherent, arising from factors such as malfunctioning equipment, power disruptions, and various other operational issues, so we have to discard everything that has more than 30% missing data, and in **Tables 5** and **6** we show a couple of examples between usable and unusable stations.

## 3.4 Data imputation

Even meticulously designed and conducted studies result in missing values. The interesting part about this is our approach to managing data that is incomplete. Over recent decades, the theory, methods, and software dedicated to addressing issues of incomplete data have seen substantial development and refinement [23].

Data imputation entails substituting missing data with an estimated value, replacing absent or incorrect values with a "likely" value derived from other available information. Mean value imputation involves substituting a missing value with the average obtained from the available observations. This method's primary benefit

| | AJU | CAM | CCA |
|---|---|---|---|
| % of missing values | 44.99 | 50.98 | 57.49 |

**Table 5.**
*Example of unusable stations.*

| | BJU | UAX | MER |
|---|---|---|---|
| % of missing values | 3.79 | 7.62 | 12.09 |

**Table 6.**
*Example of usable stations.*

is its simplicity and less computational resources, and in cases where the data lacks distinct trends or seasonal variations, it preserves the overall mean of the full dataset. However, caution is needed in situations with trends or seasonal fluctuations, as the overall mean might not accurately represent these patterns. Regression imputation is a method similar to mean value imputation, but instead of using the average value for imputation, it calculates the missing value using a predictive model, for example, a polynomial regression model as shown in **Figures 8** and **9** [24].

$$f(x) = ax^4 + bx^3 + cx^2 + dx + e \tag{2}$$

### 3.5 Data standardization

Data standardization gives the data the properties of a standard normal distribution: zero-mean and unit variance. Standardization converts the mean of each feature so that it is centered at zero, and each feature has a standard deviation of 1 [25]. In Eq. 3, we present the formula employed for the standardization of our dataset.

$$Z = \frac{X - \mu}{\sigma} \tag{3}$$

Where:

$Z$ is the Z-score, also known as the standard score. $X$ is the value you want to standardize. $\mu$ is the mean (average) of the dataset. $\sigma$ is the standard deviation of the dataset.

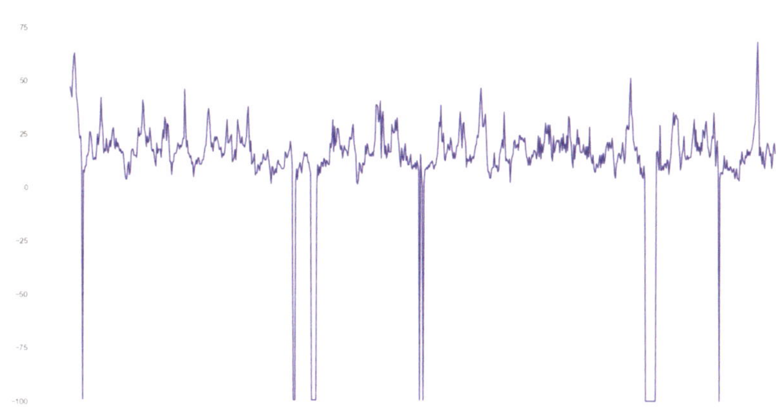


**Figure 8.**
*Data before imputation.*

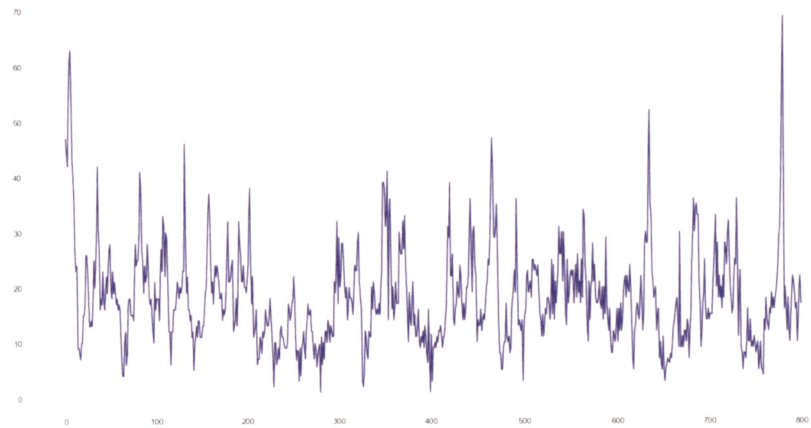


**Figure 9.**
*Data after imputation.*

## 3.6 Data division

Model evaluation needs the segregation of available data into three essential subsets: training, validation, and test. Training is conducted on the training dataset, with model evaluation (hyperparameter tunning) occurring on the validation dataset. Once the model demonstrates readiness for deployment, a conclusive assessment transpires on the test dataset, designed to closely mirror real-world production data. Subsequent to successful validation on the test set, the model is deemed fit for deployment in a production environment [14].

If the results are unsatisfactory, the network is retrained, and the validation set is tested again. This process is iteratively repeated until achieving a satisfactory classification. Only then is the model evaluated on the independent test set to assess its overall performance. It is crucial to note that a low training error and a high test error may indicate overfitting, which is especially pertinent when solely training and testing without hyperparameter tuning. When tuning hyperparameters, there is a risk of overfitting to both the training and validation sets, as adjustments are made until achieving minimal error on the validation set. It is important to be cautious of misleadingly small errors that result from the classifier learning the noise of the training set and manually adjusting hyperparameters to match the noise of the validation set. Success is determined by a proportionately small error on the test set, and if not achieved, further refinement is required. The default sizes for the train, validation, and test sets are typically set at 80, 10, and 10%, respectively, though these proportions can be adjusted based on specific requirements [26].

In this particular study, we will divide the data in three subgroups (training, validation, and test), and they will be divided as follows:

- Training—70% of the original data
- Test—20% of the original data
- Validation—Remaining data (~10%)

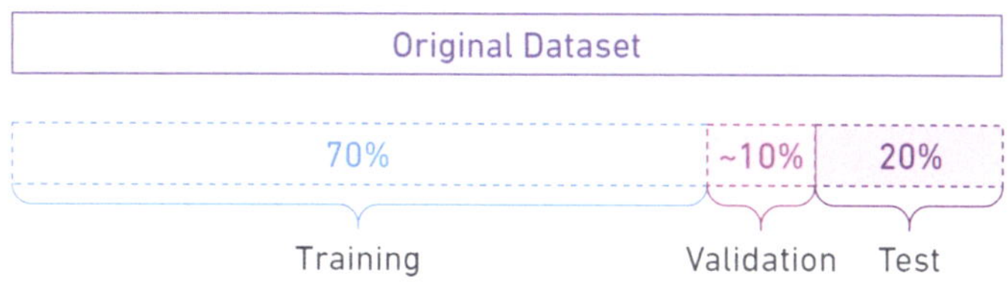


**Figure 10.**
*Data division.*

In **Figure 10**, we can clearly see how the data is divided in subsets of the original dataset.

### 3.7 Hyperparameters

Hyperparameters refer to those parameters within neural networks that cannot be learned akin to conventional parameters like weights and biases. Consequently, these parameters need manual adjustment [26].

In the course of our experiments, we systematically varied diverse hyperparameters with the objective of achieving reduced error metrics. Subsequently, we furnish a comprehensive list of the hyperparameters along with their respective values that were uniformly employed across all experimental iterations.

- Sequence length: {10, 24, 35, 50, 96, 120, 240, 480, 720}
- Training epochs: {5, 8, 10, 15, 100, 150}
- Number of attention heads: {4, 8, 10, 12, 15, 50}
- Encoder layers: {2, 4, 5}
- Decoder layers: {1, 2, 4, 5}
- Batch size: {32, 64, 128}
- Learning rate: {0.01, 0.001, 0.0001, 0.00001}
- Activation function: {GELU, RELU, LeakyRELU}

## 4. Results

To comprehensively assess the performance of our model, we will employ five distinct error metrics. These metrics offer a diverse and nuanced evaluation, allowing us to gain a more accurate and comprehensive understanding of the model's efficacy. The chosen metrics encompass a range of perspectives on prediction accuracy and include mean absolute error (MAE), mean squared error (MSE), root mean squared error (RMSE), mean absolute percentage error (MAPE), and mean squared percentage error (MSPE). By considering these varied metrics, we aim to obtain a holistic view of the model's performance across different aspects of prediction evaluation.

- MAE (Mean Absolute Error)

$$\frac{1}{n}\sum_{i=1}^{n}\left|A_i - P_i\right| \tag{4}$$

- MSE (Mean Squared Error)

$$\frac{1}{n}\sum_{i=1}^{n}\left(A_i - P_i\right)^2 \tag{5}$$

- RMSE (Root Mean Squared Error)

$$\sqrt{\frac{1}{n}\sum_{i=1}^{n}\left(A_i - P_i\right)^2} \tag{6}$$

- (Mean Absolute Percentage Error)

$$\frac{1}{n}\sum_{i=1}^{n}\left|\frac{A_i - P_i}{A_i}\right| \times 100 \tag{7}$$

- MSPE (Mean Squared Percentage Error)

$$\frac{1}{n}\sum_{i=1}^{n}\left(\frac{A_i - P_i}{A_i}\right)^2 \tag{8}$$

The results presented in this paper represent the optimal outcomes derived from a series of experiments in which we systematically varied hyperparameters within our model. It is woth mentioning that these metrics are computed subsequent to the data being reverted to its original scale, that is, prior to the standardization process.

In **Tables** 7 and **8**, the comprehensive overview of the five metrics employed in the Informer architecture is presented, including their mean, standard deviation, minimum values, and maximum values, for each one of the selected stations ("BJU" and "UAX"). Subsequently, in **Table 9**, a comparative analysis of the results between the Informer and LSTM models is provided, highlighting the superior outcomes in each

| Metric | Mean | STD | Min | Max |
|---|---|---|---|---|
| MAE | 4.6266 | 0.4153 | 4.4145 | 8.2218 |
| MSE | 40.7972 | 10.2716 | 35.7675 | 129.1333 |
| RMSE | 6.3579 | 0.6045 | 5.9805 | 11.3636 |
| MAPE | 0.2280 | 0.0228 | 0.2166 | 0.4248 |
| MSPE | 0.2247 | 0.0758 | 0.1653 | 0.8689 |

**Table 7.**
*Informer error metrics description for BJU station.*

| Metric | Mean | STD | Min | Max |
|---|---|---|---|---|
| MAE | 5.5844 | 0.1887 | 5.4241 | 6.2439 |
| MSE | 55.4009 | 3.1939 | 52.6676 | 66.3642 |
| RMSE | 7.4403 | 0.2078 | 7.2572 | 8.1464 |
| MAPE | 0.3916 | 0.0072 | 0.3774 | 0.4042 |
| MSPE | 1.6647 | 0.1526 | 1.2064 | 1.8836 |

**Table 8.**
*Informer error metrics description for UAX station.*

| | LSTM MAE | LSTM MSE | Informer MAE | Informer MSE |
|---|---|---|---|---|
| BJU | 5.6327 | 59.891 | **4.6266** | **40.7972** |
| UAX | 5.7753 | 59.9853 | **5.5844** | **55.4009** |

**Table 9.**
*Comparison MAE and MSE mean between LSTM and Informer.*

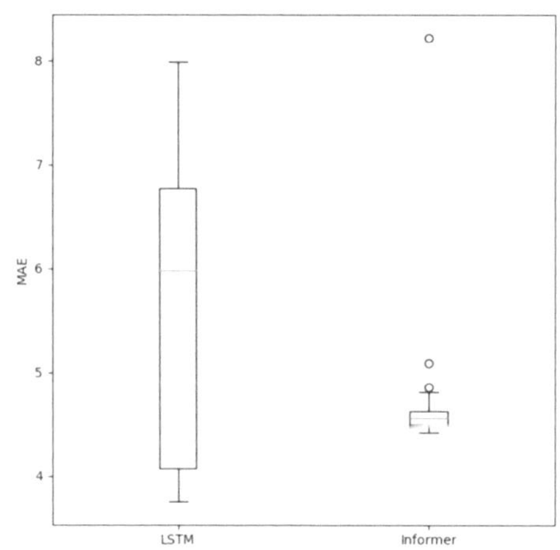


**Figure 11.**
*MAE results for BJU.*

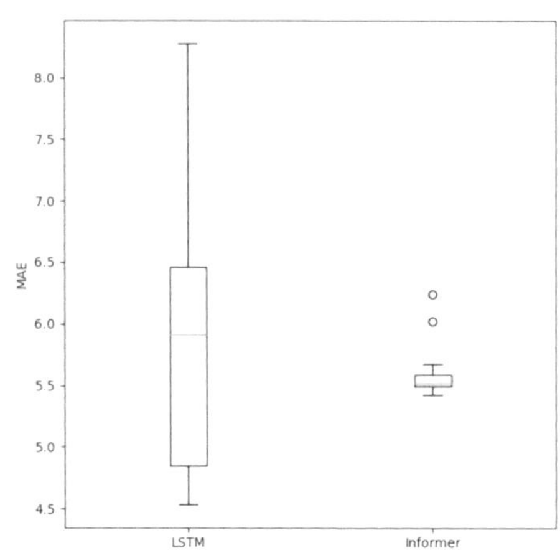


**Figure 12.**
*MAE results for UAX.*

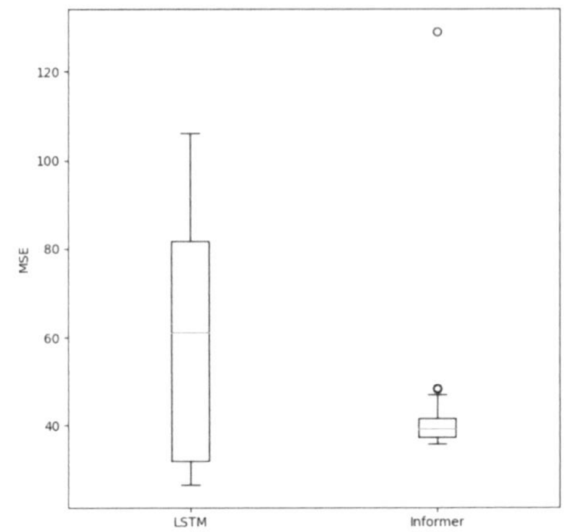


**Figure 13.**
*MSE results for BJU.*

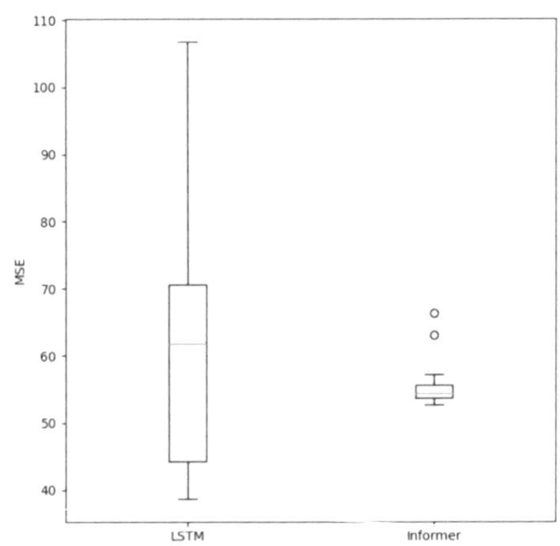


**Figure 14.**
*MSE results for UAX.*

row. For a better visualization, we present in **Figures 11–14** graphs of the MAE and MSE for each architecture (LSTM and Informer), and finally, in **Figure 15**, we observe how our implementation of the Informer model accurately models the raw data.

## 5. Discussion

By analyzing the outcomes within the Informer architecture, it is evident that optimal results were achieved when reducing the input sequence length to below 100. This adjustment implies that the model focuses on the information from the preceding 4 days relative to the predicted value. Additionally, the model demonstrated enhanced precision upon employing the LeakyReLU activation function, potentially addressing issues related to vanishing gradients, making it particularly suitable for such scenarios.

Another noteworthy observation was the improvement in model performance upon decreasing the batch size, even below 16. The model exhibited superior

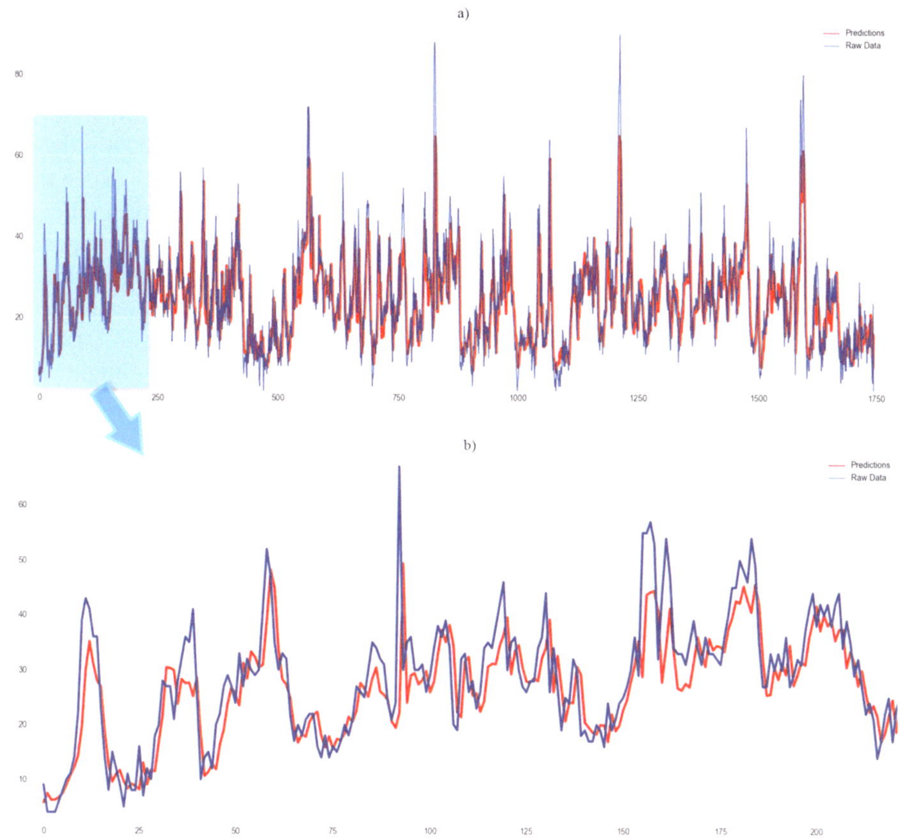


**Figure 15.**
*Final results for informer. a) Test results raw data vs. Informer prediction. b) Zoomed results for a).*

performance when hyperparameters were updated more frequently, contrasting with the use of larger batch sizes. The determination of an optimal learning rate emerged as a critical factor, with values around $1.0 \times 10^{-4}$ yielding superior results. Deviating from this range, either above or below, resulted in a deterioration of overall model performance. Similarly, the early stop mechanism, set with a patience of 3, led to training epochs typically concluding within the 7–9 range, even when a larger value, such as 100, was specified. A judicious choice appeared to be around 20–25, affording the model the flexibility to extend training if required.

It is notable that certain hyperparameter adjustments, such as encoder layers, decoder layers, and the dimension of the feed-forward network, did not yield improvements in model results when deviating from default values.

The results of transformer-based models like the Informer are quite promising, especially when compared to the long-standing state-of-the-art LSTM models in the realm of predictions. LSTM networks have been a benchmark in time-series analysis for many years. Therefore, the ability of transformer-based models to not only match but potentially surpass the LSTM in terms of error metrics represents an impressive technological advancement. This progress underscores a significant leap forward in time-series prediction and the evolving landscape of deep learning methodologies.

## 6. Conclusion

Although the Informer model has been widely used for predicting various types of real-world problems such as motor bearing vibrations [12], traffic anomalies [27], and electric vehicle charging station availability [28], it has not yet been employed for particle matter forecasting. This model's application is exemplified by its use in the Informer Architecture-Based Ionospheric foF2 Model in the Middle Latitude Region [29] and in the novel Convolutional Informer Network for deterministic and probabilistic state-of-charge estimation of lithium-ion batteries [30]. Additionally, it has been applied in load forecasting for district heating systems [31] and in the development of a data-driven long time-series electrical line trip fault prediction method using an improved stacked-Informer network [32]. These diverse applications highlight the adaptability of the Informer model in various fields, while also pointing out the areas like particle matter forecasting where its potential remains untapped.

This study delves into the application of the Informer architecture to a real-world problem, air pollution forecasting, specifically in the context of predicting PM2.5 levels. The presented results showcase the promising potential of the Informer model for addressing the challenges posed by long sequence time-series forecasting. Notably, the graphical representations not only accurately capture the underlying trends, but the associated metrics also demonstrate impressive performance.

The successful forecasting of particulate matter achieved in this study highlights the efficacy of attention models, particularly the Informer architecture, in addressing complex time-series prediction tasks. These findings underscore the model's capability to provide accurate and valuable insights into air quality forecasting.

## Author details

Jose Luis Maciel-Jacobo, Marco Antonio Aceves-Fernández*, Jesus Carlos Pedraza-Ortega and Efren Gorrostieta-Hurtado
Universidad Autónoma de Querétaro, Santiago de Querétaro, Mexico

*Address all correspondence to: marco.aceves@uaq.mx

## References

[1] Admassu M, Wubeshet M. Air Pollution: Lecture Notes for Environmental Health Science Students. Ethiopia: University of Gondar Publications; 2006:5-6

[2] Falcon-Rodriguez CI, Osornio-Vargas AR, Sada-Ovalle I, Segura-Medina P. Aeroparticles, composition, and lung diseases. Frontiers in Immunology. 2016;7:3

[3] Newby DE, Mannucci PM, Tell GS, Baccarelli AA, Brook RD, Donaldson K, et al. Expert position paper on air pollution and cardiovascular disease. European Heart Journal. 2015;**36**(2):83-93

[4] World Health Organization. Health Effects of Particulate Matter: Policy Implications for Countries in Eastern Europe, Caucasus and Central Asia. Switzerland; 2013

[5] World Health Organization. WHO Global Air Quality Guidelines: Particulate Matter (PM2. 5 and PM10), Ozone, Nitrogen Dioxide, Sulfur Dioxide and Carbon Monoxide. Switzerland: World Health Organization; 2021

[6] DOF (Diario Oficial de la Federacin), NORMA Oficial Mexicana NOM-025-SSA1-2021, 2021. [Online]. Available from: https://www.dof.gob.mx/notadetalle.php?codigo=5633855. [Accessed: November 30, 2023]

[7] Secretara de Medio Ambiente y Recursos Naturales Instituto Nacional de Ecologa. Gua metodolgica para la estimacin de emisiones de PM2. Ciudad de Mxico, Mxico: Secretara de Medio Ambiente y Recursos Naturales Instituto Nacional de Ecologa; 2011. p. 5

[8] Peixeiro M. Time Series Forecasting in Python. United States: Simon and Schuster; 2022

[9] Cowpertwait PS, Metcalfe AV. Introductory Time Series with R. Germany: Springer Science & Business Media; 2009

[10] Box GE, Jenkins GM, Reinsel GC, Ljung GM. Time Series Analysis: Forecasting and Control. United States: John Wiley & Sons; 2015

[11] Nielsen MA. Neural Networks and Deep Learning. San Francisco, CA, USA: Determination Press; 2015

[12] Yang Z, Liu L, Li N, Tian J. Time series forecasting of motor bearing vibration based on informer. Sensors. 2022;**22**(15):5858

[13] Galassi A, Lippi M, Torroni P. Attention in natural language processing. IEEE Transactions on Neural Networks and Learning Systems. 2021;**32**(10):4291-4308

[14] Chollet F. Deep Learning with Python. United States: Simon and Schuster; 2021

[15] Vaswani A et al. Attention is all you need. In: NIPS'17: Proceedings of the 31st International Conference on Neural Information Processing Systems. United States; 2017

[16] Zhang A, Lipton ZC, Li M, Smola AJ. Dive into Deep Learning. United Kingdom: Cambridge University Press; 2023

[17] Islam S, Elmekki H, Elsebai A, Bentahar J, Drawel N, Rjoub G, et al. A comprehensive survey on applications

of transformers for deep learning tasks. Expert Systems with Applications. 2023;**241**:122666

[18] Tay Y, Dehghani M, Bahri D, Metzler D. Metzler, efficient transformers: A survey. ACM Computing Surveys. 2020;**55**:109

[19] Zhou H, Zhang S, Peng J, Li J, Xiong H, Zhang W. Informer: Beyond efficient transformer for long sequence time-series forecasting. In Proceedings of the AAAI conference on artificial intelligence. Vol. 35. No. 12. 2021. pp. 11106-11115

[20] Ahmed S, Nielsen IE, Tripathi A, Siddiqui S, Ramachandran RP, Rasool G. Transformers in time-series analysis: A tutorial. Circuits, Systems, and Signal Processing. 2023;**42**(12):7433-7466

[21] Zhu Q, Han J, Chai K, Zhao C. Time series analysis based on informer algorithms: A survey. Symmetry. 2023;**15**(4):951

[22] SEDEMA, Red automtica de monitoreo atmosfrico. 2023. [Online]. Available from: https://datos.cdmx.gob.mx/d.mx/dataset/red-automatica-demonitoreo-atmosferico

[23] Van Buuren S. Flexible Imputation of Missing Data. United States: CRC Press; 2018

[24] Montgomery DC, Jennings CL, Kulahci M. Introduction to Time Series Analysis and Forecasting. United States: John Wiley & Sons; 2015

[25] Raschka S, Mirjalili V. Python Machine Learning: Machine Learning and Deep Learning with Python, Scikit-Learn, and TensorFlow 2. United Kingdom: Packt Publishing Ltd; 2019

[26] Skansi S. Introduction to Deep Learning: From Logical Calculus to Artificial Intelligence. Germany: Springer; 2018

[27] Peng X et al. Traffic anomaly detection in intelligent transport applications with time series data using informer. In: 2022 IEEE 25th International Conference on Intelligent Transportation Systems (ITSC). Canada; 2022. pp. 3309-3314

[28] Luo R, Song Y, Huang L, Zhang Y, Su R. AST-GIN: Attribute-augmented spatiotemporal graph informer network for electric vehicle Charging Station availability forecasting. Sensors. 1975;**23**(4):2023

[29] Bi C, Ren P, Yin T, Zhang Y, Li B, Xiang Z. An informer architecture-based Ionospheric foF2 model in the middle latitude region. IEEE Geoscience and Remote Sensing Letters. 2022;**19**:1-5

[30] Zou R, Duan Y, Wang Y, Pang J, Liu F, Sheikh SR. A novel convolutional informer network for deterministic and probabilistic state-of-charge estimation of lithium-ion batteries. Journal of Energy Storage. 2023;**57**:106298

[31] Gong M, Zhao Y, Sun J, Han C, Sun G, Yan B. Load forecasting of district heating system based on informer. Energy. 2022;**253**:124179

[32] Guo L, Li R, Jiang B. A data-driven long time-series electrical line trip fault prediction method using an improved stacked-informer network. Sensors. 2021;**21**(13):4466

Section 3

# Multi-Agent Systems

Chapter 6

# Algorithmic Innovations in Multi-Agent Reinforcement Learning: A Pathway for Smart Cities

*Igor Agbossou*

## Abstract

The concept of smart cities has emerged as an instrumental solution to tackle the intricate challenges associated with urbanization in the twenty-first century. Among the myriad of issues that smart cities aim to address, key concerns such as efficient traffic management, sustainable energy usage, resilient infrastructure, and enhanced public safety are at the forefront. Notably, the implementation of multi-agent reinforcement learning (MARL) has garnered significant attention for its potential role in realizing the vision of smart cities. This chapter serves as an exploration of the frontiers of algorithmic innovation within MARL and its direct applicability to address the complex challenges of urban smart grid systems. The integration of MARL principles is vital in comprehensively modeling the intricate, interdependent urban systems that underpin the smart city framework. Particularly, we emphasize the relevance of MARL in providing adaptive solutions to the intricate dynamics of the urban smart grid, ensuring effective management of energy resources and demand-side management.

**Keywords:** smart cities, multi-agent reinforcement learning, urban smart grid system, sustainable energy usage, deep deterministic policy gradient

## 1. Introduction

The rapid growth of urbanization across the globe presents a profound challenge for the design and management of modern cities. As the world's population continues to gravitate towards urban areas, there is an ever-increasing demand for cities to operate efficiently, sustainably, and intelligently. Smart cities, a vision that combines advanced technologies with data-driven decision-making, offer a promising solution to address these complex urban challenges [1, 2]. At the heart of the smart city concept [3–6] lies the ability to optimize and coordinate various urban systems in real-time, from traffic management [7] and energy distribution [8] to public safety and transportation [7]. Achieving this level of sophistication necessitates cutting-edge technologies, and among these, artificial intelligence (AI) stands out as a crucial enabler. Within the AI domain, multi-agent reinforcement learning (MARL) has emerged as a powerful paradigm for modeling and solving complex decision-making problems involving multiple autonomous agents [9]. MARL represents a fusion of reinforcement learning (RL) [10] and multi-agent systems (MAS) [11, 12] making it well-suited for addressing the intricate and interconnected challenges found in urban environments [3, 5, 6, 11, 13].

This chapter embarks on a journey into the realm of algorithmic innovation within the context of MARL, elucidating its potential as a transformative pathway for the development of smart cities. The motivation behind this exploration is rooted in the pressing need to harness the capabilities of MARL to enhance the quality of urban life. The modern cityscape is a dynamic and ever-evolving ecosystem, characterized by its complex web of interactions between diverse entities such as vehicles, buildings, infrastructure, and, most crucially, its residents. Managing these interactions optimally is a monumental task, one that has traditionally required extensive human intervention and resource allocation. Incidentally, the advent of MARL has opened new possibilities. By endowing agents, whether they are autonomous vehicles, energy management systems, or emergency response units, with the ability to learn and adapt to their environments through interactions, we can pave the way for more efficient, sustainable, and resilient urban systems. The implications extend far beyond mere automation; they encompass the potential to create cities that are responsive, data-driven, and capable of continuously optimizing their operations in real-time. The objective pursued in this chapter is at least twofold: (1) Comprehend MARL fundamentals: we will establish a solid foundation by elucidating the fundamentals of reinforcement learning and multi-agent systems, providing insights into the unique challenges and complexities of MARL in the framework of smart cities. (2) Explore algorithmic innovations: we will delve into the state-of-the-art algorithms and techniques that have emerged in the field of MARL, emphasizing their relevance and potential in the context of smart city development.

In pursuit of our goals, we will direct our attention towards the challenge of implementing intelligent automation for energy management within urban settings, employing a comprehensive multi-scalar approach that spans from individual households to the entire cityscape. It is crucial to acknowledge that the energy consumption in both residential and commercial buildings is steadily on the rise. This upward trajectory can be attributed, in part, to the escalating proliferation of household appliances, which in turn drives a substantial surge in domestic electricity demand. Consequently, effective planning for residential energy utilization becomes imperative for achieving optimal energy management within the framework of urban electricity distribution networks: smart grid. This intricate challenge is effectively addressed through the application of MARL models. The rest of the chapter is structured as follows: Section 2 focuses on the context and overview of the smart city. The Section 3 introduces the fundamentals of MARL, providing a basis for understanding its application in smart cities.

In Section 4, materials and methods, we present a comprehensive exposition on the multi-agent formalization for reinforcement learning pertaining to the automated energy management within urban buildings. This discussion is contextualized within the purview of smart grids, and it extensively expounds upon the methodological nuances underlying the modeling of diverse agents, both at the micro-level of individual buildings and at the macro-level of the entire city infrastructure. Building upon this framework, Section 5 is dedicated to an in-depth exploration of scenario testing implementation and subsequent results analysis. Here, we dissect the findings and their implications, shedding light on the intricate dynamics of urban energy management and the role played by MARL models. Finally, we conclude by emphasizing the significant potential that Collaborative Intelligence embodies in reshaping our urban landscapes, thereby contributing to the growing body of knowledge in the realm of MARL's pivotal role in shaping the cities of the future.

## 2. Background and smart cities overview

Across the globe, cities are confronting and surmounting multifaceted challenges by embracing a rich tapestry of inventive concepts [3–6]. This diverse spectrum of initiatives encompasses novel energy and transportation paradigms [7], groundbreaking innovations in residential construction [3], the proliferation of shared services [11], digitization of administrative processes [4], and a myriad of other pioneering endeavors. These groundbreaking initiatives are a collaborative effort involving cities, established corporations, nimble startups, non-profit organizations, and engaged citizens, all working collectively to advance innovative solutions. In recent years, a significant portion of these initiatives, particularly those harnessing the power of emerging information and communication technologies, have coalesced under the encompassing banner of "smart city" endeavors.

A smart city is one that methodically applies digital technologies to optimize resource utilization, elevate the quality of life for its residents, and bolster the regional economy's competitiveness in a sustainable fashion. It's a holistic approach that deploys intelligent solutions across various facets of urban life, encompassing infrastructure, energy management, housing, mobility, services, and security. These solutions are rooted in integrated sensor technology, seamless connectivity, data-driven analytics, and self-sustaining value-added processes.

However, it's important to recognize that the path to a truly smart city is not without its challenges and complexities. Smart city projects often unfold as intricate, costly, occasionally chaotic, and time-consuming endeavors. They present a unique set of demands, necessitating two distinct competencies: an astute understanding of the ramifications of embedding digital technologies within the fabric of urban development, and the capacity to conceive integrative solutions that transcend traditional departmental boundaries. Confronted by these formidable demands (**Figure 1**), many decision-makers and implementers find themselves at an impasse, unsure of where to commence or how to navigate the labyrinthine journey ahead. Consequently, a significant reservoir of untapped potential languishes on the precipice of realization.

### 2.1 The essence of smart cities

Smart cities epitomize the methodical harnessing of digital technologies' boundless potential, seamlessly interwoven with a holistic embrace of users, inhabitants, and all stakeholders alike. At its core, the smart city endeavor is driven by a grand vision: to realize urban landscapes characterized by optimized resource utilization, elevated living standards, and a sustainable boost in competitiveness. To achieve these paramount goals, a predominantly digital transformation across the domains of infrastructure, energy management, housing, mobility, services, and security becomes not just preferable, but imperative. Central to this transformation lies the concept of a city's "digital shadow" [14], a foundational element that serves as the bedrock for the city's digital evolution. It's important to distinguish this concept from the notion of a

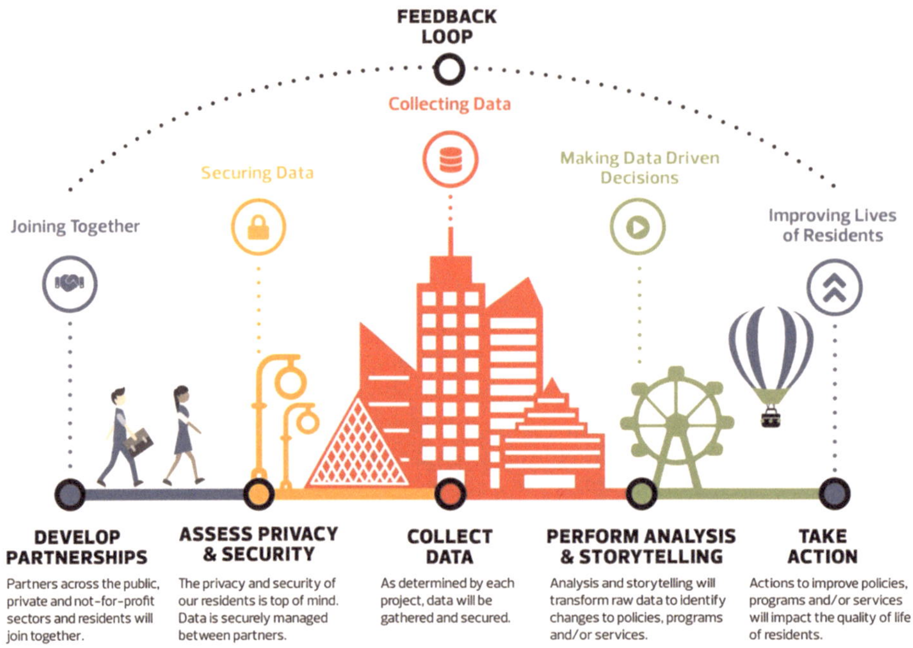


**Figure 1.**
*General framework of smart city. Source: Adapted from Ref. [13].*

"digital twin" [15]. This digital shadow is the vessel through which intelligent solutions are infused into the urban fabric. Rooted in integrated sensor technologies, seamless connectivity, adept data analysis, and self-sustaining value-added processes, the digital shadow marks the inception of a profound change. The transformation towards an intelligent, interconnected urban ecosystem commences with the transformation of physical products, processes, and services into their digital counterparts. As these entities evolve into intelligent, autonomous, and integrated entities, a digital shadow emerges, propelling ecological and social betterment into the forefront. At the vanguard of this transformation stands the Internet of Things (IoT), serving as the conduit between the digital realm and the physical world [16]. Notably, emerging technologies such as Blockchain are poised to revolutionize secure transactions and identity management within cities, fostering trust and transparency [17–20].

Powering this transformative voyage is the bedrock of modern data analytics, often encapsulated within the realm of Artificial Intelligence (AI). Through sophisticated algorithms and machine learning, AI sifts through vast datasets to uncover intricate patterns, autonomously refining systems with minimal human intervention. For instance, the intricate road system in Los Angeles has learned to optimize traffic flows through this autonomous self-improvement process, a testament to the potential unleashed by AI-driven urban innovations [11, 15, 16].

However, the digital shadow, in its nascent form, remains neutral and devoid of purpose. Therefore, it is imperative for self-learning systems to be deeply attuned to their surroundings, attentively considering the needs and aspirations of city residents. The digital shadow, while a pivotal prerequisite for smart cities, stands incomplete on its own. It is only through a laser-focused commitment to the city's holistic milieu that it can fulfill its true potential.

## 2.2 Main constituents of smart city perspective evolution

In the annals of urban development, the year 2008 marked a transformative juncture when IBM introduced the visionary "smarter planet and smart city concept" worldwide. This groundbreaking concept took root in select cities, driven by the transformative potential of Information Communication Technology (ICT). Leading the charge, nations like Japan, Singapore, and China embarked on the ambitious journey of crafting smart cities, underpinned by the prowess of ICT [17].

Over the past decade, the landscape of smart cities has undergone a remarkable metamorphosis, with ICT serving as the catalyst for change. These cities have evolved to encompass a spectrum of characteristics that together define the essence of "smart cities." These constituents are encapsulated in the following pillars: "smart governance," "smart education," "smart living," "smart mobility," "smart environment," "smart energy," "smart healthcare," and "smart citizens" [21, 22]. It is through the harmonious convergence of these elements that the symphony of a smart city comes to life. The smart city narrative continues to unfold, with technology acting as an enabler for greater intelligence and efficiency. Pioneering technologies such as the IoT, AI, and the transformative potential of big data analytics have emerged as formidable allies in the quest for smarter urban landscapes [22–25]. These technologies are the building blocks of a new urban paradigm, where data-driven insights, automation, and connectivity redefine the way cities operate and flourish. Each of these key components plays a unique role, interlocking with others to create a tapestry of innovation and progress. For a detailed breakdown of these components by domain, please refer to **Table 1**.

| Key domain | Sectors and services associated with domains | References |
|---|---|---|
| Governance | Online citizens portals, efficient and fast public services, effective resource management, innovative planning approaches, public asset management, e-services, connecting people through social media. | [4, 20, 23, 26] |
| Education | Smart infrastructure with closed-circuit television surveillance, GPS tracking of school busses, smart learning through video conferencing lectures, teacher–students management solutions, virtual labs. | [4, 20, 23, 26] |
| Living | Public security tools, safety alarms at public places at panic situations, community network management, safety of senior citizens. | [20, 21, 23, 26] |
| Mobility | A smart toll collection system, community carpooling system, charging point for electric vehicles, smart parking system, connected and autonomous vehicles | [2, 3, 20, 21, 23, 26] |
| Environment | Traffic management, vehicle monitoring, water quality management, air quality management, smart water storage and purification system Wastewater management, pollution sensors, disaster management, green and clean environment, smart waste management. | [3, 20, 21, 23, 26] |
| Energy | Smart meters, efficient utilization of energy subsystem, energy distribution through sensors. | [3, 20, 23, 26] |
| Healthcare | E-health records, diagnostic analytics portals, emergency medical services | [20, 23, 26] |
| Citizenship | Privacy and security of citizens, social engagement of the people, raising awareness of smart solutions, community interactions | [3, 20, 21, 23, 26] |

**Table 1.**
*Main required components of smart cities.*

The advent of smart cities has ushered in a paradigm shift in urban planning and management. At its core, this transformation embraces the concept of agent-based modeling (ABM), a powerful computational framework that treats various urban entities as intelligent agents. These agents, which can represent a wide spectrum of urban systems, including traffic signals, public transportation networks, energy grids, and waste management systems, interact with one another and their environment, making informed decisions to optimize their respective functions. In the context of smart cities, MARL allows agents to adapt to the ever-changing dynamics of urban environments, making decisions that lead to more efficient, sustainable, and responsive city operations [25–27].

## 3. Fundamentals of multi-agent reinforcement learning

In recent times, MARL has emerged as a focal point of research, particularly in the realm of multi-agent systems operating in expansive, large-scale environments. This surge in interest can be attributed to its remarkable success, particularly in the domain of strategic games [ … ]. At its core, Reinforcement Learning (RL) draws inspiration from the mechanisms of animal learning in psychology [ … ]. It embodies a trial-and-error learning process where an agent strives to learn an action policy that maximizes cumulative rewards over time through its interactions with an environment [ … ]. Urban environments, on the other hand, are characterized by unparalleled complexity and dynamism. They comprise a multitude of interconnected components and features, perpetually influencing one another.

### 3.1 Reinforcement learning basics

RL stands as a prominent and widely recognized subset of machine learning methods, specifically tailored to the art of acquiring the skill to accomplish specific tasks by engaging in dynamic interactions with the surrounding environment. This pivotal task often hinges on the presence of a reward mechanism, serving as a beacon guiding the intelligent agent towards optimal performance. In essence, RL casts the intelligent agent in the role of a decision-maker, requiring it to navigate a spectrum of situations by selecting actions strategically. The accumulation of rewards based on these actions functions as a compass, guiding the agent towards more proficient decision-making in the future. The overarching goal is to amass rewards as efficiently as possible over an extended period, ultimately steering the agent's behavior towards a state of optimal performance in the long term. The focal point of RL revolves around the quest to uncover a control policy capable of achieving predefined objectives. In this context, RL takes on the formalized structure of a Markov decision process [28], serving as the bedrock upon which iterative learning is built. Within each iteration, a RL agent carefully chooses an action ($a_t$) based on the prevailing policy and the current state ($s_t$). This selected action is then executed within the given environment, ushering in a transition to a new state ($s_{t+1}$) and the concomitant bestowal of a reward ($r_{t+1}$) as elucidated in **Figure 2**.

Through its continuous interaction with the environment, the policy undergoes iterative refinement via RL methodologies, all aimed at maximizing the cumulative long-term reward. To compute the optimal policy, a diverse array of techniques is at the RL practitioner's disposal, with value-based and policy-based approaches emerging as the most prominent contenders [29, 30]. When confronted with intricate

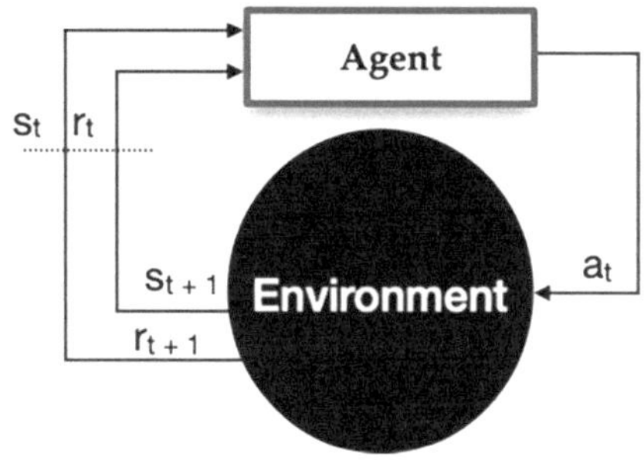


**Figure 2.**
*RL paradigm in a Markov decision process for an agent.*

challenges, such as those outlined in **Table 1**, neural networks emerge as a formidable tool, empowering RL to effectively predict the optimal policy or value function [31]. Yet, the scope of RL extends beyond individual agents tackling isolated problems. In scenarios marked by complexity and interdependency, as underscored in **Table 1**, RL seamlessly extends its domain to encompass multiple agents coexisting within the same environment. Here, these agents can engage in collaborative or competitive interactions, ushering in the realm of MARL. In the following, we will delve deeper into the intricacies of MARL and explore how these algorithmic innovations are poised to chart a transformative pathway for smart cities, where a consortium of learning agents collaboratively engages with urban environments.

### 3.2 From bellman equation to iterative policy evaluation and improvement

The quest to understand and approximate the value function of a given policy π has long been a central pursuit in the realm of RL. At its heart, this endeavor hinges on unraveling the intricate relationship between the value of a state and the values of its successor states. This foundational relationship is encapsulated by the state value function, which adheres to the following Eq. (1):

$$v_\pi(s_t) = \sum_a \pi(a_t|s_t) \sum_s P_s^a(r(s_t, a_t, s_{t+1}) + \mu v_\pi(s_{t+1}) \quad (1)$$

This equation elegantly expresses the interplay between the value of a state and the expected values of its future states. It serves as the cornerstone upon which numerous methods for computing and learning the state value function $v_\pi$ are constructed. Not to be outdone, the state-action value function qπ also adheres to a recursive relationship known as the Bellman equation [32]:

$$q_\pi(s_t, a_t) = \sum_{a_{t+1}} P_s^a((r(s_t, a_t, s_{t+1}) + \mu \sum_{a_{t+1}} \pi(a_{t+1}|s_{t+1}) q_\pi(s_{t+1}, a_{t+1}) \quad (2)$$

The Bellman equation for ($q_\pi$) embodies a similar spirit, delineating the value of a state-action pair (s, a) as a function of the rewards, transitions, and values of the ensuing states. The specific challenge of computing the state value function $v_\pi$ for a given policy, termed policy evaluation, takes center stage. To tackle this challenge, we adopt an iterative approach, bypassing direct computational methods in favor of a more computationally efficient strategy and we assume complete knowledge of the environment's dynamics, implying familiarity with the transition probabilities for each element ($s_t$, $a_t$). Below, we present the pseudo-code outlining the iterative policy evaluation algorithm:

The pursuit of computing the value function for a given policy is not merely an intellectual exercise; rather, it serves as a pivotal stepping stone towards the enhancement and optimization of existing policies. Consider a deterministic policy π for which the associated value function $v_\pi$ has been diligently calculated.

This foundational knowledge becomes a catalyst for the creation of an improved policy, denoted as $\pi'$. So, how does one transition from $\pi$ to $\pi'$? The process unfolds as follows:

$$\pi'(s_t) = argmax_a q_\pi(s_t, a_t) \tag{3}$$

The Policy Improvement Theorem [33], a fundamental result in the realm of RL, underpins the process of policy refinement. According to this theorem, the new policy $\pi'$ derived from an existing policy π is inherently superior or, at the very least, equivalent in performance. This transformative procedure, which entails evolving an old policy into a more optimal one by aligning it with the insights garnered from the value function, is formally recognized as "policy improvement." The steps to execute this method are concisely outlined below:

### 3.3 CityLearn: enabling algorithms implementation and execution

In this section, we present the fundamental implementation tools and aspects of our research through CityLearn [34]. Eqs (1)–(3) are operationalized through the pseudo-coded algorithms presented in **Tables 2** and **3**, forming the core of our agent coordination policies. In the context of MARL, these policies are the controllers. Leveraging the OpenAI Gym standard, CityLearn serves as a platform for deploying MARL algorithms for urban energy management, load-shaping, and demand response [34, 35]. CityLearn operates primarily in a decentralized control mode, which we utilized for our MARL controllers. To ensure reproducibility, we outline its four key functionalities: (1) Facilitation of MARL implementations. (2) Full customizability of the reward function, enabling the use of a multi-output function for MARL applications. (3) Modular and open-source design, accommodating diverse energy system classes, including options for user-created classes, particularly for city-scale energy systems. (4) Provision for users to generate their datasets (e.g., weather data, building

| | | |
|---|---|---|
| Initialize v(s) arbitrarily for all s ∈ S | | |
| Repeat until convergence: | | |
| | Δ ← 0 | |
| | For each s ∈ S: | |
| | | v_old ← v(s) |
| | | v(s) ← $\sum_a \pi(a_t \vert s_t) \sum_s P_s^a (r(s_t, a_t, s_{t+1}) + \mu v_\pi(s_{t+1})$ |
| | | Δ ← max(Δ, \|v_old - v(s)\|) |
| | Until Δ < θ (a small positive threshold) | |

**Table 2.**
*Iterative policy evaluation algorithm.*

| | | |
|---|---|---|
| policy-stable ← true | | |
| For each s ∈ S do | | |
| | old-action← π(s) | |
| | π(s) ← $argmax_a q_\pi(s_t, a_t)$ | |
| | if old-action ≠π(s) then | |
| | | policy-stable← false |
| | end | |
| end | | |
| if policy-stable = true | | |
| | | Stop and return π |
| end | | |
| else | | |
| | | Go to **Table 2**. |
| end | | |

**Table 3.**
*Iterative policy improvement algorithm.*

energy demand, EV schedules) and integrate them into CityLearn. Further guidelines on dataset creation can be accessed through the GitHub repository [36].

## 4. Materials and methods

MAS serve as the linchpin in a diverse array of applications within smart cities. These applications encompass a broad spectrum of technologies, including integration with the IoT and autonomous systems. Examples of such autonomous systems are intelligent robots, unmanned aerial, underwater, or surface vehicles, self-driving cars, and advanced transportation and healthcare systems. In these contexts, MAS agents engage in distributed interactions to fulfill specific tasks and objectives. In the ideal smart city scenario, MAS should exhibit robust, decentralized, and collaborative behaviors. These systems are expected to make intelligent and cognitive decisions while devising efficient solutions to data-driven challenges. Consequently, they facilitate decentralized information management and decision-making processes [37] that underpin the dynamics of smart cities. The remainder of this chapter is devoted to resolving the problem of efficient management of energy systems predicament within urban settings, employing the MARL paradigm. This section aims to dissect the complexities associated with energy resource allocation and optimization, elucidating the role of MARL in enabling efficient and effective urban smart grid management strategies.

### 4.1 Multi-agent model design for urban smart grid

One of the primary catalysts for grid decarbonization is the seamless integration of renewable energy systems (RES) into the grid's supply chain. Within the residential domain, the Home Energy Management System (HEMS) proves to be a highly effective tool for automating energy management (**Figure 3**) as illustrated.

In the realm of MARL for smart cities, the selection of appropriate sensors plays a pivotal role in the acquisition of accurate and high-quality data [38]. As technology continues to advance, an extensive array of sensors has become available for gathering geospatial data within urban environments [39–42]. In recent years, mobile sensors such as smartphones and tablets have gained significant popularity [43, 44]. The concept of demand response (DR) is central to an effective energy management strategy (**Figure 4**), offering consumers and prosumers the ability to provide the grid with the much-needed flexibility. This is achieved by reducing energy consumption through load management, shifting energy consumption to off-peak times, or generating and storing energy when grid conditions are favorable. In return, consumers and prosumers typically experience a reduction in their energy bills.

In fact, HEMS functions as a distributed intelligent agent that empowers users to partake in local energy trading and realize energy savings at the household level. By acting as a strategic agent, HEMS contributes to holistic load management, ensuring that the energy needs of each household are met in an efficient and cost-effective

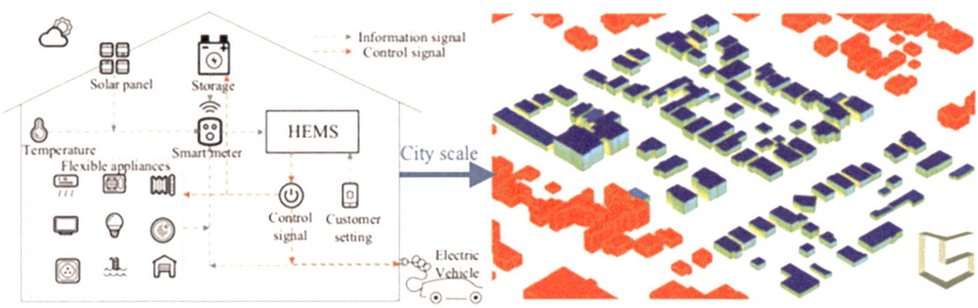


**Figure 3.**
*HEMS agent at the heart of urban smart grid.*

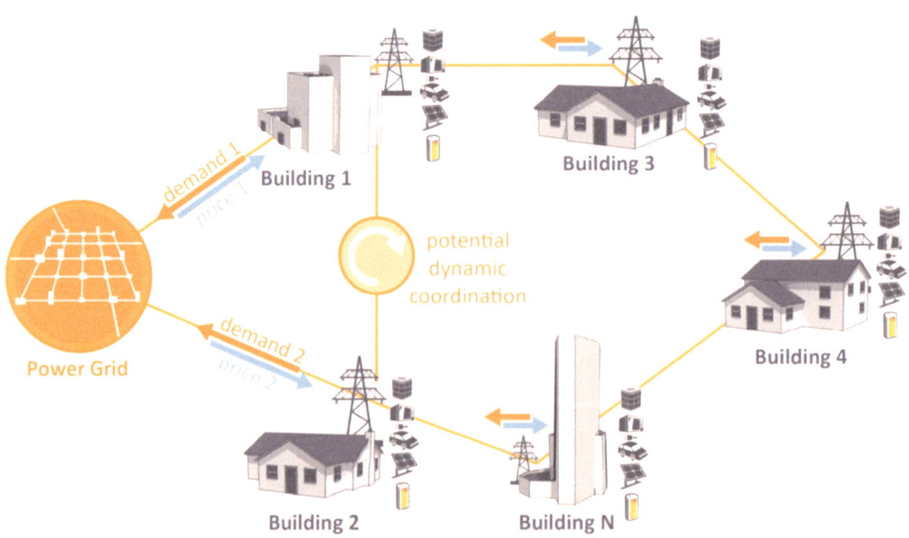


**Figure 4.**
*Multi-agent coordination in demand response within smart grid (taken from the CityLearn GitHub repository).*

manner. The HEMS system operates as an intelligent agent [45, 46] that crafts optimal energy plans for home appliances, considering individual customer energy consumption plans and comfort requirements. By adapting and learning from customer interactions, these agents become adept at predicting and optimizing individual customer decision-making patterns, thereby ensuring effective and efficient urban energy management.

### 4.2 MARL coordination policy assessment

Coordination policy takes the principles of single-agent RL and extends them to facilitate distributed decision-making at a larger scale.

- *Multi-agent training for decentralized execution:* In MARL, the challenge lies in training multiple agents to execute strategies in a decentralized manner [47]. To model this, we formulate the problem as a partially observable Markov decision problem within the framework of Deep Reinforcement Learning (DRL) [48]. However, when the environment is dynamic, the learning task becomes considerably more challenging. In such cases, each agent within a multi-agent system often perceives all other learning agents as part of the environment, creating a non-stationary scenario. This non-stationarity can lead to suboptimal policies, as they are developed in a distributed fashion and may not be sufficiently robust.

- *Addressing non-stationarity through centralized training with decentralized execution*: To mitigate the non-stationarity challenge, various approaches have been proposed [49, 50], focusing on centralized training with decentralized execution. These approaches encompass different strategies: (1) Shared Critic Networks: For actor-critic algorithms, like Multi-Agent Deep Deterministic Policy Gradient (MADDPG) [49], they involve training on an ensemble of policies that encourage more robust multi-agent policies. The shared critic network plays a crucial role in coordinating the actions of multiple agents. (2) Q-value Mixing (QMIX): QMIX [51] utilizes a network to estimate joint action values, ensuring monotonicity per agent. This guarantees tractability and consistency between centralized and decentralized policies, fostering better coordination. (3) Inter-Agent Communication: Some methods leverage communication between agents to enhance scalability. For instance, Differentiable Inter-Agent Learning (DIAL) [50] and CommNet [52] employ deep neural networks to learn end-to-end communication protocols. This is particularly useful in complex environments with partial observability. Agents in these approaches exchange information and backpropagate error derivatives, combining centralized learning with decentralized execution to improve overall performance. (4) Macro-Actions: Another approach, as introduced in [53], involves creating abstractions known as macro-actions. These abstractions help improve scalability by allowing agents to reason and plan at a higher level, thus reducing the complexity of decision-making.

## 5. Experimental settings and results

CityLearn stands out as a comprehensive and user-friendly OpenAI Gym environment tailored for the seamless implementation of MARL techniques within the intricate domain of urban energy systems. This innovative platform is designed to bring about significant transformations in the aggregated electricity demand curve by orchestrating the energy storage capabilities of a diverse array of buildings within a district [34, 35]. The primary goal of CityLearn is to simplify and standardize the evaluation of RL agents, thereby serving as an invaluable benchmarking tool for a wide spectrum of algorithms.

## 5.1 Key features of CityLearn

Key features of CityLearn are: (1) Diverse Energy Models: At the heart of CityLearn lies an extensive library of energy models, encompassing vital components such as air-to-water heat pumps, electric heaters, chilled water (CHW) systems, domestic hot water (DHW) heaters, and electricity energy storage devices. These models enable the simulation of a wide range of building energy systems, reflecting the rich heterogeneity found in real-world urban environments. (2) Building Energy Systems: Each building in the simulation is equipped with an air-to-water heat pump for cooling and an electric heater for DHW heating. Additionally, buildings have the flexibility to incorporate various combinations of CHW, DHW, and electricity storage devices. These components work collaboratively to offset cooling, DHW heating, and electrical loads drawn from the grid. (3) Storage Capacity: CityLearn introduces the concept of storage capacity, defined as multiples of the hours that storage devices can meet the maximum annual cooling and DHW demand when fully charged. This parameterization allows for precise control and optimization of energy storage strategies. (4) Grid Interaction: The framework encompasses a dynamic interaction between buildings and the main grid. Besides the energy storage devices, other electric equipment, and appliances (non-shiftable loads) also draw electricity from the grid. For sustainable energy practices, CityLearn supports the integration of Photovoltaic (PV) systems within buildings, enabling them to generate their own electricity and reduce dependency on the grid.

CityLearn has emerged as a versatile tool with a wide array of applications. Researchers have harnessed its capabilities to explore incentive-based Demand Response (DR) mechanisms [54], coordinate energy management across multiple buildings [55], and conduct rigorous benchmarking of MARL algorithms [36, 56]. Its flexibility, coupled with its diverse energy models, makes CityLearn an indispensable asset for advancing our understanding of urban energy systems and shaping the future of sustainable urban development.

## 5.2 Simulation setup for smart grid

In our research endeavor, we leverage the sophisticated CityLearn environment as a crucial testbed to rigorously assess the performance of our MARL algorithm in orchestrating the actions of multiple agents, as detailed in Section 3.2 of this chapter. Our primary objective is to delve into the behavioral dynamics of these agents concerning varying durations of offline training, relying on predefined policies. We postulate that an extended offline training period equips the agents with expert-level knowledge of optimal actions, thereby leading to enhanced overall performance when they transition to an online setting. Within the simulated smart city environment, each individual building is endowed with its dedicated Reinforcement Learning – Deep Deterministic Policy Gradient (RL-DDPG) controller. The number of these controllers aligns with the total count of buildings under consideration, a scenario featuring ten buildings in this specific case study. Notably, we explore the performance of two distinct RL controllers: the conventional DDPG controller and its multi-agent variant, known as MADPG.

Here are some key insights into our simulation setup:

- *Controller configuration*: DDPG Controller: In the DDPG setup, each agent operates in relative isolation, possessing knowledge solely of its own states and actions. This encapsulation reflects a scenario where agents are not privy to the states or actions of their peers, operating independently.

- *MADPG controller*: In contrast, the MADPG controller extends the agents' awareness to include not only their own states and actions but also those of every other agent in the system. This elevated level of information sharing fosters collaborative decision-making among the agents.

- *State representation*: As states, our framework incorporates key variables, including the hour of the day, outdoor temperature, and the state of charge within each Chilled Water (CHW) storage tank. These states provide valuable context and information for the agents to make informed decisions.

- *Action space*: The controllers' actions pertain to the energy storage and release strategies they employ during hourly intervals. These actions are pivotal in optimizing energy utilization and management within the smart city. Here is a dataset sample that captures the MARL implementation details within the CityLearn environment in **Table 4**.

Building ID specifies the unique identifier for each building within the simulation, facilitating the differentiation and tracking of individual buildings. Controller denotes the type of controller utilized in each building, indicating whether it is a DDPG or MADPG controller. The distinction between the two controllers is crucial as it influences the decision-making process and the overall behavior of the

| Building ID | Controller | Hour of the day | Outdoor temperature (°C) | CHW state (%) | Action taken |
|---|---|---|---|---|---|
| 1 | DDPG | 15:00 | 28 | 60 | Store |
| 2 | DDPG | 14:00 | 25 | 40 | Release |
| 3 | DDPG | 12:00 | 30 | 75 | Store |
| 4 | DDPG | 11:00 | 20 | 55 | Release |
| 5 | DDPG | 10:00 | 27 | 70 | Store |
| 6 | MADPG | 18:00 | 29 | 50 | Release |
| 7 | MADPG | 17:00 | 24 | 45 | Store |
| 8 | MADPG | 16:00 | 26 | 80 | Release |
| 9 | MADPG | 13:00 | 22 | 65 | Store |
| 10 | MADPG | 09:00 | 31 | 35 | Release |

**Table 4.**
*Dataset sample that captures the MARL implementation.*

building within the smart city environment. Hour of the Day represents the specific hour of the day at which the action is being taken. It provides insights into the temporal dynamics of the decision-making process, showcasing how the controllers operate at different times of the day. Outdoor Temperature signifies the outdoor temperature in Celsius, which is a crucial environmental factor impacting the energy management decisions of the buildings. It highlights the influence of external conditions on the operational strategies implemented by the controllers. CHW represents the state of the CHW storage tank within each building, depicted as a percentage. It indicates the current level of charge within the storage tank, which directly influences the decisions regarding whether to store or release energy. Action Taken specifies the action chosen by the controller in response to the current state of the CHW storage tank. The actions are categorized as "Store" or "Release," reflecting the decisions made by the controllers to either store or release energy based on the prevailing conditions and objectives.

This information is instrumental in understanding the efficacy of the MARL algorithms and their implications for optimizing energy utilization and management within the smart city context. Our study capitalizes on the CityLearn environment to conduct a meticulous investigation into the performance of MARL algorithms, with a particular focus on the impact of offline training durations.

We assess the efficacy of both individualized and collaborative decision-making strategies, shedding light on the potential advantages of multi-agent coordination in urban energy systems.

### 5.3 Policy controller results

In our comprehensive evaluation of controllers for smart grid management within the smart city context, we employed the total cooling cost as the primary performance metric to assess their effectiveness. **Figure 5** provides a visual representation of our findings, where we compared the performance of two Reinforcement Learning – Deep Deterministic Policy Gradient (RL-DDPG) controllers against two rule-based controllers (RBC).

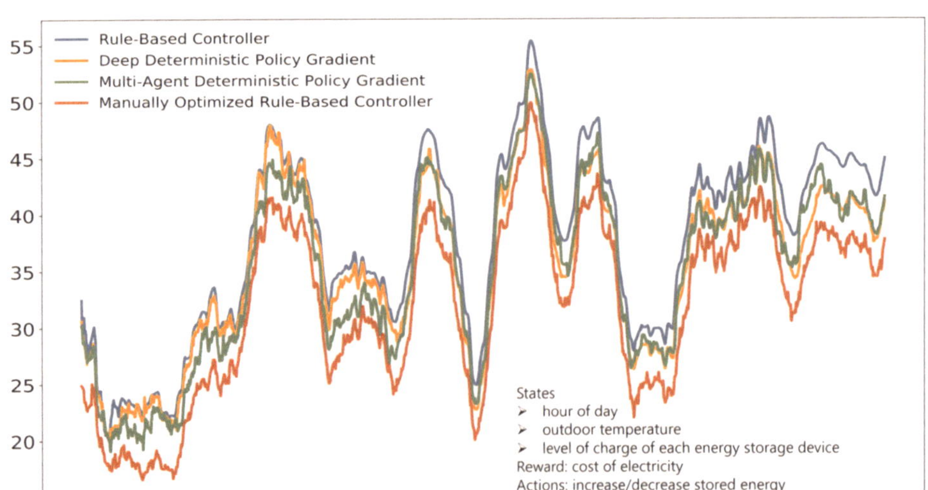


**Figure 5.**
*MARL policy evaluation for energy distribution.*

Here are the key aspects of our evaluation and observations:

*5.3.1 Controller comparison*

- *DDPG and MADPG controllers*: We subjected both the DDPG and MADPG controllers, representing advanced machine learning-driven decision-making, to a rigorous assessment. These controllers were tasked with optimizing cooling costs within the simulated environment.

- *Rule-based controllers (RBC):* To provide a benchmark for comparison, we introduced two rule-based controllers. The first RBC followed a standard rule-based approach, activating cooling when the water temperature in the tank reached a predefined maximum threshold. The second RBC was manually tuned to minimize total electricity costs, representing a more refined rule-based strategy.

*5.3.2 Performance outcomes*

- *DDPG and MADPG outperform standard RBC*: Notably, both the DDPG and MADPG controllers demonstrated superior performance compared to the standard RBC. This improvement was achieved without necessitating explicit system modeling and maintained the adaptive potential inherent to Reinforcement Learning (RL) methods.

- *Manually optimized RBC*: Interestingly, the manually optimized RBC, which was relatively straightforward to fine-tune due to the uniformity of energy systems across all buildings, outperformed both the DDPG and MADPG controllers.

The study findings, as depicted in **Figure 5**, indicate that within this specific environment, the MADPG controller did not exhibit a substantial advantage over the DDPG controller. In essence, sharing information among the agents did not yield significant performance improvements. This observation raises the question of whether coordination efforts are necessary in this context, considering that similar savings can be achieved without explicit coordination. We acknowledge that these results may vary in more complex environments characterized by diverse energy systems and potentially differing optimal policies for individual buildings. Further research is warranted to explore the dynamics of coordination in such intricate settings.

### 5.4 Evaluation metrics comparison across key algorithms

To comprehensively uncover the origins of algorithmic innovations in the pursuit of optimizing multi-agent coordination policies for addressing challenges within smart cities, it is imperative to undertake a global assessment of the performance of various algorithms employed during this research endeavor. This segment presents a thorough juxtaposition of key evaluation metrics for the Deep Deterministic Policy Gradient (DDPG) algorithm, the Multi-Agent Deterministic Policy Gradient (MADDPG) algorithm, the Rule-Based Controller (RBC) algorithm, and the Manual Optimized Rule-Based Controller (MORBC) algorithm. The comparison encompasses crucial metrics, including energy cost savings, network stability, computational

| Metric | Key algorithms | | | |
|---|---|---|---|---|
| | DDPG | MADDPG | RBC | MORBC |
| Energy cost savings | 0.921 | 0.853 | 0.652 | 0.881 |
| Grid stability | 0.854 | 0.908 | 0.603 | 0.781 |
| Computational complexity | 0.702 | 0.605 | 0.852 | 0.753 |
| Adaptability | 0.801 | 0.952 | 0.605 | 0.607 |
| Scalability | 0.903 | 0.851 | 0.804 | 0.801 |
| Decision-making complexity | 0.705 | 0.953 | 0.601 | 0.604 |
| Real-time responsiveness | 0.854 | 0.906 | 0.60 | 0.850 |
| Implementation complexity | 0.751 | 0.801 | 0.853 | 0.870 |

**Table 5.**
*Innovation metrics comparison across key algorithms.*

complexity, adaptability, scalability, decision-making intricacy, real-time responsiveness, and implementation complexity. By scrutinizing these metrics, we can elucidate the strengths and limitations inherent in each approach as applied to the simulation of smart grid management through CityLearn. **Table 5** offers a succinct overview of our comprehensive evaluation findings.

By contextualizing the evaluation within the parameters of a smart grid experimental environment, these results demonstrate insight into the performance capabilities of each algorithm, helping to highlight algorithmic innovation strategies in policy implementation. Robust multi-agent coordination adapted to efficient and sustainable smart projects.

## 6. Conclusion and future directions

MARL stands as a transformative force with the potential to revolutionize urban environments and address the multifaceted challenges that smart cities face. By facilitating decentralized decision-making processes, fostering cooperation, and introducing elements of healthy competition among agents, MARL paves the way for more efficient resource allocation and an enhanced quality of life for the denizens of urban landscapes. While the road ahead is not without its hurdles, the ongoing dedication to research and development in the field of MARL is indispensable in realizing the boundless possibilities that smart cities can offer in the future.

This chapter serves as a resounding call to action, resonating not only with researchers and technologists but also with urban visionaries, policymakers, and the architects of tomorrow's cities. It urges us to unite and harness the collective intelligence of autonomous agents, coupled with the adaptability and resilience embedded in reinforcement learning. Together, we can drive our cities forward into a future where they not only navigate the complexities of urban life but thrive as shining examples of sustainability and innovation.

In our evaluation, we have illuminated the promise of RL-based controllers in the realm of smart grid management. This has underscored the capacity of RL methods to surpass conventional rule-based strategies, particularly as the intricacy of systems escalates. Moreover, our findings beckon further exploration, especially in understanding the role of coordination within the intricate and multifaceted energy systems that characterize modern smart cities.

As we venture into the dynamic realm of smart city development, these results serve as a guiding beacon, urging us to embrace MARL as an essential instrument in sculpting the future of our urban environments.

## Author details

Igor Agbossou
University of Franche-Comté, Laboratory ThéMA UMR, IUT NFC, France

*Address all correspondence to: igor.agbossou@univ-fcomte.fr

## References

[1] Caprioli C, Bottero M. Addressing complex challenges in transformations and planning: A fuzzy spatial multicriteria analysis for identifying suitable locations for urban infrastructures. Land Use Policy. 2021, 2021;**102**:105147. DOI: 10.1016/j.landusepol.2020.105147

[2] Li J, Wu X, Fan J, Liu Y, Xu M. Overcoming driving challenges in complex urban traffic: A multi-objective eco-driving strategy via safety model based reinforcement learning. Energy. 2023, 2023;**284**:128517. DOI: 10.1016/j.energy.2023.128517

[3] Bakıcı T, Almirall E, Wareham J. A smart city initiative: The case of Barcelona. Journal of the Knowledge Economy. 2012;**4**(2013):135-148. DOI: 10.1007/s13132-012-0084-9

[4] Anthopoulo LG. Understanding Smart Cities: A Tool for Smart Government or an Industrial Trick (Public Administration and Information Technology). Vol. 22. Cham: Springer Nature; 2017. DOI: 10.1007/978-3-319-57015-0

[5] Fernandez-Anez V, Fernández-Güell JM, Giffinger R. Smart City implementation and discourses: An integrated conceptual model. The case of Vienna, Cities. 2018;**78**(2018):4-16. DOI: 10.1016/j.cities.2017.12.004

[6] Mardacany E. Smart cities characteristics: Importance of built environment components. In: Proceedings of IET Conference on Future Intelligent Cities 2014. London: ETI; 2014. pp. 1-6. DOI: 10.1049/ic.2014.0045

[7] Ali Abdul Razzaq Taresh AAR, Zghair NAK. Redesign of the communications network based on high availability of traffic management technologies to improve the communication. Measurement: Sensors. 2023;**27**(2023):100776. DOI: 10.1016/j.measen.2023.100776

[8] Hu L, Tian Q, Zou C, Huang J, Ye Y, Wu X. A study on energy distribution strategy of electric vehicle hybrid energy storage system considering driving style based on real urban driving data. Renewable and Sustainable Energy Reviews. 2022, 2022;**162**:112416. DOI: 10.1016/j.rser.2022.112416

[9] Kober J, Bagnell JA, Peters J. Reinforcement learning in robotics: A survey. The International Journal of Robotics Research. 2013;**32**(11): 1238-1274. DOI: 10.1177/0278364913495721

[10] Singh B, Kumar R, Singh VP. Reinforcement learning in robotic applications: A comprehensive survey. Artificial Intelligence Review. 2022; **55**(2):945-990. DOI: 10.1007/s10462-021-09997-9

[11] Casavola A, Franzè G, Gagliardi G, Tedesco F. A Multi-Agent Trust and Reputation Mechanisms for the Management of Smart Urban Lighting Systems. IFAC-PapersOnLine. 2022, 2022;**55**(6):545-550. DOI: 10.1016/j.ifacol.2022.07.185

[12] Sinyabe E, Kamla V, Tchappi I, Najjar Y, Galland S. Shapefile-based multi-agent geosimulation and visualization of building evacuation scenario. Procedia Computer Science. 2023;**220**(2023):519-526. DOI: 10.1016/j.procs.2023.03.066

[13] Hayes K, Ghosh S, Gnenz W, Annett J, Bryne MB. Smart city

Edmonton. In: Augusto JC, editor. Handbook of Smart Cities. Cham: Springer; 2021. DOI: 10.1007/978-3-030-69698-6_17

[14] Bergs T, Gierlings S, Auerbach T, Klink A, Schraknepper D, Augspurger T. The concept of digital twin and digital shadow in manufacturing. Procedia CIRP. 2021;**101**(2021):81-84. DOI: 10.1016/j.procir.2021.02.010

[15] Yoon S. Building digital twinning: Data, information, and models. Journal of Building Engineering. 2023, 2023;**76**: 107021. DOI: 10.1016/j.jobe.2023.107021

[16] Keegan BJ, McCarthy IP, Kietzmann J, Canhoto AI. On your marks, headset, go! Understanding the building blocks of metaverse realms. Business Horizons. 2023;**2023**. DOI: 10.1016/j.bushor.2023.09.002

[17] Guo M, Liu Y, Yu H, Hu B, Sang Z. An overview of smart city in China. Communications. 2016;**13**(5):203-211. DOI: 10.1109/CC.2016.7489987

[18] Das RK, Misra H. Smart city and E-governance: Exploring the connect in the context of local development in India. In: Fourth International Conference on eDemocracy & eGovernment (ICEDEG), Quito. Quito, Ecuador: IEEE; 2017. pp. 232-233. DOI: 10.1109/icedeg.2017.7962540

[19] Sang Z, Li K. ITU-T standardization activities on smart sustainable cities. IET Smart Cities. 2019;**1**(1):3-9. DOI: 10.1049/iet-smc.2019.0023

[20] Rehena Z, Janssen M. The smart city of Pune. Journal of Smart City Emergence. 2019;**2019**:261-282. DOI: 10.1016/B978-0-12-816169-2.00012-2

[21] Ismagilova E, Hughes L, Dwivedi YK, Raman KR. Smart cities: Advances in research—An information systems perspective. International Journal of Information Management. 2019;**47**:88-100. DOI: 10.1016/j.ijinfomgt.2019.01.004

[22] Vinod Kumar TM, Dahiya B. Smart economy in smart cities. In: Vinod Kumar T, editor. Smart Economy in Smart Cities. Advances in 21st Century Human Settlements. Singapore: Springer; 2017. DOI: 10.1007/978-981-10-1610-3_1

[23] Appio FP, Lima M, Paroutis S. Understanding smart cities: Innovation ecosystems, technological advancements, and societal challenges. Technological Forecasting and Social Change. 2019:**142**:1–14. DOI: 10.1016/j.techfore.2018.12.018

[24] Anthopoulos LG, Reddick CG. Smart city and smart government: synonymous or complementary? In: Proceedings of the 25th International Conference Companion on World Wide Web (WWW '16 Companion). Switzerland: International World Wide Web Conferences Steering Committee, Republic and Canton of Geneva; 2016. pp. 351-355. DOI: 10.1145/2872518.2888615

[25] Vinod Kumar TM. Smart metropolitan regional development. In: Book, Chapter Advances in 21st Century Human Settlements Book Series (ACHS). Berlin: Springer; 2019. DOI: 10.1007/978-981-10-8588-8

[26] Yigitcanlar T, Kamruzzaman M, Foth M, Sabatini-Marques J, da Costa E, Ioppolo G. Can cities become smart without being sustainable? A systematic review of the literature. Sustain Cities and Society. 2019;**45**:348-365. DOI: 10.1016/j.scs.2018.11.033

[27] Sarkheyli A, Sarkheyli E. Smart megaprojects in smart cities, dimensions,

and challenges. In: Chapter 19-Smart Cities Cybersecurity and Privacy. New York, NY, United States: Elsevier; 2019. pp. 269-277. DOI: 10.1016/B978-0-12-815032-0.00019-6

[28] Vázquez-Canteli JR, Nagy Z. Reinforcement learning for demand response: A review of algorithms and modeling techniques. Applied Energy. 2019;**235**(2019):1072-1089. DOI: 10.1016/j.apenergy.2018.11.002

[29] Vinyals O, Babuschkin I, Czarnecki WM, et al. 2019, grandmaster level in StarCraft II using multi-agent reinforcement learning. Nature. 2019;**575**: 350-354. DOI: 10.1038/s41586-019-1724-z

[30] Shakya AK, Pillai G, Chakrabarty S. Reinforcement learning algorithms: A brief survey. Expert Systems with Applications. 2023, 2023;**231**:120495. DOI: 10.1016/j.eswa.2023.120495

[31] Vázquez-Canteli JR, Ulyanin S, Kämpf J, Nagy Z. Fusing TensorFlow with building energy simulation for intelligent energy management in smart cities. Sustainable Cities and Society. 2019;**45**(2019):243-257. DOI: 10.1016/j.scs.2018.11.021

[32] Jones M, Peet M. A generalization of Bellman's equation with application to path planning, obstacle avoidance and invariant set estimation. Automatica. 2021, 2021;**127**:109510. DOI: 10.1016/j.automatica.2021.109510

[33] Sutton RS, Barto AG. Reinforcement Learning: An Introduction. 2nd ed. Massachusetts: MIT Press, Cambridge; 2015. Available from: https://inst.eecs.berkeley.edu/~cs188/sp20/assets/files/SuttonBartoIPRLBook2ndEd.pdf [Accessed: September 7, 2023]

[34] Github. n.d. Available from: https://github.com/intelligent-environments-lab/CityLearn

[35] Vázquez-Canteli JR, Kämpf J, Henze G, Nagy Z. CityLearn v1.0: An openai gym environment for demand response with deep reinforcement learning. In: BuildSys 2019 – Proceedings of the 6th ACM International Conference on Systems for Energy-Efficient Buildings, Cities, and Transportation. New York, NY, United States: ACM; 2019. pp. 356-357. DOI: 10.1145/3360322.3360998

[36] Dhamankar G, Vazquez-Canteli JR, Nagy Z. Benchmarking multi-agent deep reinforcement learning algorithms on a building energy demand coordination task. In: RLEM 2020 – Proceedings of the 1st International Workshop on Reinforcement Learning for Energy Management in Buildings and Cities. New York, NY, United States: ACM; 2020. pp. 15-19. DOI: 10.1145/3427773.3427870

[37] Kovařík V, Schmid M, Burch N, Bowling M, Lisý V. Artificial Intelligence. 2022;**303**(2022):103645. DOI: 10.1016/j.artint.2021.103645

[38] Biljecki F, Ledoux L, Stoter J, Vosselman G. The variants of an LOD of a 3D building model and their influence on spatial analyses. ISPRS Journal of Photogrammetry and Remote Sensing. 2016;**116**(2016):42-54. DOI: 10.1016/j.isprsjprs.2016.03.003

[39] Verma JK, Paul S, editors. Advances in Augmented Reality and Virtual Reality. Singapore: Springer; 2022. p. 312. DOI: 10.1007/978-981-16-7220-0

[40] Johannes E et al. Procedural modeling of architecture with round geometry. Computers & Graphics (Amsterdam, Netherlands). 2017;**64**: 14-25. DOI: 10.1016/j.cag.2017.01.004

[41] Peeters A, Etzion Y. Automated recognition of urban objects for

morphological urban analysis. Computers, Environment and Urban Systems. 2012;**36**(6):573-582

[42] Biljecki F, Ledoux H, Stoter J. Generating 3D city models without elevation data. Computers, Environment and Urban Systems. 2017;**64**:1-18

[43] Swathika OVG, Karthikeyan K, Padmanaban S. Smart Buildings Digitalization. Case Studies on Data Centers and Automation. CRC Press; 2022. p. 314. DOI: 10.1201/9781003240853

[44] Cherdo L. The 8 Best 3D Scanning Apps for Smartphones and IPads in 2019. 2019. Available from: https://www.aniwaa.com/buyers-guide/3d-scanners/best-3d-scanning-apps-smartphones/ [Accessed: December 5, 2022]

[45] Epstein JM. Remarks on the foundations of agent-based generative social science. In: Tesfatsion L, Judd KL, editors. Handbook of Computational Economics. Vol. 2. Stanford, CA, USA: Elsevier; 2006. pp. 1585-1604. DOI: 10.1016/S1574-0021(05)02034-4

[46] Jiang F, Ma J, Webster CJ, Chiaradia A, Zhou Y, Zhao Z, et al. Generative urban design: A systematic review on problem formulation, design generation, and decision-making. Progress in Planning. 2023;**2023**:100795. DOI: 10.1016/j.progress.2023.100795

[47] Shoham Y, Leyton-Brown K. Multiagent Systems: Algorithmic, Game-Theoretic, and Logical Foundations. Revision 1.1, Stanford University, University of British Columbia, Cambridge University; 2010. Available from: http://www.masfoundations.org/mas.pdf [Accessed: August 28, 2023]

[48] Palanisamy P. Multi-agent connected autonomous driving using deep reinforcement learning. In: 2020 International Joint Conference on Neural Networks (IJCNN). Vol. 2020. USA: IEEE; 2020. pp. 1-7. DOI: 10.48550/arXiv.1911.04175

[49] Tian Y, Kladny K-R, Wang Q, Huang Z, Fink O. Multi-agent actor-critic with time dynamical opponent model. Neurocomputing (New York, NY, United States: Cornell University). 2023;**517**:165-172. DOI: 10.48550/arXiv.2204.05576

[50] Foerster J, Assael IA, De Freitas N, Whiteson S. 2016, learning to communicate with deep multi-agent reinforcement learning. Advances in Neural Information Processing Systems. 2016;**29**:2137-2145. DOI: 10.48550/arXiv.1605.06676

[51] Rashid T, Samvelyan M, Schroeder C, Farquhar G, Foerster J, Whiteson S. Qmix: Monotonic value function factorisation for deep multi-agent reinforcement learning. In: International Conference on Machine Learning. Vol. 2018. PMLR; 2018. pp. 4295-4304. DOI: 10.48550/arXiv.1803.11485

[52] Sukhbaatar S, Fergus R, Szlam A. 2016, learning multiagent communication with backpropagation. Advances in Neural Information Processing Systems. 2016;**29**:2244-2252. DOI: 10.48550/arXiv.1605.07736

[53] Amato C, Konidaris G, Kaelbling LP, How JP. 2019, Modeling and planning with macro-actions in decentralized POMDPs. Journal of Artificial Intelligence Research. 2019;**64**:817-859. DOI: 10.1613/jair.1.11418

[54] Davide D, Davide C, Giuseppe P, MarcoSavino P, Capozzoli Alfonso C-Z. Exploring the potentialities of deep

reinforcement learning for incentive-based demand response in a cluster of small commercial buildings. Energies. 2021;**14**(10):1-25. DOI: 10.3390/en14102933

[55] Glatt RG, Silva FL, Soper B, Dawson W, Rusu E, Goldhahn R. Collaborative energy demand response with decentralized actor and centralized critic. In: Proceedings of the 8th ACM International Conference on Systems for Energy-Efficient Buildings, Cities, and Transportation. New York, NY, USA: ACM; 2021. pp. 333-337. DOI: 10.1145/3486611.3488732

[56] Qin R, Gao S, Zhang X, Xu Z, Huang S, Li Z, et al. NeoRl: A near Real-World Benchmark for Offline Reinforcement Learning. 2021. DOI: 10.48550/arXiv.2102.00714

Chapter 7

# Intelligent Multi-Agent Systems for Advanced Geotechnical Monitoring

*Ali Akbar Firoozi and Ali Asghar Firoozi*


## Abstract

Geotechnical monitoring, essential for ensuring the safety and longevity of infrastructures, has predominantly relied on centralized systems. However, as computational capabilities soar and advancements in Artificial Intelligence (AI) burgeon, the potential for decentralized solutions comes to the fore. This chapter intricately weaves the principles and applications of Multi-Agent Systems (MAS) into the fabric of geotechnical monitoring. It delves deep, elucidating the decentralized approach to monitoring aspects like soil quality and groundwater levels. Through a seamless interplay between agents, we witness real-time data acquisition, intricate analysis, and informed decision-making. While anchoring itself in theoretical foundations, the chapter also illuminates the real-world challenges and proffers potential solutions in geotechnical engineering, thereby mapping the past, present, and future of MAS in this domain.


**Keywords:** geotechnical monitoring, multi-agent systems, decentralized solutions, soil quality monitoring, groundwater level analysis, real-time data processing, artificial intelligence

## 1. Introduction

In the vast expanse of modern engineering, geotechnical monitoring stands as a sentinel, safeguarding the integrity and longevity of infrastructures that form the backbone of our urban landscapes. Ensuring the stability and safety of these structures requires intricate knowledge, a keen eye, and cutting-edge technology. Historically, monitoring techniques remained largely centralized, often offering a broader, yet sometimes less detailed, perspective. But, as we tread into an era dominated by rapid technological advances, the paradigm is shifting. The rise of Artificial Intelligence (AI) and computational prowess has paved the way for decentralized monitoring systems that promise higher precision and real-time insights. The spotlight now is on Multi-Agent Systems (MAS) — a promising integration into the geotechnical realm. This chapter embarks on an enlightening journey, diving deep into the nuances of MAS, its application in geotechnical monitoring, and the transformative potential it holds for the future.

## 1.1 Background of geotechnical monitoring

Geotechnical Monitoring, a discipline that ensures the safety and longevity of our infrastructure, stands tall as one of the pivotal components in civil engineering. Spanning centuries, civilizations have always had an innate desire to develop structures that defy time, from the Pyramids of Giza to the Great Wall of China. However, the longevity of these structures can be attributed not just to the skill of their creators but to the ground they stand upon [1]. The importance of understanding and monitoring this ground - its properties, behavior, and reactions, is precisely what geotechnical monitoring encapsulates.

Traditional geotechnical monitoring techniques often consisted of hands-on, manual measurements. These methods, rooted in time-tested principles, required an intense human workforce, frequently dealing with instruments like inclinometers, piezometers, and extensometers. They would work on field sites, collecting data, often under challenging conditions and environments. While these manual techniques brought about valuable information about the earth's subsurface, they often presented limitations in terms of accuracy, speed, and the potential for human error [1]. Furthermore, as infrastructural projects grew larger and more complex, the need for a more sophisticated, scalable, and reliable method for geotechnical monitoring became apparent.

## 1.2 Evolution of monitoring techniques

The dawn of the technological era in the twentieth century ushered in a wave of innovative methods and tools, revolutionizing the realm of geotechnical monitoring. What once was a labor-intensive, manual process beginning to metamorphose into a series of automated systems, capitalizing on electronics and early computational capacities. Centralized electronic systems were introduced, allowing data to be collected and analyzed from a singular hub [2]. These electronic systems, albeit being a significant leap from their manual predecessors, had their own set of challenges. The centralized nature meant that a single point of failure could jeopardize the entire monitoring process.

Nevertheless, the integration of technology within geotechnical monitoring did not stop there. With the proliferation of computers and advanced software in the late twentieth century, there emerged a scope for more refined, precise, and extensive data analysis. Computer-aided designs and simulations began playing a pivotal role, enabling engineers to predict geotechnical behaviors under various conditions with much more accuracy [2].

This technological transition wasn't solely about the equipment or software being used; it was reflective of a broader shift in the field of geotechnical engineering. As projects became more ambitious - think of skyscrapers piercing the clouds, or tunnels burrowing through mountains - the need for constant, real-time monitoring grew exponentially. It was no longer just about predicting how the ground would behave but actively watching it, understanding its every tremor, shift, and reaction.

## 1.3 Significance of intelligent systems in geotechnical monitoring

Enter the twenty-first century, and we find ourselves on the precipice of a new era: the Age of Artificial Intelligence (AI). With computational power increasing exponentially and data becoming the new oil, industries across the board began to explore the implications and applications of AI. Geotechnical monitoring was no exception [3].

The promise of AI is not merely in its ability to process vast amounts of data quickly but in its potential to 'learn' from this data, making predictions, and possibly, decisions autonomously. Such capabilities bear significant implications for geotechnical monitoring. Imagine a system that not only detects anomalies in soil quality or groundwater levels but also predicts potential issues, facilitating proactive interventions. These aren't mere conveniences; they could be the difference between a stable structure and a catastrophic failure.

Moreover, the recent rise in the concept of Intelligent MAS presents an even more nuanced and granular approach to monitoring. Instead of a centralized hub, imagine a decentralized network of 'agents,' each equipped with specific tasks, yet capable of collaborating, sharing data, and even making collective decisions [3]. This method offers multiple advantages over traditional systems, most notably in scalability, redundancy, and real-time data acquisition and analysis.

In conclusion, geotechnical monitoring, as a field, has continually evolved, mirroring advancements in technology and computational capabilities. From manual measurements in its nascent stages to the potential of AI-driven, decentralized MAS, the journey has been transformative. The promise of AI and MAS in this realm is vast, offering more precise, real-time, and proactive solutions, ensuring the safety and longevity of our infrastructures.

"The versatility and adaptive nature of MAS have been highlighted in numerous foundational texts, such as Balaji & Srinivasan's comprehensive guide on MAS [4]. Recent reviews, notably by Dinelli, et al. [5], underscore the significance of MAS in geotechnical infrastructure health monitoring, detailing its myriad applications and the shifts it has induced in traditional methodologies. Furthermore, as MAS becomes integral to infrastructure monitoring, establishing trust in these systems becomes paramount. Castelfranchi & Falcone [6] delve into the cognitive anatomy of trust in MAS, underscoring its social importance and mechanisms of quantification.

Effective communication protocols are essential for the functioning of MAS, especially in critical systems like geotechnical monitoring. Seminal works like that of Smith [7] have laid down the foundational principles for high-level communication within distributed problem solvers, guiding the evolution of MAS. In addition, the interaction between human stakeholders and MAS is evolving into a symbiotic relationship. As posited by Jennings et al. [8], human-agent collectives represent a frontier in MAS research, bridging human intuition with algorithmic precision."

The primary objective of this chapter is to bridge the intricate gap between traditional geotechnical monitoring methods and the burgeoning potential of MAS. We aim to delve deep into understanding the principles underpinning MAS, contextualizing its relevance and application in the domain of geotechnical monitoring. Through comprehensive exploration, this chapter will dissect the myriad advantages MAS holds over centralized systems, focusing not only on its operational efficiencies but also its real-time data acquisition, analysis, and decision-making capabilities. Furthermore, this chapter aspires to elucidate the practical challenges that come with the integration of MAS into geotechnical monitoring, offering insights into potential solutions and the future roadmap. By the end, readers should be equipped with a comprehensive understanding of MAS's theoretical underpinnings, its practical implications, and its transformative potential in revolutionizing geotechnical monitoring for the better.

## 2. Principles of multi-agent systems (MAS)

As we transition into an age where decentralized systems and collaborative intelligence play pivotal roles in resolving intricate problems, understanding the core principles of MAS becomes indispensable. MAS, with its decentralized architecture and collaborative framework, exemplifies the confluence of individual autonomy and collective intelligence. At its heart, MAS is a system where individual agents, each with its unique capabilities, come together, interacting, and collaborating to achieve a common or diverse set of objectives. These systems, thus, are not merely a manifestation of technological advancement but are reflective of a broader shift towards leveraging collective intelligence in problem-solving. In this section, we will delve deeper into the fundamental principles of MAS, exploring its defining characteristics, operational mechanisms, and the myriad advantages it offers over traditional centralized systems.

### 2.1 Definition and characteristics

A Multi-Agent System (MAS) is essentially a computerized system composed of multiple interacting intelligent agents. These agents are autonomous entities, capable of independent action and decision-making within their designed environments [9]. MAS can be used to solve problems that are difficult or impossible for an individual agent or a monolithic system to solve. A few defining characteristics of MAS include:

- *Decentralization*: Unlike traditional systems that rely on a centralized control system, MAS operates on a decentralized network, where each agent functions autonomously [9].

- *Interactivity*: Agents within MAS communicate with one another, sharing information, and collaborating on tasks. This interactivity is paramount for the system's overall functionality and efficiency [10].

- *Adaptability*: Agents in a MAS are designed to adapt to changes in their environment. This ensures the system's robustness, especially when subjected to unforeseen challenges or dynamic scenarios [11].

- *Scalability*: MAS's decentralized nature ensures it can scale seamlessly, accommodating more agents as the need arises without disrupting the system's overall functionality [11].

### 2.2 Operational mechanism

The functionality of a MAS hinges on the coordination, cooperation, and competition among agents. It's intriguing to see how agents, each designed with specific functionalities, can autonomously work together in real-world applications.

- *Initialization*: Typically, MAS starts with initializing individual agents, providing them with the necessary resources, initial conditions, and data to begin their operations. The context here can range from sensor data in geotechnical monitoring to variables from other domains [12].

- *Communication protocols*: Once initialized, agents utilize predefined communication protocols to interact with one another. These protocols enable agents to share data, request actions, and negotiate tasks among themselves [13].

- *Decision-making algorithms*: The crux of any intelligent system lies in its decision-making capabilities. In MAS, each agent employs decision-making algorithms, often rooted in machine learning or heuristic techniques, to analyze data and determine the best course of action [14].

- *Feedback mechanism*: Integral to any adaptive system, a feedback loop in MAS allows agents to learn from past experiences, recalibrating their strategies based on the outcomes of previous actions. This mechanism promotes the adaptability and resilience of the system [14].

- *Synchronization & task allocation*: Agents in MAS often have to synchronize their actions, especially when multiple agents are working towards a common goal. Sophisticated algorithms ensure that tasks are divided and executed without redundancy and inefficiencies [15].

### 2.3 Advantages of MAS over centralized systems

Centralized systems, though effective for a range of applications, have their limitations, especially when confronted with large-scale, complex scenarios that demand real-time responses. Multi-Agent Systems, with their decentralized nature, offer solutions to many of these limitations:

- *Fault tolerance and redundancy*: In a MAS, the failure of one or even several agents do not halt the entire system's operation. This distributed nature ensures that the system remains operational even when individual components face issues [16].

- *Flexibility and scalability*: As projects evolve or expand, MAS can seamlessly incorporate additional agents without significant overhauls or disruptions. This is especially beneficial in geotechnical monitoring where new monitoring points might be added or altered based on project needs [16].

- *Efficiency*: Agents, working in parallel, can process vast amounts of data simultaneously, ensuring quicker response times and real-time data processing. This parallel processing capability is a stark contrast to many centralized systems that operate sequentially [17].

- *Optimized resource allocation*: MAS, with its distributed nature, ensures optimal resource allocation, as agents can autonomously decide how to utilize available resources without central coordination [17].

- *Enhanced data acquisition*: With agents specialized in different tasks, MAS can acquire a broader spectrum of data, offering a comprehensive view of the monitored environment [16].

The essence of MAS is not merely its decentralized architecture but its ability to harness the strengths of individual agents, amplifying their collective capabilities to

| Feature | Centralized systems | MAS |
|---|---|---|
| Architecture | Single centralized control unit | Decentralized with multiple agents |
| Scalability | Limited, often requires system overhaul | High, easy to add new agents |
| Fault tolerance | Low, single point of failure | High, system remains operational even with individual agent failures |
| Data processing | Sequential | Parallel |
| Adaptability | Less flexible to environmental changes | High adaptability and dynamic response |
| Resource allocation | Fixed allocation | Dynamic and optimized based on agent decisions |

**Table 1.**
*Comparison between centralized systems and MAS.*

achieve overarching goals. This makes MAS an exciting and promising proposition, especially in domains like geotechnical monitoring.

**Table 1** succinctly captures the fundamental differences between Centralized Systems and MAS. The distinction in architecture is apparent, with centralized systems relying on a singular control unit, while MAS thrives on a decentralized structure encompassing multiple agents. This fundamental difference gives rise to various advantages for MAS, notably in scalability and fault tolerance. While the centralized approach may encounter scalability challenges requiring significant modifications, MAS facilitates the inclusion of new agents seamlessly. Similarly, the risk of system-wide failures is considerably reduced in MAS due to its distributed nature, contrasting the vulnerability of centralized systems to single points of failure. Sequential data processing in centralized systems, compared to the parallel processing in MAS, also underscores the efficiency of the latter. Finally, the adaptability and dynamic resource allocation of MAS offer unparalleled advantages in rapidly changing environments and tasks, a characteristic less prominent in their centralized counterparts.

**Figure 1**, from Russell & Norvig's renowned book [18], offers a holistic representation of how individual agents operate and interact within a defined environment. At its core, the figure emphasizes the bi-directional nature of agent-environment interactions. Agents continuously perceive their environment through sensors, allowing them to gather crucial data. In response to this perceived data, agents take actions via actuators, influencing the environment in return.

In the context of geotechnical monitoring, this interaction becomes paramount. The agents can be visualized as sensors collecting geotechnical data, such as soil quality, groundwater levels, and other relevant parameters. Upon perceiving changes in these parameters, agents, equipped with decision-making algorithms, can autonomously decide on specific actions. These actions can range from adjusting monitoring frequencies, alerting central systems, or collaborating with other agents for comprehensive data analysis.

Furthermore, the figure underscores the concept of autonomy in MAS. Each agent operates independently, yet collaboratively, drawing from its perceptions and contributing to the overall system's objectives. This autonomy, combined with the inter-agent collaboration, underscores the decentralized essence of MAS and its potential advantages over traditional centralized systems.

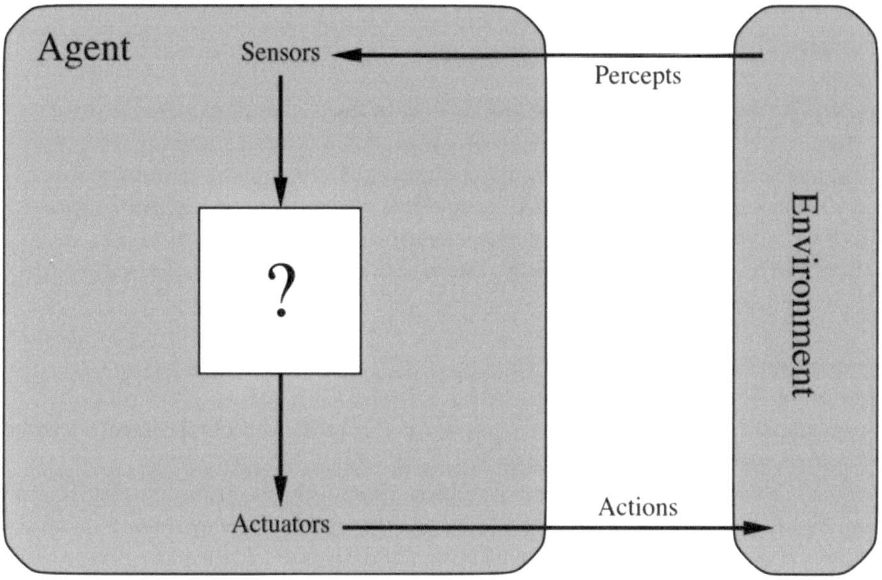


**Figure 1.**
*Operational workflow of a multi-agent system [18].*

By analyzing **Figure 1** in the context of our discussion, readers can grasp the foundational mechanics of agent-environment interactions and how these principles can be harnessed in geotechnical monitoring.

## 3. Application of multi-agent systems in geotechnical monitoring

The significance of geotechnical monitoring in ensuring infrastructure safety remains a dominant focal point in contemporary engineering. With the rising demands on infrastructure resilience and adaptability, the emergence of MAS within this discipline promises transformative solutions. This section elaborates on specific applications of MAS in geotechnical monitoring, detailing their architectural compositions, interaction mechanisms, and the tangible benefits they offer. Case studies and real-world scenarios will be referenced to provide depth and context to the discussions.

### 3.1 Soil quality monitoring

Soil quality is foundational to all civil infrastructure projects. Traditional methods, though effective, bear inherent limitations in temporal resolution and spatial accuracy.

- *MAS architecture & interactions*: For soil monitoring, the MAS architecture utilizes a hierarchical setup. Central agents receive data from peripheral sensing agents scattered across the site. Sensing agents autonomously initiate communication with adjacent agents upon detecting anomalous data. Such localized collaborations help in identifying larger patterns that might go unnoticed with isolated sensors. The underlying algorithms governing these interactions consider factors such as the degree of deviation from expected readings and historical data trends [19].

- *Outcome impact*: The real-time collaboration leads to comprehensive understanding of soil conditions. The MAS approach has been shown to detect rapid changes 30% faster than conventional methods, prompting preemptive actions and ensuring project safety [20]. A specific case in combining multi-agent systems and wireless sensor networks for monitoring crop irrigation [21] showcased how a MAS-enabled monitoring system detected soil degradation days ahead of a traditional system.

### 3.2 Groundwater level analysis

Subterranean structure stability depends on accurate groundwater level monitoring.

- *MAS architecture & interactions*: Agents here act as both individual sensing and collaborative data-sharing units. Rapid water table changes detected by an agent triggers recalibrations in nearby agents, validating or refuting the readings. This collaborative essence is facilitated by a priority-based communication protocol, ensuring rapid response to potential threats [22].

- *Outcome impact*: MAS-based systems, due to their reflexive recalibrations, offer adaptive monitoring. Studies have shown they provide warnings up to 40% faster than conventional methods, potentially saving significant repair costs [23].

### 3.3 Real-time settlement and displacement monitoring

Monitoring settlement or displacement becomes crucial with towering urban infrastructures.

- *MAS architecture & interactions*: In this MAS, agents have both sensing and actuating roles. Beyond data logging, these agents can, in real-time, activate countermeasures like adjusting tension cables or even trigger evacuation protocols based on predefined thresholds [24].

- *Outcome impact*: The proactive nature of MAS ensures minimal damage to the structure and its occupants. A case study in enhancing coordination and safety of earthwork equipment operations using MAS by Vahdatikhaki, et al. [25] discussed how a MAS reduced damage costs by 50% compared to traditional systems.

### 3.4 Tunnel and borehole stability monitoring

Tunnels and boreholes represent challenging engineering projects due to their interactions with dynamic and often unpredictable subterranean environments.

- *MAS architecture & interactions*: Within these structures, agents operate in a networked configuration. Should an agent detect, for instance, an unexpected shift in tunnel wall stress, it can alert adjacent agents to intensify their monitoring to validate this shift. Advanced MAS deployments in this context might also utilize reinforcement learning, allowing agents to refine their monitoring strategy based on prior experiences [26].

- *Outcome impact*: The collaborative and corroborative nature of MAS ensures quick detection of even minor instabilities, promoting tunnel safety and drastically reducing potential maintenance and repair costs. For instance, a project documented in wellbore stability in fractured rock by Ottesen [27] showed a 60% reduction in downtime due to the rapid response capability of a MAS.

### 3.5 Slope stability and landslide prediction

Given the devastating potential of landslides, robust real-time monitoring mechanisms are essential, especially in susceptible regions.

- *MAS architecture & interactions*: Agents deployed on slopes have dual roles: local data collection and distributed data synthesis. Through a decentralized approach, agents in critical zones initiate communication with neighbors, cross-referencing data to distinguish between local anomalies and larger-scale instabilities. Upon detecting significant shifts, a priority alert is disseminated across the network, shifting the system into a heightened monitoring mode [28].

- *Outcome impact*: The cooperative nature of MAS ensures early indicators of potential landslides are swiftly identified and assessed. Communities benefit from faster alerts, and preventive measures are enhanced, ensuring better safety and effective risk mitigation. A study in modeling agent-oriented methodologies for landslide management studied by Sugiarto et al. [29] found that MAS increased the lead time for landslide warnings by up to 45%, providing valuable additional response time for affected communities.

### 3.6 Erosion control and sediment monitoring

Unchecked erosion has profound environmental and infrastructural implications, necessitating dynamic and adaptive monitoring systems.

- *MAS architecture & interactions*: Agents assigned for erosion control operate in a continuous feedback loop with the environment. They adjust their parameters based on adjacent agents' data. For instance, if an agent detects rapid sediment loss, it alerts upstream agents to determine if this trend is localized or widespread. This synergistic MAS approach ensures a comprehensive understanding of sediment dynamics [30].

- *Outcome impact*: With MAS, erosion control moves beyond mere observation. The system offers insights that guide adaptive countermeasures. This proactive approach adjusts to changing dynamics of water flow and sediment displacement, ensuring not just reactivity but also proactiveness. An application detailed in [31] demonstrated how MAS-driven insights helped design better erosion control strategies, reducing erosion by up to 30%.

| Application area | Key parameters monitored | Advantages |
|---|---|---|
| Soil quality monitoring | Soil moisture, pH levels, compaction, organic content | Enhanced data resolution, rapid anomaly detection, predictive modeling |
| Groundwater level analysis | Water depth, salinity, temperature | Continuous monitoring, early warnings, better flood resource allocation |
| Real-time settlement and displacement monitoring | Vibrations, displacements, structural integrity | Immediate assessments, targeted interventions, emergency readiness |
| Tunnel and borehole stability | Vibrations, stress changes, water ingress | Continuous stability analysis, early issue detection, optimized maintenance |
| Slope stability and landslide prediction | Soil moisture, movement, tension cracks | Early landslide prediction, causative factor analysis, improved disaster management |
| Erosion control and sediment monitoring | Sediment levels, water flow rates, erosion rates | Continuous erosion monitoring, control measure evaluation, long-term land preservation |

**Table 2.**
*Summary of MAS applications in geotechnical monitoring.*

Wrapping up this section, MAS's integration into geotechnical monitoring is more than a technological evolution; it's a paradigm shift. By actively engaging with their environments, these systems can anticipate, adapt, and react, ensuring infrastructural integrity while reducing associated risks. The manifold advantages, as discussed and supported by various references, underscore the transformative potential of MAS in geotechnical pursuits.

**Table 2** provides a concise summary of the various geotechnical monitoring applications where MAS are making significant strides. For each application area, the table highlights the primary parameters that are monitored using MAS. Furthermore, it enumerates the advantages offered by MAS over traditional monitoring techniques. This table serves as a quick reference guide for professionals and researchers in the field, underscoring the multifaceted benefits of MAS in geotechnical endeavors.

## 4. Challenges and potential solutions in implementing multi-agent systems for geotechnical monitoring

While the applications of MAS in geotechnical monitoring show significant promise, its widespread adoption faces various challenges. In this section, we delve into these challenges and explore potential solutions, offering a balanced perspective on the practicality of MAS in the field.

### 4.1 Data overload

- *Challenge*: With numerous agents continuously collecting data, the sheer volume can lead to data overload. This makes data processing and interpretation cumbersome, potentially leading to delays in decision-making [32].

- *Solution*: Incorporating advanced data analytics and edge computing allows for processing data at the source (i.e., the agent itself). This reduces the need for transmitting vast amounts of raw data and instead only relays pertinent information or anomalies to central systems [33].

### 4.2 Inter-agent communication interference

- *Challenge*: In dense deployment scenarios, agents may face interference in communication, leading to loss of data or misinterpretations [34].

- *Solution*: Utilizing adaptive communication protocols where agents can switch communication channels or frequencies based on local traffic can mitigate this issue. Additionally, employing mesh networks ensures data transmission even if direct communication between two agents is compromised [35].

### 4.3 Power limitations

- *Challenge*: Continuous monitoring requires significant power, and frequently changing batteries or recharging agents can be impractical in remote or inaccessible areas [36].

- *Solution*: Integrating renewable energy sources like mini solar panels or vibration energy harvesters can extend the operational lifespan of agents. Additionally, agents can be designed to go into a low-power mode during periods of inactivity or less critical monitoring phases [37].

### 4.4 Environmental challenges

- *Challenge*: Geotechnical monitoring often happens in hostile environments – be it deep underground, in waterlogged areas, or regions with extreme temperatures. These conditions can impair the longevity and functionality of agents [38].

- *Solution*: Designing ruggedized agents, with protective casings and materials that can withstand environmental extremes, is essential. Moreover, self-diagnostic capabilities can enable agents to report malfunctions or degradations, prompting timely maintenance [39].

### 4.5 Integration with traditional systems

- *Challenge*: Many existing infrastructures employ traditional monitoring systems. Integrating MAS without disrupting these systems can be challenging [40].

- *Solution*: Hybrid systems, where MAS acts as an augmentation to traditional systems, can offer a solution. Over time, as the reliability and efficiency of MAS are established, a gradual transition can be undertaken [41].

These challenges, while significant, are not insurmountable. With continuous advancements in technology and a deeper understanding of geotechnical needs, MAS is poised to redefine the landscape of geotechnical monitoring in the coming years. **Table 3** concisely summarizes the primary challenges encountered in the adoption of MAS for geotechnical monitoring and offers potential solutions for each challenge. The table underscores the proactive measures that can be undertaken to mitigate challenges, ensuring the efficient and seamless functioning of MAS in varied geotechnical scenarios.

| Challenges | Potential solutions |
|---|---|
| Data overload | Advanced data analytics and edge computing for processing at source |
| Inter-agent communication interference | Adaptive communication protocols and mesh networks |
| Power limitations | Integration of renewable energy sources and low-power modes |
| Environmental challenges | Ruggedized agents and self-diagnostic capabilities |
| Integration with traditional systems | Development of hybrid systems |

**Table 3.**
*Challenges and solutions in implementing MAS for geotechnical monitoring.*

## 5. Real-world case studies of MAS in geotechnical monitoring

Understanding the theory and potential of MAS is vital. However, its real-world application offers a true testament to its efficacy. In this section, we delve into several case studies from diverse geotechnical monitoring projects around the world that have benefited from the successful employment of MAS.

**Table 4** elucidates how MAS has been a vital asset across various geotechnical domains. By focusing on the methodologies employed, the tangible outcomes, and the broader implications, we see a recurring theme: MAS, with its adaptability and precision, offers transformative solutions to complex geotechnical challenges, ensuring both safety and sustainability.

## 6. The future of MAS in geotechnical monitoring

The landscape of geotechnical monitoring is poised for transformation, with the continuous evolution of MAS capabilities. As we look towards the future, several emerging trends and innovations stand out, promising even more efficient, robust, and versatile monitoring solutions.

### 6.1 Integration with quantum computing

Quantum computing, with its unparalleled computational power, offers a potential leap in the processing capabilities of MAS [46]. By integrating MAS with quantum processors, we can expect:

- Rapid data analysis, even with vast datasets from expansive geotechnical sites.
- Enhanced prediction accuracy by analyzing a multitude of parameters simultaneously.

### 6.2 Augmented reality (AR) interfaces

With AR technology maturing, it's plausible that future geotechnical engineers could use AR glasses or displays to visualize MAS data in real-time over actual terrains [47]. This could lead to:

| Case study | Location | Background & challenges | Key methodologies | Primary results & achievements | Implications & broader impact | Citation |
|---|---|---|---|---|---|---|
| Soil quality monitoring in farmlands | Southern France | Vast agricultural regions in Southern France faced inconsistent soil quality due to diverse topography and climatic shifts. Traditional methods could not capture the intricacies required for optimal farming. | MAS equipped with soil sensors were strategically placed across farmlands to monitor vital parameters like soil moisture, pH levels, and organic content. The real-time communication setup provided a comprehensive soil health map. | A notable 15% crop yield increase in the initial year of MAS deployment. Early identification of soil degradation and nutrient deficiencies, aiding in precise irrigation and fertilization. | Emphasizes the transformative power of MAS in agriculture, converting data into actionable insights leading to enhanced yield and sustainable farming practices. | [42] |
| Groundwater level analysis in urban settings | Tokyo, Japan | Rapid urbanization in Tokyo mandated real-time groundwater monitoring. Variations in water consumption and construction patterns presented challenges. | MAS, equipped with underground pressure transducers, gauged groundwater levels. This data, along with rainfall and urban water usage stats, fed into a predictive model for forecasting. | High precision in predicting and tracking groundwater fluctuations. The data significantly informed the city's disaster mitigation strategies, especially during monsoons. | Demonstrates the essential role of MAS in urban setups for ensuring safety and facilitating efficient water resource management. | [43] |
| Tunnel stability monitoring in subway systems | New York City, USA | The expansive and aged infrastructure of NYC's subway system demanded proactive monitoring to detect potential structural vulnerabilities. | Acoustic emission sensors, integrated into the MAS, were installed within subway tunnels. Continuous monitoring of sound waves helped pinpoint anomalies suggestive of structural issues. | Proactive identification of potential structural weaknesses, facilitating timely repairs and ensuring subway safety. | Highlights the continuous monitoring potential of MAS, critical for safeguarding urban infrastructures. | [44] |
| Slope stability in mountainous regions | Himalayan Region | The Himalayan terrain, prone to landslides due to rainfalls and tectonic activities, posed severe threats to human settlements and infrastructure. | MAS agents with geotechnical sensors embedded in high-risk areas monitored crucial parameters: soil moisture, displacement, and seismic events. | Detection of landslide precursors days before any major occurrence, enabling early warning systems and timely evacuations. | Underlines the life-saving potential of MAS, especially in regions vulnerable to natural disasters, ensuring prompt response mechanisms. | [45] |

**Table 4.**
*Detailed overview of MAS applications in geotechnical monitoring.*

- Immediate on-site decisions based on live data feeds.
- Enhanced understanding of geotechnical parameters with immersive visual representations.

### 6.3 Self-healing and autonomous agents

The next generation of agents might be equipped with self-diagnostic and self-healing capabilities [48]. This means:

- Agents could autonomously detect faults or damages and undertake basic repair actions.
- Reduced maintenance overheads and prolonged agent lifespans.

### 6.4 Eco-friendly and biodegradable agents

Given the increasing focus on environmental sustainability, future agents could be designed to be eco-friendly and eventually biodegrade [49]. This has two significant implications:

- Reduced environmental impact even if agents are left in monitoring sites post their operational lifespan.
- Facilitation of MAS deployment in ecologically sensitive zones without environmental concerns.

### 6.5 Enhanced inter-agent communication protocols

With advancements in communication technologies, agents of the future might employ more sophisticated communication techniques for better data exchange and decision-making processes [50]. This might result in:

- Reduced data transfer times.
- Minimized chances of communication interference, even in dense agent deployments.

### 6.6 Broader integration with infrastructure systems

MAS could become a standard component of infrastructure projects, fully integrated into building and civil engineering processes [51]. This will lead to:

- Proactive geotechnical monitoring from the very inception of infrastructure projects.
- Enhanced safety standards across urban and rural constructions.

The prospective landscape of MAS in geotechnical monitoring is vibrant and full of potential. With the convergence of various technologies and a deeper understanding of geotechnical needs, the role of MAS is set to expand and become even more pivotal in the coming decades. **Table 4** offers a structured overview of the anticipated developments in the domain of MAS and their applications in geotechnical monitoring. The table is segmented into three primary columns:

- *Advancement*: This column details the emerging technological advancements and innovations projected to refine the efficiency, accuracy, and versatility of MAS in geotechnical contexts.
- *Description*: Offering a brief elucidation, this section explains the essence of each technological evolution. From quantum computing's superior data processing capabilities to the integration of AR interfaces, the descriptions provide a succinct snapshot of what each advancement entails.
- *Expected implication*: Perhaps the most significant column, this section demystifies the practical ramifications of each advancement. It explicates how each evolution will potentially redefine the contours of geotechnical monitoring, emphasizing the benefits and the transformative potential.

In essence, **Table 5** functions as a roadmap, steering readers through the future trajectory of MAS in geotechnical monitoring. By juxtaposing technological innovations with their tangible implications, the table fosters a clear understanding of the forthcoming changes and their potential to reshape the realm of geotechnical monitoring.

### 6.7 Implications and future research directions

The findings of our review underscore the transformative potential of Multi-Agent Systems (MAS) in geotechnical monitoring. The capabilities of MAS characterized by their dynamic adaptability, real-time responsiveness, and collaborative

| Advancement | Description | Expected implication |
|---|---|---|
| Integration with quantum computing | Utilization of quantum processors in MAS for data processing. | Rapid data analysis even with vast datasets; heightened prediction accuracy. |
| Augmented Reality (AR) interfaces | Deployment of AR for real-time visualization of MAS data on terrains. | Immediate on-site decisions; immersive visual representation of geotechnical parameters. |
| Self-healing and autonomous agents | Agents equipped with self-diagnostic and repair capabilities. | Autonomic fault detection and basic repair actions; reduced maintenance overheads. |
| Eco-friendly and biodegradable Agents | Designing agents that have minimal environmental impact and can biodegrade. | Reduced environmental footprints; deployment in sensitive zones without concerns. |
| Enhanced inter-agent communication protocols | Advanced techniques for agent-agent communication to improve data exchange. | Quick data transfer times; minimized communication interference. |
| Integration with infrastructure systems | Standardizing MAS components in infrastructure projects. | Proactive geotechnical monitoring from project inception; heightened safety standards. |

**Table 5.**
*Future advancements and implications of MAS in geotechnical monitoring.*

interactions – have found resonance in the intricacies of geotechnical challenges, leading to enhanced safety, efficacy, and sustainability.

However, as with any evolving interdisciplinary domain, there are still challenges to be addressed and gaps to be bridged:

- *Scalability of MAS*: As geotechnical projects continue to grow in scale and complexity, there is a pressing need for research into the scalability of MAS, ensuring they remain efficient and effective in larger operational environments.

- *Integration with advanced technologies*: The synergy between MAS and emerging technologies like Artificial Intelligence, Internet of Things (IoT), and Blockchain remains largely untapped. Exploring these intersections could lead to more robust and versatile geotechnical monitoring solutions.

- *Standardization and protocols*: There's a palpable lack of standard protocols guiding the design and deployment of MAS in geotechnical endeavors. Future research could focus on developing these standards, ensuring consistency and interoperability.

- *Environmental and ethical considerations*: As MAS become more integrated into geotechnical projects, it's vital to consider the environmental footprint of these systems and the ethical implications of their widespread deployment.

In conclusion, while MAS have undoubtedly revolutionized geotechnical monitoring, the journey has just begun. The road ahead, replete with challenges and opportunities, promises exciting times for researchers, practitioners, and stakeholders in this domain.

## 7. Concluding remarks

In the growing realm of geotechnical monitoring, the adoption and integration of MAS marks a revolutionary stride. The journey, as mapped out in this chapter, commenced from understanding the rudiments of MAS, extending to its profound implications when juxtaposed with geotechnical monitoring processes.

The realm of geotechnical monitoring, once dominated by traditional, centralized systems, is now on the cusp of a transformation. The granular and decentralized approach promised by MAS not only enhances monitoring precision but also enriches real-time data acquisition and analysis capabilities. The profound synergy of agents, both in cooperative and competitive scenarios, is set to redefine the benchmarks of data collection, analysis, and predictive accuracy in geotechnical domains.

Case studies, as detailed earlier, serve as testament to the profound impact and efficacy of MAS in real-world scenarios. They underscore the tangible benefits and also shine a light on the challenges that engineers, and decision-makers might grapple with, forging a path for continual refinement and innovation.

Peeking into the future, evolution seems not just promising but transformative. From the integration of quantum computing to the advent of self-healing agents, the horizon of MAS in geotechnical monitoring is expansive. While challenges will inevitably arise, the convergence of technology, innovation, and need will undoubtedly charter a course for solutions.

To conclude, the future of geotechnical monitoring, augmented by MAS, promises safer infrastructures, enriched data accuracy, and streamlined monitoring processes. The confluence of technological prowess with the timeless principles of geotechnical science marks the dawn of a new era. An era where technology not only supports but propels the objectives of geotechnical engineering to unprecedented heights.

## Acknowledgements

We express our profound gratitude to the Geotechnical Engineering community for their relentless pursuit of knowledge and innovation. Special thanks are extended to the editorial team and reviewers for their invaluable feedback and insights that have enriched this chapter. Our heartfelt appreciation goes to all the researchers and scholars whose work formed the foundation of this study. Their contributions to the realm of MAS and geotechnical monitoring have been pivotal. Lastly, we thank our families and colleagues for their unwavering support throughout the creation of this chapter.

## Conflict of interest

The authors declare that there are no conflicts of interest concerning the research, authorship, and publication of this chapter. All findings and assertions presented here are based on objective analysis and have not been influenced by any external entity or funding agency.

## Author details

Ali Akbar Firoozi* and Ali Asghar Firoozi
Faculty of Engineering and Technology, Department of Civil Engineering, University of Botswana, Gaborone, Botswana

*Address all correspondence to: a.firoozi@gmail.com

## References

[1] Clarkson L, Williams D. An overview of conventional tailings dam geotechnical failure mechanisms. Mining, Metallurgy & Exploration. 2021;**38**(3):1305-1328. DOI: 10.1007/s42461-021-00381-3

[2] Confuorto P, Di Martire D, Centolanza G, Iglesias R, Mallorqui JJ, Novellino A, et al. Post-failure evolution analysis of a rainfall-triggered landslide by multi-temporal interferometry SAR approaches integrated with geotechnical analysis. Remote Sensing of Environment. 2017;**188**:51-72. DOI: 10.1016/j.rse.2016.11.002

[3] Baghbani A, Choudhury T, Costa S, Reiner J. Application of artificial intelligence in geotechnical engineering: A state-of-the-art review. Earth-Science Reviews. 2022;**228**:103991. DOI: 10.1016/j.earscirev.2022.103991

[4] Balaji PG, Srinivasan D. An introduction to multi-agent systems. Innovations in Multi-Agent Systems and Applications-1. 2010;**1**:1-27. DOI: 10.1007/978-3-642-14435-6_1

[5] Dinelli C, Racette J, Escarcega M, Lotero S, Gordon J, Montoya J, et al. Configurations and applications of multi-agent hybrid drone/unmanned ground vehicle for underground environments: A review. Drones. 2023;**7**(2):136. DOI: 10.3390/drones7020136

[6] Castelfranchi C, Falcone R. Principles of trust for MAS: Cognitive anatomy, social importance, and quantification. In: Proceedings International Conference on Multi Agent Systems (Cat. No. 98EX160). Piscataway, NJ, USA: IEEE; 1998. pp. 72-79. DOI: 10.1109/ICMAS.1998.699034

[7] Smith RG. The contract net protocol: High-level communication and control in a distributed problem solver. IEEE Transactions on Computers. 1980;**29**(12):1104-1113. DOI: 10.1109/TC.1980.1675516

[8] Jennings NR, Moreau L, Nicholson D, Ramchurn S, Roberts S, Rodden T, et al. Human-agent collectives. Communications of the ACM. 2014;**57**(12):80-88. DOI: 10.1145/2629559

[9] Wooldridge M. An Introduction to Multiagent Systems. Hoboken, NJ, USA: John Wiley & Sons; 2009

[10] Hanga KM, Kovalchuk Y. Machine learning and multi-agent systems in oil and gas industry applications: A survey. Computer Science Review. 2019;**34**:100191. DOI: 10.1016/j.cosrev.2019.08.002

[11] Pimenov DY, Bustillo A, Wojciechowski S, Sharma VS, Gupta MK, Kuntoğlu M. Artificial intelligence systems for tool condition monitoring in machining: Analysis and critical review. Journal of Intelligent Manufacturing. 2023;**34**(5):2079-2121. DOI: 10.1007/s10845-022-01923-2

[12] Deng Z, Chen T. Distributed algorithm design for constrained resource allocation problems with high-order multi-agent systems. Automatica. 2022;**144**:110492. DOI: 10.1016/j.automatica.2022.110492

[13] Vlassis N. A Concise Introduction to Multiagent Systems and Distributed Artificial Intelligence. Berlin, Germany: Springer Nature; 2022

[14] Abate A, Gutierrez J, Hammond L, Harrenstein P, Kwiatkowska M, Najib M, et al. Rational verification: Game-theoretic verification of

multi-agent systems. Applied Intelligence. 2021;**51**(9):6569-6584. DOI: 10.1007/s10489-021-02658-y

[15] Kim YG, Lee S, Son J, Bae H, Do Chung B. Multi-agent system and reinforcement learning approach for distributed intelligence in a flexible smart manufacturing system. Journal of Manufacturing Systems. 2020;**57**:440-450. DOI: 10.1016/j.jmsy.2020.11.004

[16] Wooldridge M, Jennings NR. Intelligent agents: Theory and practice. The Knowledge Engineering Review. 1995;**10**(2):115-152. DOI: 10.1017/S0269888900008122

[17] Duan S, Wang D, Ren J, Lyu F, Zhang Y, Wu H, et al. Distributed artificial intelligence empowered by end-edge-cloud computing: A survey. IEEE Communications Surveys & Tutorials. 2022;**25**(1):591-624. DOI: 10.1109/COMST.2022.3218527

[18] Russell SJ. Artificial Intelligence a Modern Approach. London, UK: Pearson Education, Inc; 2010

[19] Thomaz EL, Araujo-Junior CF, Vendrame PR, de Melo TR. Mechanisms of aggregate breakdown in (sub) tropical soils: Effects of the hierarchical resistance. Catena. 2022;**216**:106377. DOI: 10.1016/j.catena.2022.106377

[20] González-Briones A, Castellanos-Garzón JA, Mezquita-Martín Y, Prieto J, Corchado JM. A multi-agent system framework for autonomous crop irrigation. In: 2019 2nd International Conference on Computer Applications & Information Security (ICCAIS). Piscataway, NJ, USA: IEEE; 2019. pp. 1-6. DOI: 10.1109/CAIS.2019.8769456

[21] Villarrubia G, De Paz JF, De La Iglesia DH, Bajo J. Combining multi-agent systems and wireless sensor networks for monitoring crop irrigation. Sensors. 2017;**17**(8):1775. DOI: 10.3390/s17081775

[22] Zhang Q, Hu T, Zeng X, Yang P, Wang X. Exploring the effects of physical and social networks on urban water system's supply-demand dynamics through a hybrid agent-based modeling framework. Journal of Hydrology. 2023;**617**:129108. DOI: 10.1016/j.jhydrol.2023.129108

[23] Elkamel M, Valencia A, Zhang W, Zheng QP, Chang NB. Multi-agent modeling for linking a green transportation system with an urban agriculture network in a food-energy-water nexus. Sustainable Cities and Society. 2023;**89**:104354. DOI: 10.1016/j.scs.2022.104354

[24] Boje C, Guerriero A, Kubicki S, Rezgui Y. Towards a semantic construction digital twin: Directions for future research. Automation in Construction. 2020;**114**:103179. DOI: 10.1016/j.autcon.2020.103179

[25] Vahdatikhaki F, Langari SM, Taher A, El Ammari K, Hammad A. Enhancing coordination and safety of earthwork equipment operations using multi-agent system. Automation in Construction. 2017;**81**:267-285. DOI: 10.1016/j.autcon.2017.04.008

[26] Xi L, Chen J, Huang Y, Xu Y, Liu L, Zhou Y, et al. Smart generation control based on multi-agent reinforcement learning with the idea of the time tunnel. Energy. 2018;**153**:977-987. DOI: 10.1016/j.energy.2018.04.042

[27] Ottesen S. Wellbore stability in fractured rock. In: IADC/SPE Drilling Conference and Exhibition. New Orleans, Louisiana, USA: OnePetro; 2010

[28] Guthrie R, Befus A. DebrisFlow predictor: An agent-based runout program for shallow landslides. Natural Hazards and Earth System Sciences. 2021;**21**(3):1029-1049. DOI: 10.5194/nhess-21-1029-2021

[29] Sugiarto V, Ramdani F, Bachtiar F. Modeling agent-oriented methodologies for landslide management. Journal of Information Technology and Computer Science. 2019;**4**(2):193-201. DOI: 10.25126/jitecs.201942129

[30] Badmos BK, Agodzo SK, Villamor GB, Odai SN. An approach for simulating soil loss from an agro-ecosystem using multi-agent simulation: A case study for semi-arid Ghana. Land. 2015;**4**(3):607-626. DOI: 10.3390/land4030607

[31] Elzwayie A, Afan HA, Allawi MF, El-Shafie A. Heavy metal monitoring, analysis and prediction in lakes and rivers: State of the art. Environmental Science and Pollution Research. 2017;**24**:12104-12117. DOI: 10.1007/s11356-017-8715-0

[32] Dorri A, Kanhere SS, Jurdak R. Multi-agent systems: A survey. IEEE Access. 2018;**6**:28573-28593. DOI: 10.1109/ACCESS.2018.2831228

[33] Liu X, Yu J, Feng Z, Gao Y. Multi-agent reinforcement learning for resource allocation in IoT networks with edge computing. China Communications. 2020;**17**(9):220-236. DOI: 10.23919/JCC.2020.09.017

[34] Sharma N, Magarini M, Jayakody DNK, Sharma V, Li J. On-demand ultra-dense cloud drone networks: Opportunities, challenges and benefits. IEEE Communications Magazine. 2018;**56**(8):85-91. DOI: 10.1109/MCOM.2018.1701001

[35] Chen C, Xie K, Lewis FL, Xie S, Fierro R. Adaptive synchronization of multi-agent systems with resilience to communication link faults. Automatica. 2020;**111**:108636. DOI: 10.1016/j.automatica.2019.108636

[36] Brandi S, Piscitelli MS, Martellacci M, Capozzoli A. Deep reinforcement learning to optimise indoor temperature control and heating energy consumption in buildings. Energy and Buildings. 2020;**224**:110225. DOI: 10.1016/j.enbuild.2020.110225

[37] Alishavandi AM, Moghaddas-Tafreshi SM. Interactive decentralized operation with effective presence of renewable energies using multi-agent systems. International Journal of Electrical Power & Energy Systems. 2019;**112**:36-48. DOI: 10.1016/j.ijepes.2019.04.023

[38] Gaddam A, Wilkin T, Angelova M, Gaddam J. Detecting sensor faults, anomalies and outliers in the internet of things: A survey on the challenges and solutions. Electronics. 2020;**9**(3):511. DOI: 10.3390/electronics9030511

[39] Billen P, Mazzotti M, Pandelaers L, Zhao W, Liu Z, Redus J, et al. Melt ceramics from coal ash: Constitutive product design using thermal and flow properties. Resources, Conservation and Recycling. 2018;**132**:168-177. DOI: 10.1016/j.resconrec.2018.01.035

[40] Sanchez M, Exposito E, Aguilar J. Industry 4.0: Survey from a system integration perspective. International Journal of Computer Integrated Manufacturing. 2020;**33**(10-11):1017-1041. DOI: 10.1080/0951192X.2020.1775295

[41] Minutolo V, Cerri E, Coscetta A, Damiano E, De Cristofaro M,

Di Gennaro L, et al. NSHT: New smart hybrid transducer for structural and geotechnical applications. Applied Sciences. 2020;**10**(13):4498. DOI: 10.3390/app10134498

[42] Gros M, Mas-Pla J, Boy-Roura M, Geli I, Domingo F, Petrović M. Veterinary pharmaceuticals and antibiotics in manure and slurry and their fate in amended agricultural soils: Findings from an experimental field site (Baix Empordà, NE Catalonia). Science of the Total Environment. 2019;**654**:1337-1349. DOI: 10.1016/j.scitotenv.2018.11.061

[43] Zhang C, Zhao Z, Guo D, Gong D, Chen Y. Optimization of spatial layouts for deep underground infrastructure in central business districts based on a multi-agent system model. Tunnelling and Underground Space Technology. 2023;**135**:105046. DOI: 10.1016/j.tust.2023.105046

[44] Zhou Y, Li S, Zhou C, Luo H. Intelligent approach based on random forest for safety risk prediction of deep foundation pit in subway stations. Journal of Computing in Civil Engineering. 2019;**33**(1):05018004. DOI: 10.1061/(ASCE)CP.1943-5487.0000796

[45] Chowdhuri I, Pal SC, Saha A, Chakrabortty R, Roy P. Mapping of earthquake hotspot and coldspot zones for identifying potential landslide hotspot areas in the Himalayan region. Bulletin of Engineering Geology and the Environment. 2022;**81**(7):257. DOI: 10.1007/s10064-022-02761-5

[46] Cho CH, Chen CY, Chen KC, Huang TW, Hsu MC, Cao NP, et al. Quantum computation: Algorithms and applications. Chinese Journal of Physics. 2021;**72**:248-269. DOI: 10.1016/j.cjph.2021.05.001

[47] Zhang CC, Zhu HH, Shi B, She JK, Zhang D. Performance evaluation of soil-embedded plastic optical fiber sensors for geotechnical monitoring. Smart Structures and Systems. 2016;**17**(2):297-311. DOI: 10.12989/sss.2016.17.2.297

[48] Cervantes JA, Rodríguez LF, López S, Ramos F, Robles F. Autonomous agents and ethical decision-making. Cognitive Computation. 2016;**8**:278-296. DOI: 10.1007/s12559-015-9362-8

[49] Wu H, Yao C, Li C, Miao M, Zhong Y, Lu Y, et al. Review of application and innovation of geotextiles in geotechnical engineering. Materials. 2020;**13**(7):1774. DOI: 10.3390/ma13071774

[50] Ma D, Lan G, Hassan M, Hu W, Das SK. Sensing, computing, and communications for energy harvesting IoTs: A survey. IEEE Communications Surveys & Tutorials. 2019;**22**(2):1222-1250. DOI: 10.1109/COMST.2019.2962526

[51] Attaran H, Kheibari N, Bahrepour D. Toward integrated smart city: A new model for implementation and design challenges. GeoJournal. 2022;**87**(Suppl. 4):511-526. DOI: 10.1007/s10708-021-10560-w